FIRE ON ICE

FIRE ON ICE

JEREMY C. HOLM

CFI
An Imprint of Cedar Fort, Inc.
Springville, Utah

ISBN 13: 978-1-4621-1367-5

Published by CFI, an imprint of Cedar Fort, Inc.
2373 W. 700 S., Springville, UT 84663
Distributed by Cedar Fort, Inc., www.cedarfort.com

LIBRARY OF CONGRESS CATALOGING-IN-PUBLICATION DATA

Holm, Jeremy C., 1980- author.
Fire on ice : gospel lessons learned from a lifetime of sports / Jeremy C. Holm.
pages cm
ISBN 978-1-4621-1367-5
1. Christian life--Mormon authors. 2. Holm, Jeremy C., 1980- I. Title.

BX8656.H6575 2013
248.4'89332--dc23

2013033361

Cover design by Shawnda T. Craig
Cover design © 2014 Lyle Mortimer
Edited and typeset by Emily S. Chambers

Printed in the United States of America

10 9 8 7 6 5 4 3 2 1

CONTENTS

FOREWORD

What does it mean to stand as a champion of the Lord? Throughout my life as an Olympic gymnast and collegiate coach for Brigham Young University, and as a convert to the Church, I have wondered how best to answer that question.

In my experience, not everyone who wins a medal has the heart of a champion, and not everyone who loses lacks the spirit of a victor. Similarly, not everyone who makes mistakes or occasionally loses a "game" in life should be viewed as a loser.

In the most basic sense, a champion is someone who excels, who rises above, and who never gives up. Is a medal, a calling, or a certificate required before this title can be given? Of course not! We can all be champions of the Lord in our lives.

During my career as a gymnast, I traveled to and competed in forty-nine states and thirty-nine foreign countries. After five years on the US National Team, I made it to the 1972 Olympic Summer Games held in Munich, Germany, where I competed in the vault, uneven bars, balance beam, and floor exercises. My team and I came in fourth, barely edged out by Russia, Hungary, and Czechoslovakia. Some would argue that since we did not medal we were not champions. But let me tell you something—something the mainstream media fails to correctly portray today—anyone who goes after their dreams with all their heart and soul, who sweats and bleeds and gives everything he or she has to make a goal a reality, is a champion. The girls I trained and competed alongside may not have come home with medals, but we all came home with our heads held high. We were better athletes and better people at the end of the day because of our experiences in pursuing our dreams.

After I was introduced to the gospel of Jesus Christ and baptized into the Church, I had the pleasure and honor of living with the self-respect that comes from continually striving to live as a champion of the Lord in everything I do, say, or think. Does it take discipline? Of course! But nothing worth having comes easily, which you will discover as you seek to apply the principles found in *Fire and Ice*. The guidelines and challenges found in this book are winning values that can help each of us reach our highest potential, something that Jeremy Holm is good at helping people do.

In 2004, I was one of the most desperate people in the state of Utah. I was ill and headed for surgery. I was teaching school full time, attending classes, and trying to manage the Utah Olympic Alumni Association. I came home with a sick headache bred from a long, hard day of teaching, a long commute, and the disappointment and worry about what to do with a diminishing group of Olympians who had longed to serve the state of Utah and in some way inspire others to reach their goals.

Two days before my surgery at the Mayo Clinic in Minnesota, I turned over my responsibilities for the Utah Olympians to Blaine Lindgren, a silver medalist in the 110-meter high hurdles in the 1964 Tokyo, Japan, Summer Olympic Games. One day before I left for Minnesota, I received a phone call from Jeremy Holm, a bobsledder training in Park City, Utah. We agreed to meet in my classroom at the end of the next day. Jeremy was passionate about serving others, and he had great timing since I needed all the help I could get.

Now, several years later, Jeremy has put together a recipe, if you will, for reaching eternal goals. The steps are a reminder of what we already know. This book is a plan that, if practiced, can make you a champion of the Lord in all walks of life. Thank you Jeremy, for once again sharing your time, faith, and passion to inspire others.

—Debra Stark-Clark
1972 US Olympic Team, gymnastics

INTRODUCTION

"Ok, God, you have one week to give me a reason to live."

Uttering the ultimatum, I stared quietly at the large knife in my bedpost. I didn't want to die; I just didn't know how to go on living. After half-a-lifetime on the roller-coaster ride of mortality I had hit bottom.

Fire on Ice is a glimpse into the ups and downs of my life in and out of sport, including the battles with anxiety and depression that led to my "knife in the bedpost" moment. In it you will see the hand of the Lord in my life, and I pray you find the flame of your faith kindled as I pass along the lessons that he taught me along the way.

But just like a team's run down the bobsled track, a book is never the work of just one person. A huge thank you is in order to my book "coaches," Catherine Christensen and Emily Chambers and their staff for their corrections and suggestions, to Shawnda Craig for the beautiful cover design, and to Cedar Fort for taking a leap of faith with my manuscript.

To all the athletes who pushed me on and off the ice to become my best self, I owe a deep debt. Lane, Matt, Adam, Don, Dave, Dan, Mark, Nick, Steve, Joe, Cody, Brad, and the list continues to grow: thank you for being the best teammates a guy could ask for.

And to all the athletes, world champions, Olympians, administrators, and coaches who have taught me the Champion's Way, thank you for influencing my life for the good.

My life would be incomplete if not for all the Honduras San Pedro Sula Mission "teammates" I had along with all the Church "coaches" and "officials" who have taught me the rules of the Lord and helped me play the game of life according to his rules and pointing me in the direction of the eternal finish line.

Finally, to my family and friends who have seen me at my best and my worst and have never stopped cheering me along the way. Whether I came in first or last, you loved me for doing my best.

I never went to the Games. There are athletes who were more successful and talented than I in our sport, but I felt the Lord's voice calling me to share the lessons and faith found within this book. I pray it helps you deepen your testimonies of him. Olympic "Silver and gold have I none; but such as I have give I thee" (Acts 3:6).

Dream big, my friends, and never forget that there is always hope!

HOPE: THE SUBSTANCE OF GOLD MEDALS UNSEEN

Are you ready for this?" I had been asking myself that question during the forty-five minute drive from Sandy to Park City, Utah. As we drove up through Parley's Canyon on February 5, 1997, I thought that of all the things I had imagined for my life, what I was about to do never crossed my mind. I was about to take a four-man bobsled ride down the 2002 Olympic track.

All I knew about bobsled was (a) apparently the Jamaicans aren't terrible at it, and (b) the course looks like a crazy roller coaster on ice except this ride doesn't have safety bars or guide rails and you can fall out, get ice burns, break bones, and even die. Plus, what's with the skintight superhero suits?

I had seen the sport up close on January 25, 1997, at the track's grand opening. The start area was a madhouse of spectators, politicians, camera crews, reporters, athletes, and sport administrators. The snow was coming down pretty heavy that afternoon, but I remember watching my future coach, three-time Olympian Randy Will, and his brakeman, Chris Coleman, push and load into a two-man bobsled. I never imagined that a week and a half later I'd be riding down the same course.

Arriving at what was then known as the Bear Hollow Winter Sports Park, we drove through the old gate at the top of the track and parked. Introductions were made, and the ensuing safety speech sounded like the rules of a roller coaster, which is ironic considering I hated those things growing up (proof that heaven has a sense of humor). Basically, "Please keep all arms, legs, and heads inside the sled at all times. Stay in your seat (like that would be a problem at four Gs) and enjoy the ride!" That ride changed my life.

So how did this Pennsylvania-born- Oklahoma-raised boy of sixteen end up experiencing what has been called "The Champagne of Thrills"? I blame my parents.

Dad's company, High Performance Coatings, Inc. (HPC), had recently become a sponsor for the US Olympic Bobsled Team. Because of the sponsorship, the director for the program at the Park City track set up a four-man bobsled ride for my dad. But the ride was for two, and when my mother quickly declined, I agreed to take her spot. Only later did I think, "Wait, what did I just agree to?"

I felt calm as I watched the staff pull a cherry-red four-man sled to the starting line, the same sled I would drive a decade later. If this had been a theme park, I would have had a stomach full of butterflies by now, but instead I felt a surreal peace, one that I later understood to indicate that this was something special. Not special in a worldly view, although the sport is amazingly cool. No, I knew in some part of my soul that bobsled was part of my life's mission. This experience was for me.

Pulling on my helmet, I climbed into the number-three spot and tried to contort my legs around my dad, who sat in front of me. I pushed my feet against tiny metal pegs on the sled's frame and wrapped my arms around myself so I could grab the handles by my sides. I did the "bobsled shrug," which means shrugging your shoulders to lock your head and helmet in place—which in theory was supposed to allow us to watch the ride, but reality had other plans (when we hit the first major curve on the track, I turned into a bobsled bobble-head).

"Are you ready for this?" I asked myself. With a nod we were slow-walked to the crest of the track and released. Back then there were no start buildings or covers over the track. All we could see was a tunnel that dropped down and curved to the left. We began to pick up speed and I thought, "Okay, this isn't so bad." Then gravity laughed in my face.

People always ask what going down the track feels like. Well, take your favorite roller coaster, blend in a fighter jet, then add what astronauts feel on takeoff—all done while whipping through turns at over eighty miles per hour as you are smashed down like there are four of you sitting on your shoulders. It's awesome.

After the ride, we exited the sled at the bottom, where Mom was waiting to make sure we had survived. When she asked what I thought of the experience, I responded, "Forget soccer (my sport of choice since age five). This is what I'm going to do!"

I've heard that your life flashes before your eyes right before you die.

Maybe that's why as bobsled pilots, we visualize the track in our mind before we drive, because despite the countless safety precautions, that tiny chance you might not make it off the hill alive is always there. I recently read through one of the track waivers that I've signed over the years, and my favorite part says, "I understand that by signing this Release, I will forever preclude from suing or otherwise claiming against any of the Sponsoring Parties, for any . . . death I may sustain while participating in any of the activities." Because, you know, suing a place after you're dead is at the top of your list.

I'm not trying to make it sound more dramatic. I'm just trying to make a point. We are thrill-seekers. I mean, who in their right mind throws themselves down an icy chute at faster-than-freeway speeds in a fiberglass or carbon fiber sled without a seat belt, air bags, or drag chute while wearing spandex uniforms and specialized shoes that cost a couple hundred dollars a pair?

We do, and we do it because we have three things: (1) competitive natures, (2) a craving for the thrill of our sport, and (3) faith. Faith in bobsled? Absolutely.

Faith in sports is described as confidence, optimism, or a winning attitude. These attributes are an athlete's lifeblood, and without them, he or she won't have the emotional, mental, or physical strength and stamina to meet the requirements for success. The pursuit of excellence in sport, or any chosen field, requires a healthy dose of consistent effort, hard work, adaptability (the capacity to learn new habits and skills and eliminate bad ones), and often great sacrifices. What is it that allows a competitor to give that much, try that hard, and put it all on the line on the day of the big event? Faith.

"Faith is the substance of things hoped for, the evidence of things not seen" (Hebrews 11:1), and it is what helps an athlete have dreams and goals. The Bible Dictionary teaches that "faith is a principle of action and of power." But spiritual faith and athletic faith both have to start somewhere.

The ancient Greeks had a word, *pistein,* which means "to believe" or "I know." But what do we believe in? Another Greek word, *notitia,* means "to believe in the information" or the topic, doctrine, philosophy, and so on. For faith to be faith, it must be faith in something or someone. The first step to diligently seeking God is to have *pistein,* or belief, that he exists. Once we have this belief, then we will have *notitia,* or belief in the information and teachings that comes through his servants (Doctrine and Covenants 1:38).

Once this occurs, we will give *assenus*, or "our consent." We choose to accept and believe, which is a decision that can be confirmed through the Holy Ghost (Moroni 10:3–5).

But is belief alone enough for exaltation, or is confidence enough to win the gold medal? Not a chance. Many well-meaning religions teach that we are saved merely by believing in Jesus Christ. However, when we dig deeper into the roots of faith, we find that belief alone won't save us. No athletes, no matter how much they believe they can win, will win without putting in the work.

Plus, true faith—the kind that gets winning results—must be based on true principles. For this reason, "a man is saved no faster than he gets knowledge" (*History of the Church* 4:588). How can we be baptized in the correct manner if we have never been taught? How can we drive a bobsled correctly unless we are coached? As Paul asked, "How shall [we] believe [in truth that we] have not heard? and how shall [we] hear without a preacher?" (Romans 10:14). As an athlete, you spend a lot of time listening to and acting upon the words of your coach—your preacher as Paul said—and at the end of the day, you hope and pray they are teaching you the truths that will help you win the game and take home the gold medal. That takes faith.

I think that as Latter-day Saints we forget how blessed we are to have the knowledge of true principles and doctrines that help us win the eternal game. We don't have to guess; we don't have to wonder. When we develop faith in our Savior, we can "henceforth be no more children, tossed to and fro, and carried about with every wind of doctrine, by the sleight of men, and cunning craftiness, whereby they lie in wait to deceive" (Ephesians 4:14). We have the winning game plan!

The necessity for basing faith on true principles is essential for athletes as well. Imagine what would happen if your coach trained you all summer like a sprinter when the goal was to compete in the marathon. Or what if you truly believed that eating a gallon of ice cream along with a chocolate cake right before a soccer match would improve your performance? In sports there is a reason for all the research to discover new techniques, nutritional improvements, and more effective training: correct knowledge applied correctly is power. Incorrect knowledge, even if applied correctly, brings about a loss of power. This is why Olympic Training Centers, college athletic departments, and professional sports teams are filled with some of the greatest minds in strength and conditioning, sports medicine, sports psychology, nutrition, kinesiology/biomechanical analysis, physical therapy, and other related fields. The discovery of true principles, that when followed can improve athletic performance, is worth gold! Well, gold medals at least (or trophies or championship rings if that's your thing).

When I began coaching the US Adaptive Bobsled Team program in the winter of 2010, one of my first tasks was to educate myself on the levels of disability of each participant. Were they above-knee amputees (AKs) or below-knee amputees (BKs), and what was the level of spinal injury for our seated (wheelchair) drivers? Most of the athletes were open and patiently answered my ignorant questions. It was a new world for me, but the information was crucial as it allowed me to move on to the next step: translating all that data into the procedures necessary for success. I needed to evaluate their biomechanics (movement of their bodies) and the mechanical limitations of their prosthetics and then figure out how best to adapt bobsled techniques to match. I took what I knew worked for able-bodied athletes (ABAs), athletes with no disability, and changed those methods and procedures to serve athletes with physical disabilities. For example, during a push start involving an ABA brakeman, the athlete would stand behind the sled and drop into a crouch with their hands on the back handles. Their hips would be low, their back straight, and their feet would be on top of the push block so that when they leaned forward they would roll over the block's edge, thus providing a solid base.

But let's take a look at one of our above-knee amputees, Cody Reese, who ended up an amazing driver but began as a brakeman. Cody's prosthetic fit into a special socket at his hip, but since the prosthetic did not have a full hip joint, he had a little trouble getting as low as a brakeman normally does. So we tried several different angles to see if his push would be faster this way or that way. In the end, when Cody received a new J-foot (a lower-leg prosthetic shaped like a big "J"), he tried putting the curved prosthetic behind the push block and shoving off with his beastly strong natural leg, which ended up taking over a tenth of a second off the push time.

This condensed version gives you an idea of the revolutionary efforts we made together in our search for "the truth," or the truest form of a brakeman's push for his unique situation. Cody truly was a pioneer in the field of adaptive bobsled, and I feel blessed to have been there for his journey. However, that doesn't mean that another above knee amputee athlete and their coach won't come up with a better technique in the future. When that happens, the technique we developed will no longer be a "saving" principle. We will have to put our faith in and act upon the newer, more current "truth."

This example demonstrates the huge difference between having faith in mortal "truths" and trusting in those found within the gospel. Worldly opinions change all the time, but the doctrines of salvation are eternal. We need not worry that what leads us toward the spiritual gold today (exaltation) will be discredited tomorrow (though occasionally the Lord may ask us to change some things).

Do we realize the great endowment of knowledge that our eternal coach, even our Father in Heaven, has provided through the saving truths of the gospel for "the perfecting of the saints, for the work of the ministry, for the edifying of the body of Christ" (Ephesians 14:12–13)? Since our coach has given us these game winning truths, we can have full *fiducia*.

Fiducia is the Greek term for "commitment" or dedication to a cause. We call it conversion, but when we reach the *fiducia* stage of belief, we begin to experience the power of faith, which I believe is tied directly to the meaning of religion. The word *religion* comes from the Latin word *religare*, which means "to bind." When we have faith in Jesus Christ and his gospel, we become bound to it, not by force, but by choice and covenant. Once that occurs, faith becomes a powerful source of motivation, which is something that both champions in sport and the champions of the Lord need to succeed.

One of the first things you learn in a sport like bobsled is that you must have faith. The pursuit of excellence on the ice requires *pistein*, or belief, in your goals and in yourself. Once you have that fundamental faith, you need to seek out trustworthy and experienced coaches and trainers who are willing to share their knowledge and experience. If their teachings about the sport are true, then you can have *notitia* in them, or trust and confidence. When this happens we give our coaches our *assenus*, our consent. We embrace our athletic pursuits and dreams and give them our *fiducia*, our complete commitment. But we can't stop there; the battle is just beginning and it is faith that will see us through to the medals podium finish . . . if we act accordingly.

The Apostle James said it best: "Faith, if it hath not works, is dead" (James 2:17). What good does it do an athlete to seek out a great coach and then ignore their counsel? Faith alone, belief alone, even knowledge alone cannot save or earn them the gold medal unless it is acted upon in the correct manner. Faith, like dedication to a sport, is a way of life.

The ancient Greeks believed that by obeying their religious and philosophical dogmas, they would be living "enthusiastically," which means "to be filled with the gods." As Latter-day Saints, we believe that by having faith in Jesus Christ and remaining true to the principles of the gospel and the covenants we make, we can live "enthusiastically," but we will be filled with the Spirit of God, and that is even better (1 Corinthians 2:9–12).

Whether as a bobsled athlete or a Latter-day Saint (or both), we can learn the meaning of faith by using a simple reverse formula. Without a desire to believe, a teacher will not matter. Without a teacher, there can be no knowledge to trust in. Without that trust, there will be no motivating power to act. And without action, there can be no results. Ultimately our level of conversion and dedication to the gospel is in direct correlation to our level of faith and obedience.

Hold to your faith, cling to your faith, stand firm in your faith. As the motto of the Athlete Outreach Project (www.athleteoutreach.com) that I founded states, "There Is Always Hope." Why is there always hope? Because we have an eternal coach who knows how to win, wants to help us win, and is willing to share every moment of our journey with us. That is the stuff that spiritual gold medals are made of. As long as our faith is based in the Lord Jesus Christ, there is always hope.

FIRST, FAITH IN OUR COACH, JESUS CHRIST

When you're a young rookie athlete, you constantly look for opportunities to learn and grow, which means you take a lot of things on faith. While you hope that the sources you're listening to help you become a better competitor, sometimes even new athletes wonder when faith is being misplaced.

On December 23, 1997, a fire destroyed an auto-body shop in West Valley, Utah, wherein lay a beautiful $30,000 four-man bobsled belonging to decorated sled pilot Bruce Roselli. Bruce and his team spent Christmas with their loved ones only to find their hopes for competing in the upcoming US Olympic Trials literally burned to ashes. Or were they? This group of dedicated athletes rallied together and, with the help of numerous donors and sponsors, were able to obtain a replacement sled. No matter the adversity, Bruce always knew where to place his faith. He always had "Luke 1:37" displayed on his sleds, which reads, "With God all things are possible."

But remember what I said about wondering when faith is misplaced? When Bruce received his new sled, he brought it to the Park City track, and I got to ride in it. Was my faith misplaced in Bruce as a driver? Absolutely not; I trusted Bruce completely, but my faith in the newbies who were riding with us was rather thin. I was to act as the brakeman for the group while Bruce drove, but the two guys he brought up to push and load from the sides had never ridden in a sled before. A push start for a four-man team is a bit of a process, and I worried these two would not make it in.

Surprisingly, they made it into the proper positions for the number-two and number-three seats. *Okay, not so bad,* I thought. I tucked down in the brakeman's seat, counting the turns as we made our way smoothly down the track. As we crossed the finish line, I sat up quickly and tapped the number-three guy on the back, which is the sport's universal sign for "Get your behind off the brake handles."

Only he didn't budge. In a four-man sled, once you cross the finish line the number-three guy normally pulls himself up out of his seat so the brakeman can have full access to the brake handles. With this guy still tucked, I had to reach around trying to find the handles and pull them out from underneath him, all while watching the finish area come rushing toward us. I managed to find and pull one handle while trying to shove this guy forward to get him up. The brakes were starting to dig into the ice and slow us down but not fast enough. We flew past the finish area's take-out point and into a pile of half-snow-half-ice that lay beyond. At the end of the day, hope and trust are only as good as the sources in which they are founded, and unfortunately on that occasion, the number-three guy fell a little short.

Luckily, as Latter-day Saints we know a better object for our faith since we believe that the first principle and ordinance of the gospel is "Faith in the Lord Jesus Christ" (fourth article of faith). What other being or "thing" in the entire universe is worthy of such trust, outside of our Father in Heaven? Part of the reason the Israelites—and all of us for that matter—were commanded to "have no other gods before [him]" (Exodus 20:3) is there are no other gods made by man's hands or his mind that can save us from our sins and physical death (John 14:6) or in whom we can have complete trust (1 Nephi 21:14–16).

Jesus Christ is the perfect teammate. He is Holy One of Israel, (Isaiah 1:4), the Prince of Peace (Isaiah 9:6), our Advocate with the Father (Doctrine and Covenants 45:3), and most important of all, our Redeemer (Job 19:25). It is because of Christ that we can "lay aside every weight, and the sin which doth so easily beset us, and let us run with patience the race that is set before us, looking unto Jesus the author and finisher of our faith" (Hebrews 12:1–2).

Without faith we will ignore his invitation to come unto him (Matthew 11:28) and follow his teachings (Mark 8:34). Without faith we will miss all the temporal, spiritual, and eternal blessings, "which God hath prepared for them that love him" (1 Corinthians 2:9). Unless we embrace the Lord as our Savior, our spiritual gold-medal desires are going to fall short because he is the only true source of strength, comfort, peace, and forgiveness. He is the only coach that never fails.

For an athlete to have complete faith in a coach, that coach needs to have (1) proper credentials (certification), (2) correct knowledge, (3) good communication style, (4) shared goals, and (5) mutual respect. When these attributes exist within the coach-athlete dynamic, the athlete has a much higher opportunity for success. I have seen and had coaches that met each of these qualities, and the results were constructive. On the flip side, I have seen coaches who lacked some of these traits, and the desired results were harder to come by. It is difficult to maintain faith in your coach when you feel they do not know, do not care, and do not try.

So let's apply these five coaching qualities to our eternal coach, Jesus Christ.

1. Proper Credentials

When you look for a coach, you want one who has credentials, which indicates he or she has the experience or training required to meet the demands of the coaching position. This certification usually comes from a governing body for the sport—an organization that you can trust. The Savior's credentials began with the declaration in the Council in Heaven when our Father selected Jesus to be the Lamb of God (Abraham 3:27) and were eternally cemented in place through his atoning sacrifices in Gethsemane and on Golgotha. We can have complete faith in Christ's "credentials" because there is no other (credentialed) name given under heaven wherein we can be saved (Acts 4:12).

2. Correct Knowledge

In sports, to do your best you need a coach who understands the game and comprehends how to coach you to your highest potential. Without faith that your coach knows what he or she is talking about, it can be difficult to apply yourself to the teaching. The Savior's knowledge of the game of life is perfect. Because of his experience in the Garden of Gethsemane, Jesus understands our lives completely and knows best how to coach us on the "field" of life (Alma 7:11–12) and help us reach our highest potential.

3. Good Communication Style

Good communication is a game changer. Without it a coach cannot transfer his or her knowledge and winning techniques and game plans. The Savior established his Church so we can receive his instructions and coaching through the mouths of his "assistant coaches," our Church leaders (Doctrine and Covenants 1:38). We also have the gift of the Holy Ghost, which communicates the Lord's desires for us personally (Doctrine and Covenants 8:2–3) while we are playing the game. The Savior has an open-door policy for each and every one of us, no matter where, when, or what. We just need reach out to find him waiting for us with open arms.

4. Shared Goals

To be able to put faith in your coach, you need to know that they share or respect your goals enough to help you achieve them. This can be crucial when we feel discouraged, and our coach(es) must step in to help us get back on track. Our coach Jesus Christ loves us more than we can comprehend, and his greatest desire is to help us lead a life full of blessings and joys. He shares our goal of exaltation so much that he gave his life and suffered in Gethsemane so we could repent of our sins and return to our Heavenly Father's kingdom (3 Nephi 27:14–16). He will be there when we want to give up on our dreams or even ourselves (Isaiah 49:14–16). On days when the game gets rough, Jesus will rush onto the field when we need him.

5. Mutual Respect

A coach's ability to instill confidence in his or her athletes can mean the difference between victory and defeat. This power of inspiration is based heavily on the respect the athletes have for said coach and vice versa. Without mutual respect, team chemistry, and cohesion begin to break down. When it comes to the Savior, the amount of respect and love he has for us cannot be measured. The Lord reveres us even when we do not respect ourselves, and our potential is constantly before his eyes. He may chasten, but he never berates, belittles, or betrays that respect.

It's important to comprehend these aspects of the Savior's personality and divine role because to have faith means we must first believe that he exists and have a correct understanding of his character. Without this knowledge and faith, we can never find the eternal results that we so hunger after. Jesus said, "I am the bread of life: he that cometh to me shall never hunger; and he that believeth on me shall never thirst" (John 6:35).

Just as a coach is the center point of a sports team, Jesus Christ is the foundation we must build on if we want to enjoy eternal victory. He is the standard of our faith that we must look to if we are to stand on the celestial medals podium.

The Olympic flag made its official debut in 1920 during the Antwerp, Belgium, Olympiad. Created in 1913, the flag, with its iconic five rings, has become a standard for the Olympic movement. It represents the ideals of Olympism, that we should seek a balanced development of the mind, body, and character, and that we should find joy in our efforts, or as Latter-day Saints we would say, "joy in the journey." It reminds us that we should value the opportunity to be a good role model for others, to "let our light so shine" and treat others with a spirit of brotherhood, tolerance, and friendship. There is something beautiful about seeing those five rings on a sea of white floating in the breeze.

Just as the Olympic flag and the five rings are central symbols of the modern Olympic movement, our Savior and his Atonement are the central points of our religion. He is the symbol of our faith and the reason we have hope for eternal life (John 3:14–15).

Likewise, Christ is the guiding light that can lead us through this life and safely back to God's presence. Jesus proclaimed, "I am the light of the world: he that followeth me shall not walk in darkness, but shall have the light of life" (John 8:12).

On February 5, 2003, I attended a relighting ceremony for the 2002 Olympic cauldron at Utah's Rice Eccles Stadium, the site of the opening and closing ceremonies for the Salt Lake City Games. The event was fantastic. I considered it a bit of a consolation prize since I missed the Utah Olympics while I was serving in the Honduras San Pedro Sula Mission.

Anyone who has witnessed an Olympic cauldron being lit or already lit can tell you that it is an awesome sight. There is a spirit to the torch, a fire that does more than warm the air around it (Salt Lake's cauldron burned at 900°F); it warms the heart, something I find completely appropriate for the Utah cauldron since the motto for the 2002 Games was "Light the Fire Within." But the difference between the Olympic flame and the Light of the World is that while one is only lit and then extinguished every two years, Jesus is "a light that is endless, that can never be darkened" (Mosiah 16:9). Our goal is to make our faith so strong that it becomes less like the Olympic torch, able to be extinguished, and more like the light of Christ: endless and so strong that it can never be darkened.

I know of no coach more supportive, more respectful, more credentialed, more knowledgeable or more loving than Jesus Christ (Ephesians 3:19). He is our mentor, our brother, and our friend. Have faith. Trust him. Believe in him. Accept his instruction. Come unto Christ and be coached, be healed, be lifted, and be saved.

THE MUSCLE OF FAITH GROWS THROUGH EXERCISING IT

One of my mother's frustrating recollections of my early bobsled years was the nigh-impossible task of taking a picture of a sled roaring past at full speed. This was the late nineties, so consumer-focused digital cameras were new and expensive. Mom used the tried-and-true method of shooting a roll of film and then having a photo lab develop it to see if you actually got anything good.

Here's the problem. Your average film-loaded camera had a slower shutter speed, which means they took pictures at a slower rate. As Mom and many spectators can attest, by the time you pushed the button to take a photo, the sled was heading into the next turn. All you got was a picture of blank ice, or, if you're lucky, maybe a blurry image. Mom said the trick was to time it just right. You listened for the bobsled, and when it is was at a certain point in the turn ahead of you, you started to push the button. Also, you pulled your eyes away from the camera's viewing window so you could watch the track.

The process of developing faith can be a bit like taking a picture of a moving bobsled. At first, things may feel a bit blurry as we learn and grow and struggle through life. Other times we miss the mark completely. And sometimes we need to step back and look at the big picture and focus on Jesus Christ. I want to suggest a few ways that we can all develop a richer, more fulfilling faith. Let's take our faith from a "desire to believe" (Alma 32:27) and turn it into a gold-medal conviction.

For me, trying to train for bobsled while dealing with the real battles of anxiety and depression and their cohort self-doubt was a serious challenge for my body and mind. That being said, while I haven't been perfect at it, I have done my best over the years to prepare for the demands of my sport.

Since a lot of people ask what kind of training we do, I thought I'd share a few routines from days gone by, and then compare it to having faith in Jesus Christ.

Days 1 & 4: Lower Body
Warm-ups
Power Cleans: 4 sets, 2–3 reps
Front Squats: 5 sets, 6 reps
Bulgarian Split Squats: 3 sets x 10 reps per side
Barbell Hip Thrusts: 4 sets, 8 reps
Static Flexibility & cold bath

Days 2 & 5: Upper Body
Warm-ups
Close-Grip Bench Press: 4 sets, 4–6 reps
Barbell Row: 4 sets, 6 reps
Standing Barbell Press: 4 sets, 6–8 reps
Neutral Grip Chin Ups: 4 sets, 10 reps
Dumbbell Incline Press: 3 sets, 10 reps
Dumbbell Laterals: 3 sets, 10 reps

As you can see, bobsled athletes put in a fair amount of work based on their faith, or their hopes and dreams. They may not lift as much weight as they want to today, but they have faith that, through work, they can tomorrow. They may not be as fast as they want to be today, but they have hope that if they keep training, they can be soon. An exercise program, like the gospel, is only as effective as the faith-based efforts we put into it. "By the sweat of [our] brow" (Genesis 3:19) our muscles grow through work and proper nutrition. Faith in Jesus Christ works the same way; faith in Christ grows by exercising it and through proper spiritual nourishment.

We say that faith is a power and a gift; it is a power that leads to action, and it is a gift from our Heavenly Father. As Elder Bruce R. McConkie taught, "Faith is a gift of God bestowed as a reward for personal righteousness."[1] The more obedient we are, the higher our level of faith.

But faith is also a developed attribute; it grows as we exercise and rely on it. Like an athlete's body, faith must be nurtured and sometimes pushed to its limits in order to mature and grow. Faith is a line-upon-line, precept-upon-precept (2 Nephi 28:30) principle, so its development is a process. Let's say you get a new coach for your team—a really good one. If we follow Alma's explanation of faith in Alma 32, you might "desire to believe" (verse 27) in your new coach. With your desire comes a willingness to listen to and act upon their teachings. When that happens, the seed of faith begins to grow (verse 28), and we can start to see the fruits of our faith (verse 30); you become a better athlete. As long as we do not cast out the seed and we continue to nurture and act upon it, we can enjoy "the fruit thereof [victory on the field], which is most precious, which is sweet above all that is sweet . . . and ye shall feast upon this fruit even until ye are filled, that ye hunger not, neither shall ye thirst" (verse 42).

I love those words: "feast upon this fruit until ye are filled." Proper nutrition for an athlete is everything. I've had friends preparing for the Olympics who had their meals planned out four months in advance. Making sure you have enough calories to meet your developmental and performance needs is key, but you have to make sure you are giving your body the right nutrients. Since every athlete is different, a personalized diet plan is golden, and smart athletes adhere to their diet as if it were gospel (mostly) because they're going to get out of their bodies on game day what they've been putting into it. Put in the correct nutritional fuel and you're going to feel and perform at the top of your game.

Faith in Jesus Christ requires similar discipline since what we put into it is proportionate to what we get out of it. Whether the discipline is repenting of our sins, obeying the commandments, or simply relying on the Lord's care, we need to do the work and nurture our faith in order to enjoy the benefits thereof. We learn by doing, and our faith grows by action, even if someone else (the Lord) volunteers us to take those actions.

In February 1999, a group of us took a trip to the Calgary, Canada, track. After two days of training on the 1988 Winter Olympic track, Pat, our coach, told my teammate Jared and me that some local four-man teams were looking for brakemen for that night's session. He suggested we try it, and we agreed. Pat vouched for the skill level of the teams and that was enough for us.

Both of us had experience as brakeman, but understandably the Canadian teams wanted to practice dry-land loads with us before we took to the ice. Half an hour later we parted ways until the training session began. I met up with my new teammates and helped get the sled to the line. Was I nervous? Sure. I had ridden in the back of four-man sleds on the Park City track numerous times, but this was Calgary, a track I had only been down about ten times.

So let's pause and apply the story so far to the principle of faith. First, I honestly desired to experience the Calgary track in the back of a four-man sled, and I of course hoped to do so in safety. I had to trust in the skills of the pilot I would be riding with and have faith that he would guide us all the way to the finish line. With all that in mind, I decided to act on my trust and faith.

We called our cadence and then pushed off and sprinted down the start ramp. The pilot hopped in, and then the number-two and number-three pushers followed. After a few more steps, I kicked into the sled, made sure the side push bars were closed, and shouted, "Down!" so the number-three guy knew to sit down (he was holding himself up slightly so my shoes could slide in). From there the ride was awesome, quite a bit different than the two-man sleds we used earlier in the day. Four-man sleds are different because riders move further back in the sled from nose to rear, and that makes the trip more violent. I smashed into my seat through turn after turn until we cruised through the finish line, and then I pulled back on the brake handles for all I was worth, grateful that my faith in the pilot had not been misplaced.

Through this experience I grew in both knowledge and confidence in my abilities in the sport. My initial desires turned into a more sure knowledge of faith as a result of the actions I took. Those actions led to progression.

There is a reason top athletes spend so much time applying their faith through practice. As they become familiar with the techniques necessary to win, their confidence grows. Self-doubt melts away, and a reduced anxiety level about the competition leads to smoother performance. Muscle memory develops, which allows for quicker reaction times on the field so no "heat of the moment" hesitations exist. The stipulation to all this faith is that it only works if athletes practices proper technique (basing their "faith" and works on correct principles). Nourishing our faith through acting on the "good techniques" of scripture study, prayer, fasting, obedience to the commandments, and regular church attendance is crucial.

One of the greatest ways we can exercise faith in the Savior is to repent of our sins. Repentance begins with a desire to be forgiven and healed. If you want to develop a personal relationship with Christ, turn to him often. When we accept his invitation to "return unto [him], and repent of [our] sins, and be converted, that [he] may heal [us]" (3 Nephi 9:13), we will be blessed. Our faith that Jesus loves us and is our personal Savior will become instinctive because our "knowledge is perfect in that thing" (Alma 32:34).

Experiencing the cleansing power of repentance is a potent way to nourish our faith.

We often say that the Atonement allows us to be reconciled to God when we have fallen away. Many people don't realize that the Olympics themselves fell away beginning in AD 393. The ancient Games were dedicated to the Greek gods, particularly Zeus, which gave the competitors and the people a strong connection to old religious beliefs. However, Christian Emperor Theodosius I of the Eastern Roman Empire (Byzantium) felt that the Games were too pagan, so he outlawed them in AD 393. The site of Olympia became lost to the world as time, earthquakes, flooding, storms, and war left the site buried—similar to what happens to our spirits when we sin. The birthplace of the Games lay dormant until the modern Olympic movement was rekindled in 1896 under the guiding hands of Baron Pierre de Coubertin, who founded the International Olympic Committee in 1890. Coubertin and his comrades' actions restored not only the healing and inspiring power of the Games to the world, but they also eventually returned, even reconciled, the first contemporary Olympics to their birthplace of Athens, Greece. So if you ever feel like you have fallen away from the gospel, know that—like the Olympic Games—you can return to your inherent glory. And it's all because of faith in Jesus Christ.

Another way to develop faith in Christ is to rely on his grace and mercy during times of adversity. Discovering that he truly loves us and wants to succor us as we strive to endure the heartaches of mortality can be one of the most spiritually enlightening experiences of our lives. I testify that as we exercise faith in Christ during times of trouble, we will "renew [our] strength; [we] shall mount up with wings as eagles; [we] shall run, and not be weary; and [we] shall walk, and not faint" (Isaiah 40:31).

It may be through halting steps like a warm-up walk or through a full-on spiritual sprint, but whatever we do to strengthen, nourish, and exercise our trust in Jesus Christ will help our faith grow and develop, and we must continue in that path until the end (3 Nephi 15:9). That being said, there certainly are ways to starve faith along the way.

That fear is the opposite of faith is a principle that holds true in sport as well as spiritual matters. Thoughts or actions based on fear, discouragement, disbelief, doubt, uncertainty, and apprehension can sap our motivation and leave us feeling despair or disaffected. I'm not saying we won't struggle, but there is a difference between feeding our faith and feeding our fears. When times of difficulty arise, champions of Christ may wrestle with demons, but they ultimately choose faith. As Elder Jeffrey R. Holland reminds us, "even as the Lord avoids sugary rhetoric, he rebukes faithlessness and he deplores pessimism. He expects us to believe!"[2]

Over the years I have taken apart, repaired, cleaned, and reassembled the steering system of bobsleds time and time again. An obvious reason for my labors is that a bobsled is a precision instrument, and I want my steering to work perfectly. Would you want to step up to the starting line with a sled that wasn't functioning properly? Why, then, do we discount the value of our faith by neglecting proper spiritual maintenance? We should constantly clean out or repair any thoughts, fears, habits, or problems that are holding us back from enjoying a fruitful relationship with the Savior and maintaining a strong conviction of his gospel. That means vigilant work, daily work, even hourly work, but a labor for something so wonderful is no sacrifice. Championship faith is 24/7.

It's hard to train for an event during a competition, so develop faith before adversity comes. Yes, the races of life will challenge the strength of our souls, but we should preserve a constant relationship with the Savior rather than sporadically and desperately reaching out for his help when we are brought low to the dust.

But let's be honest: even elite athletes get tired. Sometimes the trials of life, those exercises of the soul, feel overwhelming. I have found that within moments of discouragement and adversity one of the greatest ways to find peace and hope is through serving our mortal teammates. In addition, Christlike service is an excellent way to develop faith in our Savior. Together we can do amazing things and lift the heavy loads off of each other's hearts and shoulders.

As we nourish our faith through obedience, repentance, sacrifice, and service, we will see the hand of the Lord in our lives. Sometimes my conviction has wavered, but I testify that when we exercise what faith we have, even if it be as tiny as a mustard seed (Luke 17:6), marvelous things can happen. As Nephi so boldly declared, "the Lord is able to do all things according to his will, for the children of men, if it so be that they exercise faith in him. . . . Wherefore, let us be faithful to him" (1 Nephi 7:12).

While writing this book, I began fundraisings for a new two-man bobsled since my personal sled was damaged by two athletes I had been helping (I knew the risk when I let them use the sled). But I wanted to do something special; I wanted to use the sled to inspire others, to motivate them to embrace life and to forgive themselves for past mistakes. I wanted to spread hope wherever the sled went, so I called it *The Phoenix* after the mythical bird that rose from the ashes to soar again. It would take faith to get the money, but I had that faith. The Lord had helped me so many times in the past in my bobsled pursuits, and I trusted he would assist me again.

I knew the economy was in pretty bad shape and that many companies were withdrawing sponsorship support, cutting their workforces, and reducing expenses. On top of that, many families faced financial difficulties, so donations were going to be hard to come by. But I had faith that miracles could happen.

Utilizing my design skills, we created a website for the project, www.teamphoenixbobsled.com, and produced a sponsorship and donation packet to distribute. I had a desire and faith that it would work out, and you know what? As we went to work, the support poured in. I spent one morning thinking that I needed heaven's help to make the project a success, and then a company I produced some graphic design work for came to my mind. Half an hour later I had a pledge of economic support.

The Phoenix is now parked in my parent's garage, waiting for the next season (dad's garage has all the tools I need for sled work). What started with a desire took effort and faith to come to pass, but in the end the Lord's tender mercies made it happen.

My dear friends, nourish your faith. Exercise it daily. Cherish it like an Olympic gold medal because faith in the Savior is far more valuable. Don't worry if that faith has wavered in the past. Choose today as the day you will strengthen and maintain it. I promise that the Savior will always be there for us; we need only trust him. He has promised that if we "will have faith in [him, we] shall have power to do whatsoever thing is expedient in [him]" (Moroni 7:33).

TALK TO THE COACH; THERE'S NO DATA LIMIT ON PRAYER

Fun fact: when you're roaring down the track at eighty to ninety miles per hour, it is somewhat difficult to maintain a complete view of the "big picture."

When you're inside the course and driving a sled, the view is mostly limited to the turn in front of you. While we maintain an understanding of where we are on the course, our perspective is rather narrow when compared to what spectators see on TV, but that is where a coach comes in.

Spectators are often surprised to see coaches standing on the side of the track during training sessions and races. It does seem illogical since there are signs posted everywhere that say "Stay off the track," but if you ever watch a sledding event in person and you see coaches on the course, don't worry. They are there to help the athletes, and they know what they are doing.

While standing on the edge of the track a coach can see much more than the sled's pilot. The coach has a wider view, which allows him or her to watch where the sled is coming from, how the pilot is driving as they pass, and where the sled goes as it heads down the track. It's a skill that takes practice to develop since the sleds are passing at such high speeds, but coaches watch for the direction of the sled's nose, runners, timing on the entrances and exits, any flops out of turns, skids, and so on. As a coach, all those details help you understand what the pilot of the sled is doing. Did they steer too much or too little, too late or too soon, were they too high or too low in the turn—that sort of thing. By combining what you see with what you know about the sport, you can help the sled's pilot improve his or her skills and have a faster run next time. But as you can imagine, it's a little tough to hold a conversation when the athletes are passing at 80 mph. Technology to the rescue.

After a team crosses the finish line and heads into the finish area, the driver grabs a handheld radio sitting nearby. He or she can then talk to their coach who has a twin radio in hand. The conversation is usually just a quick exchange of words, but a coach may say something like "Ease up on the entrance of the turn," "Go about three inches higher before your first check," or "Don't steer so early at the exit; let it run a little bit longer." Bobsled pilots needs to trust their coach's knowledge, and in faith they need to take their coach's suggestions to the top of the track and experiment on their word (Alma 32:27) during the next run.

Now athletes talk to their coach before a session starts as well to help themselves prepare for the ice. Similarly, we had sweet communion with our Father in Heaven before we started our "run" of mortality. We saw his face and listened to his voice. When God sent us to earth to be tried and to prove ourselves (Abraham 3:1–3), he knew we would need his help to win eternal victory.

After all, life can easily be compared to an exciting bobsled ride. Mortality has its ups and downs, fast areas and slow areas, and there are plenty of "driving" decisions to be made. One thing is certain: we all need help from a coach with more experience, greater understanding, and a desire to help us improve.

As sled pilots, we can't communicate face to face with our coaches when they are out on the track and we are in the finish area. Similarly, as mortal beings we have left Heavenly Father's presence to come to earth. With the veil drawn over our minds, we cannot see him on the sidelines of our lives, but we know he is attentive to everything that happens to us (Psalm 8:4–5). Because of his perfect knowledge and divine understanding, God is the only source we can completely confide in for guidance and correction in this life. He is a loving coach who knows everything about the race of life.

How grateful I am for the knowledge that he isn't a deaf god who stands idly by as we make our way in this world. Just as a coach focuses on helping his or her athletes reach their full potential, God helps us become the best we can be through his encouragement, support and divine direction. Since his objective is to help us return home in honor and glory and achieve exaltation (Moses 1:39), he is a great motivator, quick to send affirmations of his love and his belief in us. More than anything God wants us to be happy. So how do we reach our eternal coach? He's "out there on the track" and we are down here.

In his tree of life vision in 1 Nephi 8, Lehi found himself wandering "for the space of many hours in darkness" before he "began to pray unto the Lord that he would have mercy on [him], according to the multitude of his tender mercies" (verse 8). As soon as he prayed, Lehi was directed out of darkness and toward the tree of life, which through Nephi we learn represents "the love of God; . . . wherefore, it is the most desirable above all things" (1 Nephi 11:22).

We learn from Lehi's account that no matter where we find ourselves as we race through life, prayer can always lead us to the love of God. The Bible Dictionary states, "As soon as we learn the true relationship in which we stand toward God (namely, God is our Father, and we are his children), then at once prayer becomes natural and instinctive on our part."[3]

Prayer can be defined as solemn communication between God and man. Prayer is to be directed to God and no one else, including man-made images (Exodus 20:3–5). We know that prayer has been a commandment since Adam and Eve were first expelled from the Garden of Eden (Moses 5:4). The Lord himself reminded us that, "Ye must always pray unto the Father in my name" (3 Nephi 18:19). True prayer, then, the kind that opens the heavens and strengthens our souls must be based on faith "in God, the Eternal Father, and in His Son, Jesus Christ" (first article of faith). Prayer is the radio we use to talk to our Father in Heaven.

In our modern era of technological marvels, mankind finds numerous mortal equivalents to prayer. We can instantly communicate with another person without even seeing their face via text, instant messaging, fax, email, phone calls, portable radios, and so on. The concept of speaking and being heard by a being, a deity no less, becomes more feasible with every passing day. If we as human beings can figure out how to communicate with space probes tens of thousands of miles from earth, the question of God hearing our prayers quickly becomes moot.

Coaching helped me better understand why God commands us to pray. Standing on the side of the track really gave me greater perspective since I can see more than the athletes in the sled can. Plus, my years of experience allowed me to understand what they are doing right or wrong. Having that little radio in my pocket allows me to quickly aid them with helpful instruction, correction, or guidance. Just like prayer.

Not every athlete wanted help, however. Some chose to ignore the communication option and go back to the start without talking to me. How's that for a metaphor of those who return to heaven without talking to God in mortality? As a sled pilot, I couldn't believe they would forgo the available help and teaching I could provide. It wasn't about ego; I just knew that if a pilot really wanted to improve, he or she needed to listen to coaching and change whatever needed to be changed. Without listening to the coach, the pilot couldn't or wouldn't progress, and he or she would keep on making the same mistakes. It is sad, but it helped me understand why we should take the time to grab the spiritual radio and communicate with God. Without prayer we are left to our own devices on this earth, and, like those athletes who chose not to communicate with me as their coach, we will be free to make the same mistakes over and over again. Additionally, without heaven's guidance we have to rely on our own limited decision-making processes for life's toughest questions and rely on our feeble mortal strength to resist temptation and endure adversity. Not the smartest play in the book.

Elder J. Devn Cornish of the Seventy taught, "because [God] will not infringe upon our agency, we must ask for His help. . . . Prayer is one of the most precious gifts of God to man."[4] Are we taking advantage of this gift? Do we open the channel of communication often? Remember, there are no minute or data limitations on our conversations with the divine.

Some days it can be easy to say, "I don't have time for prayer." We keep so busy with hundreds of different things that one more responsibility feels like the straw that broke the camel's back. With the strains of family and social life, plus work and church responsibilities mixed with the necessity of caring for our bodies and minds along with the pursuit of personal goals, no wonder we find our schedules pushed to the limit.

The problem is that skipping daily prayer is the spiritual equivalent of skipping breakfast: we end up hungry and weaker, and we can't think as clearly. And if breakfast is the most important meal of the day, then we can say that prayer is the most important activity of starting the day. No matter how hectic the game of life gets, we cannot afford to skip this spiritual "meal" and instruction session with our coach on high.

Sometimes after a run down the track as pilots, we don't have time to talk to our coach in the finish area, so we talk on the radio during the truck ride to the start. Similarly, we carry the opportunity to pray with us wherever we go, day and night. We can pray in our minds on the drive to work or bow our heads momentarily while the kids play. We can pray in our hearts during class or even during a mid-morning job or bike ride. Even if all we can do is follow the example of President George Albert Smith, who once prayed after a full day of conference meetings: "Heavenly Father bless all good people, Thy servant George A. is tired. In the name of Jesus Christ, Amen," we will feel the difference.[5]

The funny thing about prayer is that the more we do it, the more we realize how much we need the advice and guidance of our eternal coach.

After my first season coaching the US Adaptive Bobsled group, I wanted to organize a special summer push camp for current and potential athletes. To my knowledge it would be the first adaptive bobsled summer push camp ever. Our director agreed with the plan, so we got to work. We all wanted to see the sport grow and gain further traction in international competition, and to make that happen we needed to increase our own programs here in the United States.

I began planning the itinerary for the three-day camp with a list of ideas for activities and lectures that I felt were crucial to the growth of our veteran athletes as well as the instruction of new recruits. I wanted the athletes and volunteers to feel inspired and experience powerful growth as a group, but I also wanted to review the importance of sportsmanship, discipline, and respect. Most of all, I wanted all the athletes to know how committed I was to helping them succeed. But something was missing.

I felt responsible for the camp's success or failure (familiar territory for a coach). So I knelt down and thanked Heavenly Father for this unique opportunity. Then I expressed my concerns about its outcome. I pled for guidance so that I could be a guiding light for the participants and know how to assist them in their athletic endeavors.

The ideas poured into my mind, and I began a complete rewrite of the camp itinerary. I kept a heavy emphasis on principles and techniques, but I wanted to make sure there was equal time for team building and play. I also planned one-on-one interviews with each athlete so I could get to know them better.

The camp went fantastically. We had athletes from all across the United States with varied backgrounds. Together we passed the days in lunches and lectures, physical testing, and push practice. I even threw in a photo shoot followed by a group barbecue. We spent time studying track videos and discussing the theories of sled piloting. The list of activities goes on, but I know much of our success was because the Lord was willing to guide me as their coach. He knew what these athletes and volunteers needed and had helped me be an instrument, but it wouldn't have been possible without prayer.

One athlete was able to show his daughter what Daddy did on the ice. Another began her path to becoming the first seated female bobsled pilot in the world. Another confessed that his newfound passion for the sport would help him leave a life of drugs behind. Another told me he had been depressed after losing his leg in an accident, and that bobsled camp, with its team atmosphere, had given him a new perspective and hope. To this day I consider the camp one of the greatest accomplishments of my life. It may not have made the news, but we felt we were making history, and I knew I made a difference.

Now, God may not answer our spiritual calls in the time or way we hoped, but he will always bless us for seeking him through prayer. While coaching, I've had to make a driver wait after his or her run because I was watching another sled come down, conversing with a volunteer, or using the video camera. So sometimes I couldn't answer the radio right away, but I would respond as quickly as possible. God is always "online" and eager to talk, but in his infinite wisdom he will give us what we need (not always what we want) in the right circumstances. We need to have faith in his timing.

Can we really go one day without the kneeling before a loving God? Can we really go one day without talking to our "coach" who desires to guide, teach and support us? Heavenly Father is in the perfect position to instruct, correct and encourage us. All we have to do is pick up the spiritual radio of prayer; God is always listening on the other end. As we have been promised, "Draw near unto me and I will draw near unto you; seek me diligently and ye shall find me; ask, and ye shall receive; knock, and it shall be opened unto you" (Doctrine and Covenants 88:63).

IN-GAME STRATEGY FOR SUCCESSFUL PRAYERS

I never learned how powerful prayer is until I got into bobsled. It wasn't just the blessings that came into my athletic endeavors through prayer (although there were many). No, it was out on that track in freezing temperatures that I really felt the burning warmth of the Spirit.

Even the greatest athletes would admit that sometimes it's just nice to have someone there to support you. Although my family and friends have always been supportive, they couldn't attend every practice and competition. So during my first season in bobsled I sensed the Spirit prompting me to pray for strength, guidance, encouragement, clarity of mind, and countless other blessings that I deeply needed. Like Enos, "my soul hungered" (Enos 1:4). Every time I got to the track I felt like Heavenly Father wanted me to reach out to him through prayer.

Before every practice or race I would find a quiet place where I could be alone. Most days, this occurred during my track walk when I walked the course to inspect the ice and visualize myself driving each turn. While I was walking the track to get my mental bearings, I was opening my heart to God so he could help me get my spiritual bearings.

I would kneel down in the middle of a turn and express all my hopes, fears, and faith through prayer. I would ask for help to do my best, pleading that I would be guided as I, in turn, guided the sled. It was during those prayers that I felt a powerful peace. My concerns melted away, and I knew without a doubt that Heavenly Father had heard my cries out there on the track. I cannot express the comfort and confidence that that knowledge brought to me both on the ice and in life.

My friends often comment that when they come to see me race or train, I have a different aura around me. I am calmer, more focused, and more determined. They tell me that I'm "in my world, where I was born to be." I know this change happens, in part, because of my love for the sport, but I testify that it occurs more as a result of my prayers. I felt God's presence during the training sessions or races that followed. That is why I have such a special place in my heart for various turns on different tracks. They have become special places to me where I had such sweet communion with God.

Addressing Prayers to God

Elder Bruce R. McConkie said that "to pray is to speak with God, either vocally or by forming the thoughts involved in the mind."[6] Sometimes our hearts are so full that we can't put our desires into words, but our Heavenly Father will always understand the things our spirit is shouting that our lips can't say. But how should we talk to him?

Whenever I'm coaching, I strive to maintain a warm relationship with the athletes, but I also encourage a professional and courteous atmosphere. While there is always plenty of razzing from both sides, when we are at a race, a public event, or conversing with officials or sponsors, we use a different approach to our communications. The camaraderie is still there, but the language changes to a more respectful tone.

Similarly, we have been counseled to use a respectful tone when speaking with deity. Using "thee," "thou," and "thine" are encouraged, and an underlying reverence should always guide our thoughts and feelings during prayer. When athletes approach me they usually address me as "Coach" out of respect. Likewise, the Savior taught us to begin our prayers with a respectful salutation (Matthew 6:9). By beginning our prayers with an acknowledgment for "Our Father, which art in Heaven," we set the reverent tone for our petitions and conversations. We are a pretty lucky people because we know which "coach" to listen to, unlike the Greek Athenians, whom Paul chastened for worshipping "The unknown god" (Acts 17:23).

I have seen something similar out on the bobsled track when athletes start working with a new coach. They can be initially hesitant, but that isn't because the athletes don't respect the coach's position; they just haven't developed full trust. In some ways their coach is "The unknown god," and the athlete-coach relationship hasn't grown to fruition.

Another scenario that taught me the importance of knowing whom we pray to involves athletes talking to multiple coaches on the track. While this can be extremely helpful for veteran drivers, for newer athletes it can be detrimental. I can think of one new athlete who did this. When he got back to the top of the track, he barely remembered anything the coaches had instructed him to do. Athletes in this situation may not know which voice to focus on and follow. Instead of progressing, they end up less effective.

No wonder we have been commanded to only "pray to [our] Father which is in secret" (Matthew 6:6). We cannot direct our prayers to any other source (Exodus 20:3). As Elder Lawrence Corbridge taught, "Only God can bless us. Only he can sustain us. Only he can cause our hearts to beat and give us breath. Only he can preserve and protect us. Only he can give us strength to bear up the burdens of life. Only he can give us power, knowledge, peace, and joy. Only he can forgive our sins. Only he can heal us. Only he can change us and forge a godly soul. Only he can bring us back into His presence."[7]

Giving Thanks

In 2008, I started The Athlete Outreach Project (www.athleteout-reach.com), a philanthropic organization that uses sport to inspire others. The AOP has allowed me to work with some of the greatest athletes in the Olympic and world-class arena as we participated in countless hospital visits, youth club afternoons, fundraisers, school assemblies, conservation activities, parades, seminars, humanitarian trips, and more. The opportunity to serve others provides tremendous satisfaction, but it's also a lot of work. Sometimes I feel like the project is a full-time job. Is it all worth it?

A few years ago, after a big service activity that I had spent weeks organizing, another athlete—a two-time Olympian—came up to thank me for making outreach events like that one possible. Her kind words of genuine gratitude struck me and motivated me to plan even more events. It also reminded me that gratitude never goes out of style.

Gratitude is an integral part of prayer. The *For the Strength of Youth* pamphlet teaches, "In your prayers, before you ask for blessings, pour out your heart to God in thanks for the blessings you have already received. Thank Him for your family, for friends and loved ones, for leaders and teachers, for the gospel, and for His Son, Jesus Christ." Indeed the Lord taught that "in nothing doth man offend God, or against none is his wrath kindled, save those who confess not his hand in all things" (Doctrine and Covenants 59:21). As King Benjamin said, "O how you ought to thank your heavenly King!" (Mosiah 2:19). When we kneel before our Father in Heaven we should remember to express gratitude for all that he has given us, even the challenges. God's blessings represent his love, while the challenges represent his desire to coach us. Both are necessary to live a championship life.

Expressing gratitude can open our eyes to the blessings that God has given us. It eliminates pride because we will focus more on what we have instead of what others possess. I know athletes that were happier with a sixth place finish than a bronze medal because they were just grateful for the experience.

By expressing gratitude through prayer, we will draw closer to our eternal coach and feel happier. I promise that as you do so, you will learn to feel and recognize his hand and his love in your life even more.

Petitions and Requests

In bobsled you get used to a life of requests of all types. They can come from sponsors, coaches, trainers, officials, teammates, organizations, event-planners, journalists, and everyday fans. And not all the requests are incoming, because as an athlete you have plenty of requests for money, new equipment, track time, health supplements, race entrances, time off from work, and so on. When you dedicate your life to a sport (or any serious goal), you must hold fast to the hope that your goal-driven requests will help you reach your dream.

Prayer is the conduit by which we humbly state our needs to our Father in Heaven. Righteous requests are nothing less than faith-driven petitions for our lives and loved ones. During his visit among the Nephites, the Savior demonstrated this significant ingredient to prayer when he said, "Father, I pray that thou wilt give," "I pray unto thee for them," and "I pray not for the world, but for those who thou hast given me out of the world" (3 Nephi 19:21, 23, 29).

A word of caution: any good coach knows that sometimes he or she has to tell your athletes, assistant coaches, school officials, team parents, sponsors or even the media, "No." Sometimes not giving people what they want can be the best thing for them. They may not understand it at the time, but withholding one thing they desire from them because there is something even better in store is a gift.

Some athletes who suffer injuries and want to get back on the field to play need to be told "no" so they avoid further, perhaps permanent, damage. Maybe an athlete who wants to try doubling the weight of their one-rep max in squats, or maybe a new pilot wants to drive from the top of the track in their first on-ice session. They're great requests and desires, but the coach has to do what is right for the player in the long run.

God has a flawless view of the long run of our lives, and, as the perfect coach, he knows when to say "yes" and when to decline. We should never take a "no" as sign that he does not care about our prayerful petitions; rather, a no demonstrates his magnificent love. It reminds us that our lives are part of his game plan and that he is the head coach here. That may sound harsh at first, but so, too, does a coach saying "no" to the injured athlete who desires to play. Such requests are easily dismissed by people with greater knowledge and experience because they understand that saying "no" is of greater benefit to the game's outcome than saying "yes."

For our prayerful petitions to be efficacious, they must be founded on faith and humility—faith that God cares and can bless us according to our needs, and humility that although "[we] know that he loveth his children; nevertheless, [we] do not know the meaning of all things" (1 Nephi 11:17). Our requests, no matter how heartfelt, must be based on faith in our coach's greater knowledge and the humility to accept his will, even when he says no.

Close in Christ's Name

There's a certain chain of command, a hierarchy, when it comes to bobsled. Push athletes and brakemen usually work with and follow the directions of their pilot while the team captain or athlete representative leads beyond the pilot. The ultimate power for what happens on the ice lies with the coaches and finally the head coach (I'm simplifying here). No matter how long an athlete has been on the ice, coaches have the final word.

While this may sound authoritarian, there's a method to the madness. Just like any sports team or business organization, the pecking order of authority helps everyone understand who makes decisions, who grants requests, and who has the knowledge and credentials to instruct. Can you imagine the chaos that would ensue if you had an entire team of athletes with no coaching, structure, rules, or guiding force to follow? Who would help them improve their skills? Who would put the teams together? Who would have the authority to speak directly to the million-dollar sponsors? Who decides how that money is divided up and used? Who would tell the race jury the athletes are qualified for the competition or that a team has sufficient skills to run from the top of a course?

A chain of command clarifies who has what responsibility and authority. When it comes to prayer, we are blessed because we know that God is our head coach who loves us and has the ultimate say and power over our lives.

So there is an actual chain of command that defines whom we pray to (our Father in Heaven) and who we pray through (our Savior). Jesus taught his disciples that he is "the way, the truth, and the life: no man cometh unto the Father, but by [him]" (John 14:6). These eighteen words remind us that while we can always talk to our eternal head coach, we can do so because Jesus is our Mediator with the Father (Doctrine and Covenants 45:3). That our prayers ascend unto heaven in Jesus's name was a principle taught during his visit with the Nephites (3 Nephi 18:19) and reiterated during the Restoration (Doctrine and Covenants 24:5). As Timothy boldly testified, "there is . . . one mediator between God and men . . . Christ Jesus" (1 Timothy 2:5). When we receive any blessing or answer to prayer, it is through him.

We are greatly blessed to know that God has promised to listen to our prayers wherever and whenever we offer them. I testify that our eternal coach is there and will always listen and bless us during the game of life.

A NECESSITY FOR ALL SEASONS

While we should "let [our] hearts be full, drawn out in prayer unto [God] continually (Alma 34:27), the need and desire for prayer may arise at any time. Whether we are preparing to drive a bobsled down the track or kneeling by our bedside, a deep longing to open our hearts can come for an infinite number of reasons.

February 2009 was a mixed bag for me. My four-man team and I were improving our times (we set a new team best on the fourth); I had enjoyed a relatively good season; my social life was going well (minus being single); and my health was in top form—which is usually when the bottom falls out.

I had been working for a good-sized travel company as a graphic and web designer for a few years. The people were great, the pay was good, and the flexibility was perfect for bobsled and school. And then I was laid off. The economic downturn in the United States was not kind to the travel industry. People understandably put basic needs like food and housing over vacations when they lost their jobs. I survived the first round of layoffs, but not the second. Amy, my supervisor, did not want me to go, but the decision had not been hers to make. She cried when I cleaned out my desk, but, as you'll see, she had my back the whole time.

Like most Americans who found themselves unexpectedly unemployed, I was concerned. The paychecks stopped, but the bills kept coming. I lived off my savings for a bit, but even that began to dry up after a while. I found some sporadic design jobs, but the reality of grown-up life was catching up. I worried about losing my insurance and my car. Some days I worried if I would have food to eat. I was never destitute, but I also knew the upcoming season would be difficult if I couldn't find the necessary funds. One Saturday, I found myself looking at my two-man bobsled, safely stored for the summer in my parents' garage, wondering if I would get to take her out on the ice next October. What was I going to do?

I felt a strong urge to pray, so I bowed my head and offered some heartfelt pleas. I humbly asked God for help, laying out my worries that I might default on my financial responsibilities and be unable to sled (donations and sponsorships fell off because of the economy). Could he help me? Would he help me?

I don't remember why, but I walked out the back door and around the side of their shed. To my surprise, there was a large rusty coin sitting right in the middle of the sidewalk. Intrigued, I picked it up and turned it over in my hands. Later we discovered that it was an old one-dollar piece from 1845. As I sat there wondering how it even got there, I felt a warmth flow into my heart. The Spirit seemed to whisper that the coin was a reassurance from our Heavenly Father that he would help me during my financially difficult time and that he cared about my concerns and fears. A few months later my old supervisor, Amy, called and asked me to come back. I still have that coin and no, I've never cleaned it. I want to keep it just the way I found it that jobless Saturday afternoon.

The need for prayer can be spurred by desired guidance, emotional comfort, blessings of safety, a need for help, forgiveness of a sin, or heaven's assistance with some other challenging problem. But when the need or desire arises, don't hesitate to pray. If there is one thing that bobsled has taught me, it's that prayer is available all the time.

The apostle James counseled, "If any of you lack wisdom, let him ask of God, that giveth to all men liberally, and upbraideth not; and it shall be given him" (James 1:5). It's nice knowing we have a coach who will never upbraid our heartfelt desires! As Zenos, a great prophet of Old Testament times, proclaimed, "Yea, and [he is] merciful unto [his] children when they cry unto [him]" (Alma 33:68).

What is the first thing that goes through your mind when adversity shows up? Maybe it's the day of the big game and you feel nervous, or maybe you feel shy on the first day of school. Did you think to pray? The next time you're struggling, pray first. I promise that you will find peace, comfort, and strength to make it through anything.

Zenos's words remind us that God is a merciful and loving coach who wants us to turn to him whenever we need help on the field. He helped me when I learned to drive four-man bobsleds.

While the basic principles of driving a four-man bobsled are the same as a two-man sled, there are some differences. Four-man sleds are heavier, which causes them to reach higher speeds. The sleds are also longer: twelve and a half feet versus the eight and a half of a two-man sled. These differences lead to the reality that if you make a mistake in a four-man sled, your errors can be harder to correct. When you watch bobsled competitions, you will probably see more crashes in the four-man races.

After being invited to attend a special four-man driving course in 2004, I was excited and nervous. It was an opportunity that would open new doors in the sport for me and for my teammates, but like so many of life's big breaks, this one initially created some anxiety-induced hesitation. Not only would I be learning to drive four-man sleds, but I would also have to take turns riding as a passenger while others drove. That concerned me the most because some drivers were new and inexperienced.

Over the next few weeks leading up to our first day, I prayed often about my concerns, safety, and desires regarding the course. I felt the Spirit's calming influence, and I knew that God was listening and would answer my prayers.

When I stepped onto the ice for the first day of four-man training, the fear and concerns were gone. I smiled as I put on my helmet before my first run. This might sound funny, but I could almost sense Heavenly Father there on the side of the track, watching and cheering me on. I got into that sled knowing that everything was going to be okay.

The ability to pray, whenever and wherever we need to, is a great blessing and a winning technique for life. The ancient Greeks went to great lengths to put on huge ceremonies surrounding their "prayers" to the different gods. But the knowledge that our eternal coach, even God, is always willing to listen to even the simplest of prayers should give us tremendous strength to face our daily competitions with faith. Prayer, like training for the Olympics, is an everyday thing. That's how spiritual gold medals are won.

PREGAME PREPARATION FOR PRAYER

If you ever come to the bobsled track before a competition, one of the first things you'll notice is how busy the start area is. Athletes warm up, trucks run to and fro, and officials walk around and check everything. When you throw in the journalists, cameras, fans, and track crew, the top of the track is a hive of activity. Perhaps the strangest thing you will see, though, is a pre-race ritual that many sled pilots perform before the competition begins.

Pilots who prep before a competition find a quiet place to stand and hold their hands in front of them as though driving an imaginary sled. With closed eyes, they turn around in circles or half circles while imagining that they are flying down the track at full speed. In their minds they picture pushing off the start block, loading into the sled, and then driving a perfect run down the course.

It looks funny, but this is an important pre-race technique for a driver. It's called "mental imagery," which is simply going through an activity in your mind before you perform the deed physically. In sports psychology we learn that correct imagery involves full immersion in the scene unfolding in the mind's eye. Drivers imagine the sounds of the crowd, the crunch of the ice, the pressures their bodies will feel as they go through the turns, and what they'll feel emotionally when they win or have a great run.

The benefits of mental imagery are obliging for competitive success. Running through a routine in their minds before "stepping up to the plate" can help athletes develop greater confidence, focus their attention on the task at hand, and establish an appropriate level of mental and physical excitement. Bobsled pilots want to be physically primed to push the sled, but their minds need to be clear once they sit down and start driving. I always say, "Push like an animal; drive like a fighter pilot." By reviewing what will happen once you step on the starting line, you can eliminate some of the psychological background noise caused by nerves or fear.

Mental imagery is everywhere in sports. Gymnasts run through their floor routine before stepping onto the mat, golfers sink the putt in their mind before they touch the club, and batters imagine hitting the ball with ease before they face the pitcher. Mental imagery is even used in bowling, fishing, badminton, and curling. Yes, curling.

When you want to win gold you need your body, mind, and soul ready for game day. To paraphrase President Monson, when the time for action arrives, the time for preparation is past.[8] Mental imagery provides that important preparation. That's why sports psychology is such a serious science and why teams and athletes pay big money from experts in sports psychology.

So what does mental imagery have to do with prayer? While we all may not use imagery the way athletes do, we have been counseled to regularly use its sister technique, meditation. As Job was instructed, "prepare thine heart, and stretch out thine hands toward him" (Job 11:13). How do we prepare our hearts before we stretch out our hands toward heaven? We do so through mental imagery, such as meditation.

We can define *meditation* as continued or extended thought, reflection, or contemplative spiritual introspection. The word comes from the Latin *meditationem*, which means "to meditate, to think over, or to consider."

But what do we meditate on for prayer? As bobsled pilots at the top of the track we think about what we are going to do in each turn and straightaway. Before praying, to help our minds and spirits become more in tune, we can ponder the things that are troubling us or review the blessings we have been given. We can quietly consider the things we need and take stock of our own spiritual standing before the Lord. Through meditation we can raise our attitude to a more humble plane and exercise our faith by remembering our dependence upon God.

Just as mental imagery helps athletes calm their bodies and minds, meditation helps us overcome the "natural man" and bring us into alignment with the Spirit. Scripture study and fasting are also powerful ways to get into the proper mind-set and help us place the spiritual above the physical. Then, with our minds in tune, we can approach God with humble hearts and a greater sense of reverence and worship. In this way we will have more enriching and spiritually rewarding experiences with prayer as we open up our hearts to receive the guidance and strength we may be seeking. As

President David O. McKay taught, "Meditation is one of the most secret, most sacred doors through which we pass into the presence of the Lord."[9]

As sled pilots, imaging gets our minds "in the zone" so we can focus while driving down the track. Spiritually speaking, active and reflective meditation puts our hearts, minds, and spirits into the right state to receive the guidance and blessings we seek as we "drive" the track of life. President Gordon B. Hinckley wrote, "The trouble with most of our prayers is that we give them as if we were picking up the telephone and ordering groceries—we place our order and hang up. We need to meditate, contemplate, think of what we are praying about and for and then speak to the Lord as one man speaketh to another."[10]

Mental imagery was one of the first things I reviewed with the adaptive bobsled pilots I coached because I could tell which drivers never ran through the track in their minds before getting into the sled. I observed that athletes who did not practice imaging before a race were not mentally—and therefore physically—ready to drive. While coaching from the side of the track, I could tell they were "behind the sled," a phrase that means their driving was more about reacting than guiding. Since they weren't mentally prepared, they were fighting to make it down the track upright. I could see it in their eyes too—a fear that they were barely maintaining control. Mental imagery would have allowed them to drive in a relaxed manner and focus on piloting the sled in a way that would provide a winning time. A lack of preparation left them ill-equipped mentally and physically to obtain the results they desired.

Once the athletes were taught how to use mental meditation to drive the track in their minds before a run, they approached the ice more confidently. Over time I could see they no longer drove haphazardly; instead, they were mentally focused, which improved their piloting.

For prayer, meditation helps put us "in the zone," spiritually speaking, by inviting the Holy Ghost to be our companion throughout the experience. This is an important aspect of prayer because only through a spiritual mind-set can we receive the guidance and comfort we seek. As Paul taught, "the natural man receiveth not the things of the Spirit of God: for they are foolishness unto him: neither can he know them, because they are spiritually discerned" (1 Corinthians 2:14). Meditation can help us better understand the answers and promptings the Lord would give us.

Nephi reminds us that the Spirit "teacheth a man to pray" (2 Nephi 32:8), but we know the Holy Ghost can also teach us how to pray and help us know what to pray for. As spiritual beings having a mortal experience, part of our responsibility is to work through our own natural desires, fears, and thoughts and learn to pray in tune with the Spirit. In this way, we will not "ask anything that is not expedient for [us]," that "it shall turn unto [our] condemnation" (Doctrine and Covenants 88:65).

I love the powerful account of the prayers offered by Jesus's disciples on the American continent. In 3 Nephi 19, we read that "they did still continue without ceasing, to pray unto [God]; and they did not multiply many words, for it was given unto them what they should pray, and they were filled with desire" (verse 24). What a glorious experience to have our personal petitions guided by the voice of the Spirit, to have our hearts drawn out in prayer, and to feel that beautiful connection with our Heavenly Father.

I had such an experience on January 28, 1998. Randy, my coach, sat in turn twelve at the Park City track and watched me drive a terrible run down the course. I don't know what was going on; I just couldn't get my mind in the game, so we brushed the sidewalls out of a few turns and fishtailed in one of the straightaways. We crossed the finish line with a less-than-pleasing time, and I was disappointed with my performance. Randy could tell. He knew when to push, when to instruct, and when to let his athletes learn the hard way. We weren't using radios that day, so I had to jog down to where Randy was standing and talk to him face to face. He was nice about everything, but he did point out a few of the many mistakes I had made.

After our conversation, I walked toward the track's control tower and plopped down on a cement barrier to wait for the sled truck. As I sat and stewed and grumbled, I felt the Spirit whisper a simple invitation: "Pray."

Pray? After an awful run down the track? Pray in the middle of a snow-covered Park City valley about a sport that was driving me crazy? Why would God care about that? I hesitated, but the invitation came with a deep sense of parental care. I knew our Father in Heaven is mindful of his children and the things they care about, so I took a deep breath and told him how bad my last run was, explained how frustrated I felt, and asked for his help to improve. I've never asked him to help me win, but I've always felt confident asking him to help me do my best, and my last run was not my best.

As I sat on that cold cement wall, my breath crystallizing in the air, I felt a peaceful warmth come over my entire body, like I was being enveloped in pure love. The frustration melted away, and my mind instantly cleared. I got up, climbed into the truck, got back to the top, and drove my second run perfectly. It felt like my hands were guided as I piloted the sled. I remember crossing the finish line feeling so alive. I got out of the sled and felt an overwhelming sense of gratitude.

Now some would argue that I was just "in the zone," but I knew Heavenly Father heard my prayer. I also knew that the Spirit guided my prayer. I'll never forget it.

By preparing ourselves for prayer, we will have more soul-refreshing experiences like the one I described. With the help of the Holy Ghost, we will pray for that which is expedient for us and see the Lord's promise that, "Whatsoever ye shall ask the Father in my name, which is right, believing ye shall receive, behold it shall be given unto you" (3 Nephi 18:20).

But our preparations need to go beyond our minds and hearts alone. For prayer to be a true conversation with our eternal coach, we need to listen for the answers the Lord gives. I have had athletes ask me for advice or instruction, only to have them ignore everything I said. Why ask if you won't do?

In this modern day of instant communication, we have become accustomed to sending a message (text, email, instant message, and so on) and then waiting for a response to come back. We go about our day, putting the conversation out of our minds until the phone rings or an email pops up when the person has responded. It can be easy for this mind-set to affect our prayers. We send up our "prayer orders" then go about our business without listening or looking for a response.

Some bobsled, luge, and skeleton athletes make careful notes following their post-run conversations with their coaches. They write down things they did right and should do again and things they did wrong that their coach wants them to correct. Some entries may contain details about the way they set up their sled for the session or competition, what runners they used, the ice and air temperatures, weather conditions, time of day, and so on. These notebooks become important sources of information for athletes as they continue to track their progress. They also demonstrate that the individual is willing to listen to and learn from their coaches, thus leading to greater growth as an athlete.

In prayer, a sincere willingness to listen and learn maintains an open avenue of communication with the Spirit. Instead of mentally typing out a prayer and clicking "send" before we jump into bed or rush out the door, we should spend a few minutes quietly listening for the Lord's answers. Preparation for prayer isn't just about the before; it is also about the after.

Some people, like bobsled athletes, find it helpful to carry a small notebook throughout the day to jot down the ideas and feelings that come through the Spirit. Others write in a journal at the end of the day about the specific answers they received. Whatever method you choose, find a way to demonstrate to the Lord that you are ready and willing to take note of his answers. This willingness to listen for your coach's voice will demonstrate a humility and faith that will deeply enrich your experiences with prayer.

Additionally, if we truly desire to prepare ourselves for prayer then we must do our part to make the requested blessings come to pass. As President David O. McKay taught, "Sincere praying implies that when we ask for any virtue or blessing, we should work for the blessing and cultivate the virtue." An athlete can ask his or her coach for a chance to play, but he or she has to work for it if he or she wants it to happen.

Also, while the channels of prayer are always open, we should find a private place to converse with the Lord when possible (Alma 34:26). The scriptures are full of the examples of faithful men and women who sought the solitude of a mountaintop or the privacy of a tent in which to converse with God. The solitude afforded by our secret places can provide a quiet place to focus on becoming more in tune with the Spirit.

One of my secret places to pray is the bobsled track itself. I know that sounds odd given the public nature of the facility, especially during a competition. But I have found the inside of the track to be a quiet and comforting place to kneel on the ice and pray. Some days I didn't have time to pray while walking the track, so I would find a quiet place near the top of the track, even if it meant slipping into the equipment room to be alone. Could I have prayed while sitting with all the other athletes or while walking around the start area crowd? Sure, but by taking the time to find a quiet place where I could focus on my conversation with my Heavenly Father, I found my heart and mind much clearer and the peace and comfort of the Spirit to be greater. By finding a secluded place to pray, we can better prepare ourselves to receive the Spirit and the uplift we seek.

We can also work to find answers to the questions that we pray about. As the Lord reminded Oliver Cowdery, we cannot expect guidance "when [we take] no thought save it [is] to ask [the Lord]" (Doctrine and Covenants 9:7). As we search the scriptures, discuss our concerns with family or friends, and study the problems out in our minds, we are doing our part and preparing ourselves for guidance. The Lord knows the value of self-sufficiency.

As a coach, I could tell the athletes everything I know about every technique of our sport. But all parents, teachers, and coaches know some things are better learned by experience, trial, and error. I've had to explain certain principles over and over again to drivers because they weren't getting it. At first I thought I wasn't being clear enough, so I tried rephrasing my words. Still nothing. Finally, I realized these pilots were unwilling to do their part to apply their own mental faculties. Their lack of effort made it difficult to come to an understanding.

In contrast, some drivers constantly used their creative and critical thinking to deepen their comprehension of the techniques required to excel. We met in the middle because I brought my knowledge and experience to the table while they brought a desire to learn and dissect everything about our sport. They asked me to help them progress, but they also used their agency to figure things out on their own.

The principles surrounding the necessity of effort on our part are clearly demonstrated in "Moroni's promise." Moroni counsels interested parties to first read the Book of Mormon and ponder (meditate) upon its truths. They need to think, really think, about what they have read and decide how they feel about it. Only then can they enjoy Moroni's promise that if they ask God with faith and full purpose of heart, he will manifest the truth of the book through the Holy Ghost (Moroni 10:3–5).

One last lesson. As a bobsled pilot, I don't wear gloves when driving. I know this sounds crazy considering (a) bobsled is a winter sport, which means cold temperatures, and (b) the implied dangers of ice burns on my bare skin. But there is a method to my madness.

I drive bare-handed because I can better feel the response of the sled's steering system on the ice. Since we drive bobsleds by holding on to metal rings shaped like a big "D" (surprisingly called D-rings), I find that gloves softened the sensations. Bare-handed driving allows me to better feel what happens on the ice, what the surface conditions feel like, what pressures the sled's runner feels, and so forth. Some pilots love their gloves, but I prefer to feel everything I can even if it means suffering a little cold air.

I bring this up because if we are to fully prepare ourselves for prayer, one of the most important things we can do is approach our Father in Heaven with clean hands. Please don't misunderstand; I'm not saying we should stop praying if we are struggling with sin. In fact, we should pray more when we are struggling. But just as driving bare-handed allows me to better feel the vibrations and movement of the steering system, so too will praying with a pure heart help us better feel the whisperings of the Spirit. The spirit-dulling sensation of sin, like the padding of a thick winter glove, will be absent and we will have full access to the guidance of the Holy Ghost.

Whatever our situation may be, I know that by taking the time to prepare our hearts and minds for prayer, we will enjoy a deeper connection with God and a closer relationship with the Savior. The Spirit will become a close companion, and our desires will fall in line with the will of the Lord. Like progress on the bobsled track, it may come little by little, but the Lord will bless us for every effort we make to have richer and more spiritual prayers. And we don't even have to spin around in circles and wear spandex to do it.

1, 2, WHAT DO WE PRAY FOR? ABSOLUTELY ANYTHING.

I'll say it again: as a bobsled athlete you do a fair share of asking (begging) during your career. If you go into a sliding sport to become a fast millionaire, I'm going to dash your hopes right now. Many Olympic athletes struggle to make ends meet, and since bobsled is the second most expensive sport in the Olympic field, the financial bottom line becomes an all-controlling master in many ways. Luckily, many supportive people give what they can to help American athletes pay those bills, and I can tell you that every dollar helps.

In 1999, a few months before I left for my mission, my brakeman and I decided to participate in one final race. Since it was my last "big show" for two years, I wanted to make it an experience to remember, so I sought the ever-appreciated financial support to purchase new uniforms, helmets, and other equipment. My father helped me create a sponsorship package to send out to companies, including one called Quality Quilters out of Texas. I met the owner, Bill Bishop, years before at an automotive race in California, and I believe the nicest word I would have used to describe him was *cantankerous*. When we met, the first thing he pointed out was my obvious struggle with teenage acne—not my first choice of conversation topics.

I know, I know: "thou shalt not judge." But in order for you to truly appreciate the next part of the story, I couldn't leave any of this out.

A week or so after the sponsorship packages went out, my dad received a call from Mr. Bishop asking about "the bobsled thing." Dad explained what I was doing and what the money would be used for. When he told Mr. Bishop the price for the top-level sponsorship, Bill said he would take two—as in two gold-level sponsorships. Was there more benefit to him to take two? No, but this man—whom I thought to be crusty and rough around the edges, believed in me and my dreams enough to give double the required amount. And it only happened because I asked.

The story doesn't end there. I made sure to send Mr. Bishop a letter containing my gratitude and thoughts, including a summation of my change of heart concerning his character. I never forgot his kindness, but the letter slipped from my mind until later on my mission. This man who taught me that a heart of gold may be hidden behind a rough exterior passed away shortly after he chose to support my dreams. I felt his loss but was grateful for my knowledge of the plan of salvation. I imagined Bill was entertaining those on the other side of the veil with his dry wit.

My parents really dropped the bomb when they wrote to say that Bill's family chose to share my thank-you letter during his funeral. I guess my note impacted him so much and explained Mr. Bishop's spirit so well that it became a central point in the service.

I was humbled. This man whose depth of soul matched the depths of his pockets, who was associated with world-famous racing teams, and who took the time to support a young man's athletic dreams was touched by a simple, heartfelt letter sent by a missionary. In turn, his kindness left a deep impression upon my own soul, and I have tried to live up to the trust and belief he had in me as an athlete and a person.

But beyond financial support, as a bobsled athlete you become accustomed to asking for knowledge as well. No competitor claims to know everything (though it may sound that way), so athletes must reach out to those who know or who are studying to know more. You seek out knowledge of the best health and diet plans, fitness regimes, mental training programs, and so forth. Knowledge is power, and in sports that power can mean the difference between victory and loss.

You also ask for support—yes, financial support, but also emotional and mental support. You ask for the best equipment to train and compete with. You ask your coaches for opportunities to progress and, most of all, for the chance to follow your dreams as far as your coaches, hard work, and potential can take you. And you have to ask yourself for the power and motivation to dig deep and push your mind, heart, and body even further.

We rightfully cheer the victory of the athlete on the medals podium, but we often forget the countless supporters who helped mold that competitor into the champion they have become. The truth is champion status can happen only if an athlete will ask for and then accept help. Without this humility (or desperation), many athletes' careers would end before they even began.

In the spiritual sense, prayer is the greatest avenue for help that we have access to in mortality. Like athletes, we can ask for the knowledge, support, and blessings we need to succeed. Through prayer we can open the windows of heaven and receive strength, renewal, and comfort, but first we must ask. Indeed, no scriptural message is repeated more often than the invitation to pray to a loving Father in Heaven who wants the best for his children.

The Lord reminded us of this eternal fact when he said, "Or what man is there of you, whom if his son ask bread, will he give him a stone? Or if he ask a fish, will he give him a serpent? If ye then, being evil [imperfect beings], know how to give good gifts unto your children, how much more shall your Father which is in heaven give good things to them that ask him?" (Matthew 7:9–11).

No good-intentioned coach would ever give his or her athlete a "stone" or "serpent." He or she would do his or her best to help his or her athletes in any way professionally possible. The Savior reminds us that our heavenly coach is always ready to help us progress in body, mind, and spirit if we humbly solicit his help. When Adam and Eve were expelled from the Garden of Eden, the first commandment they received was to pray (Abraham 3:25). Seeking God's support has been man's prerogative ever since.

What, then, do we ask for, and how should we ask? President Joseph F. Smith counseled, "We should not ask the Lord for that which is unnecessary or which would not be beneficial to us. We should ask for that which we need, and we should ask in faith."[11]

Whenever athletes ask for financial support, most people want to know what the money will be used for—they want to know if our need is sincere. Donated funds may go toward a new sled, travel costs, higher-quality runners, and so on. But sincere need and faith are perhaps two of the most fundamental aspects of our prayerful petitions. How sincere are we in our asking, and how much faith do we have in God's ability to provide? The good news is having just a "particle of faith" or a "desire to believe" (Alma 32:27) can be enough to open the windows of heaven. The scriptures are full of countless examples of men and women who sincerely asked in faith and received blessings untold.

As a coach, I had the opportunity to work with athletes possessing various levels of commitment. Some came to training sessions with a less-than-enthusiastic heart, while others demonstrated a real hunger to progress. This latter group were the athletes who sincerely asked and gratefully accepted the knowledge, equipment, and opportunities provided.

Sometimes athletes would ask for something, such as an opportunity to forerun (hill-test) for a race, but I could think of a handful of their teammates who had been showing double, triple, or even quadruple their amount of effort. These athletes wanted the glory of the experience, but their work ethic was lacking. They were neither sincere nor dedicated to their proclaimed desires to become competitors of the highest caliber and to represent their country in the future. Given our limited list of equipment, training time, and opportunities, I had to make decisions about who was really sincere and ready for such opportunities and who was not. It wasn't easy or fun to make those choices, but every once in a while the occasion called for it.

Unlike a lowly bobsled coach, however, our Father in Heaven has limitless power and blessings available if we but ask. That being said, he has set up parameters defining what he asks of us before we can ask of him.

As coach, I was more prone to work with those athletes who had sincere desires and who had humility to learn. The more I experienced this transfer of knowledge or necessary opportunities to sincere athletes, the more I came to understand our responsibilities regarding prayerful petition. Not only must we bend our will to the Lord's so we won't find ourselves "ask[ing] amiss" that we may consume the blessing "upon [our] lusts" (James 4:3), but we must, as Moroni counseled, "ask with a sincere heart, [and] with real intent" (Moroni 10:4). Maybe the easiest way to know if we are sincere is to examine our motives. Is our request (a) in line with the principles of the gospel; (b) something that will bring us closer to God, the Church, and our family; and (c) something that we sincerely need? Maybe that's why I never received the lightsaber I prayed for when I was six.

The list of what we should pray for is as varied as the sands of the sea, but as long as the need and desire is real and as long as we believe God can indeed bless us, what we pray for is open to the circumstances we find ourselves in.

The following list is far from conclusive, but I hope it will provide a basic foundation that can strengthen and enrich your own personal prayers.

Spiritual and Emotional Comfort

I wish I could tell you that my bobsled years have always been sunshine and rainbows. I'd like to give you a glossy, Hollywood version full of incredible highs, successes, and happiness. But I'd be lying.

Because of my battles with depression and anxiety, which led to feelings of low self-esteem and a controlling desire for perfection, my journey has been full of humbling lows to stretch my faith, hope, and endurance at times to what I believed was my breaking point. I do not say this to evoke sympathy or sorrow, but rather to remind us all that mortal life is a test, and what test would truly suffice for the eternities if it didn't push us to our limit?

In trying times, prayer has become a teammate that provides comfort and strength. I didn't always have a conscious thought to pray; often there was just a deep, inner desire to speak to God, to bare my soul and inner feelings to a coach who is always listening. I know now that those feelings are often invitations from the Spirit for us to turn to he who notices a sparrow's fall. The Lord knows the needs of our hearts, even when we feel like we are at the end of our rope.

We all have days when the burdens are so heavy we fall to our knees. Prayer is the key to this deliverance and to the comfort we seek, even when our mouths can't say what our hearts feel. God understands our pain. Just as he has delivered me time and time again from the darkness, so too will he comfort you in the midst of your afflictions and deliver you when the time is right.

A few years after my mission, I dated a female skeleton athlete (break out the tissues). We met over the summer and found ourselves dating as the bobsled season began, so we had some good times around the track and Park City.

As the season progressed, however, she spent more and more time with another male bobsled athlete, and though she assured me they were just friends, I wasn't sure. Note: listen to your instincts. A few months later, she dumped me and started dating him. Okay, big group "aw." And this was after she talked me into riding down the Park City track with this kid the first time he drove a four-man bobsled when I knew he was going to crash (which he did).

It was a heartbreak that came at an already tough time. I was struggling to keep up with my workload, schoolwork, training, family life, and Church responsibilities. Plus, my anxiety was not really helping. I had one of those moments where you look to heaven and ask, "God are you still up there?"

I know this heartache is nothing compared to the suffering so many face, but I hope the rest of the story helps. During this period, I spent a lot of time in prayer because sometimes I felt I had nowhere else to go to. I testify to you that God did know my needs and hurts, and he sent comfort through the Spirit and the support of good friends. I know that he hears our prayers in our times of need and will answer them with the comfort and support that we need if we but ask.

If you are struggling, I implore you to seek the comfort and strength to be gained through prayer. I know that if you do, you will feel God saying to you, as he said to Alma and his people, "Lift up you heads and be of good comfort, for I know of the covenant which ye have made unto me. . . . And I will also ease the burdens which are put upon your shoulders, that even you cannot feel them upon your backs, even while you are in bondage; and this will I do . . . that ye may know of a surety that I, the Lord God, do visit my people in their afflictions" (Mosiah 24:13–13).

Forgiveness

"I'm sorry." You won't hear those words often in the world of sports. It's not that athletes don't feel bad about the mistakes they make on the field; they just usually have a healthy understanding that no one is perfect, that mistakes can be good teachers, and that they can try again tomorrow.

I learned that lesson during a race in February 1998. We had just returned from a trip to the Calgary, Canada, track, and our season had about a week left, so Coach decided to have one last competition before summer break. At the time, an interesting hodge-podge of practice sleds with some athletes driving from the top and others driving from lower starts made up our program, so Coach chose to make it a consistency race. Whichever driver had the two closest times after two runs won.

I was excited. I was just coming off a post-Canada kick and the thought of ending the season with a win was a highlight I looked forward to, a highlight that unfortunately I would miss.

For the race we partnered up with another program participant who would brake for us, then we would brake for him, then rinse and repeat so we both received two runs. The athlete I was put with—I'll call him Aaron—had also attended the Canadian training camp, but his performance on the Calgary track hadn't been impressive. Not wanting to be negative or cause a scene, however, I hopped into the driver's seat and we took off.

When Aaron took his turn in the driver's seat, I was uneasy. I felt he was not 100 percent ready to be back on the ice. But, again, wanting to do the right thing, I sat in the brakeman's seat and prepared myself. I could tell it was going to be exciting after the first three turns: Aaron drove all over the place. I knew a crash was probably on its way.

After nine more curves we headed for turn thirteen, the sled-eater of the Park City track. I tried to get as low in my seat as possible. As we roared out of turn twelve and into thirteen, I thought, "This is it!" Moments later, an eerie silence descended before the sled rolled out of the turn and onto its side, which sounded like a car grinding against a steel barrier. I saw Aaron pull into the nose of the sled and look at me with eyes as wide as dinner plates. My first reaction was anger that I was in the situation, but as I tucked lower to avoid having my shoulder burn on the ice, I realized anger was pointless. We all make mistakes. I'd made a few mistakes during my first race too.

We stopped at the bottom of the course, and the track crew and EMTs helped us out of the sled. Neither of us was hurt, and the track crew cleared the sled for use, so we hopped into a truck and went back to the top for my second and final run.

I could have given Aaron a hard time for flipping us, but I knew that if I wanted to do my best I needed to forgive him for his driving errors and forgive myself for mine. The irony of it all was this was a consistency race. In order to win, I needed to purposely drive rough so I could match my first poor downtime.

That's if I wanted to win, which I no longer did. I knew that forgiveness was worth more than gold in this situation, so I apologized to my coach for the errors made on my first run and to Aaron for giving him a few bumps on the way down the track. I also mentally forgave Aaron for crashing us. After all, I couldn't change the past, but I could affect the future. I made mistakes on my first run during the competition, but I wasn't about to relive or to dwell on them. I wanted do better no matter what.

It turns out I drove one of the cleanest runs I had all season with the downtime to prove it. Unfortunately, the difference between my bad first run and my killer second one put me at the bottom of the consistency race results, but I didn't care. I considered the second run a clean slate for me to build upon the next season.

In the competition of life we will all make mistakes, even some that appear to "lose the game" as it were. But like elite athletes, we must constantly remind ourselves that we learn from our errors and can come back stronger and better if we want to. Because of the Atonement of Jesus Christ, our mistakes on the playing field of life do not affect the final scoreboard in the sky.

While we discuss repentance in later chapters, prayer is a crucial step in the forgiveness process. As Elder Bruce R. McConkie taught, "A sinner must always confess all sins, great and small, to the Lord."[12] Before his marvelous experience with the angel Moroni, Joseph Smith said, "I betook myself to prayer and supplication to Almighty God for forgiveness of all my sins and folly, and also for a manifestation to me, that I might know of my state and standing before him."[13] A prayerful petition for forgiveness can cause miracles, which include a cleansing and a healing of our souls.

I know that if we will approach our Father in Heaven in prayer with broken hearts and contrite spirits, he will forgive our mistakes and heal our broken hearts, and we can then feel that "[our] sins are forgiven [us]" (Enos 1:5).

Guidance

When I started driving sleds, my coaches taught us about specific points on the track called pressure points, which are spots on a turn that you adjust your steering in or toward. How a pilot drives at these points can make or break a competition run, not to mention that missing a pressure point can lead to a hard hit or a crash.

When you enter a large turn, the sled is traveling in a forward bearing. While the turn curves around, the sled wants to keep going in that forward direction (thank you, Newton's law of Physics). If you don't make a steering adjustment at that "pressure point," you will go straight to the top of the turn (ouch). At the second pressure point, if you don't steer out, you will stay on the turn too long and flip over at the exit (also ouch).

These pressure points are crucial to guiding a bobsled quickly down the track, plus the way you steer out of one turn affects the point in which you enter the next. Think of it as a big game of connect the dots played at eighty to ninety miles per hour. In life we have "pressure points" or guiding moments that come into our lives, and how we drive through them will affect the rest of our run down the track of mortality. Which college we should attend, who we should marry, which career we should pursue, where we should live, and so on. The list of guiding "pressure points" is endless, but the principle holds true: where we "drive" our lives at these crucial points will determine where we are headed.

I remember walking the Park City track one morning and whistling in amazement when I reached turn six. A fairly new women's team from Canada had trained the previous day and must have enjoyed a wild ride. They completely missed the first pressure point so up they went—*BAM!*—right to the top of the turn. They came down in the middle of the turn and back up at the second pressure point. *BAM*! Another hit. I don't know how they made it through without crashing, but I bet they both walked away with some good bumps and bruises.

Our Heavenly Father knows where those crucial "pressure points" are in our lives, and he wants to help us drive safely through them. Just as our bobsled coaches would illuminate the points on each turn, God can point out which direction we should go when an important decision is laid before us. No wonder Alma told his son Helaman to "counsel with the Lord in all thy doings, and he will direct thee for good" (Alma 37:37). When we humbly bring a problem before the Lord, we can have faith that he will help us make the right choice.

But there's a caveat to this promise. Just like when I study the bobsled track before driving it, our Heavenly Father expects us to do our part in the decision-making process by studying the options or question out in our mind and coming to a decision of our own first (Doctrine and Covenants 9:8). Figuring out as much information as we can, including the pros and cons of each outcome, will allow us to make a decision based on our limited understanding. Then we can take our decision to the Lord and ask for ratification.

A powerful example of doing our part in praying for guidance is found in Ether 2:16–18. The Jaredites built their ships according to the Lord's instructions, but there were two issues: (1) there was no internal light for the people to see with, and (2) since they were watertight ships, they were also airtight (verse 19). So, the Brother of Jared simply asked what to do, and the Lord instructed him to make stoppable air holes in the top and the bottom of the vessels. One problem solved, but then the Lord asked this mighty prophet to come up with a solution for the light dilemma. The Lord could have told him what to do, so why did he give the Brother of Jared the task?

Perhaps for the same reason, he asks us to study our problems and circumstances and make a decision before asking for guidance. "It is not meet that [the Lord] should command in all things" (Doctrine and Covenants 58:26). Like the perfect coach that he is, our Father in Heaven knows that we need to learn and develop through trial and error, success and failure, and effort and inspiration. For faith to be saving, it must include good works or efforts (James 2:20), and faithful prayers are no different.

As President Harold B. Lee taught, "It was as though the Lord were saying to [the Brother of Jared], 'Look, I gave you a mind to think with, and I gave you agency to use it. Now you do all you can to help yourself with this problem; and then, after you've done all you can, I'll step in to help you.' . . . This is the principle in action."[14]

It took creativity and effort for the Brother of Jared to molten those rocks out of the mountainside. Can we expect the Lord to touch our minds with light like he did those stones without laboring on our own behalf? The Lord will bless us with guidance and inspiration, but only "after all we can do" (1 Nephi 2:25). Sometimes the "all we can do" part isn't much, but let's do what we can.

When you drive a bobsled on the correct line through a turn, you just know it. You feel it with the speed, the acceleration, and the pressure. Similarly, if the decision we bring to the Lord is correct, the Holy Ghost will ratify our decision through peace and a burning in our bosom. If it is wrong, we will have a stupor of thought (Doctrine and Covenants 9:8–9).

It is my hope that we can have the faith to take our important choices to the Lord so he can coach us to gold medal experience in life. Many times we use the excuse that we didn't know which way to go or what direction to take, but in those moments we should remember the question that Nephi asked his brothers: "Have ye inquired of the Lord?" (1 Nephi 15:8).

Our coach is always ready to instruct, and I testify that if we exercise faith through our efforts to come to a decision on our own before seeking heavenly confirmation, he will guide us to a championship life. Through prayer we can find those perfect "pressure points" on the bobsled track of life and discover all the Olympic-level wonders and blessings that the Lord has in store for us.

Praying for Others

While preparing to help with a race during the beginning of the 2006–2007 season, I found myself a bit uneasy. I had been asked to forerun, which means my team and I tested the hill before the competition. I was already feeling overwhelmed with school, work, dating, and a few health problems, so I kept asking myself, "Should I take this on? My plate is kind of full." I had to completely rearrange my work schedule so I could make all the training and race sessions, and I found myself a little burned out. I know Satan used this time to make me feel anxious.

I mentioned my situation to a couple of friends, and soon enough I began to hear "You're in my prayers." Was this a life-or-death situation? No, but I cannot express how much it meant to have loved ones praying for me. There is something incredibly strengthening and comforting about hearing a teammate in life say, "I'm praying for you." The race worked out perfectly, and we had a wonderful time. I know I was able to do all I needed to during that busy week because of the heartfelt prayers of others.

Praying for those around us can be such a wonderful experience. We are all part of the gospel team, after all. Praying for those you love is one of the greatest gifts you can give. We should pray "for [our] welfare, and also for the welfare of those who are around [us]" (Alma 34:27), especially our families (3 Nephi 18:21).

The Olympic Games represent a movement designed to unify the world through brotherhood and camaraderie. Can you imagine how different things would be if more people embraced that spirit and prayed instead of persecuted, supported instead of slandered? So many people around us face illness, loneliness, financial problems, or some other adversity. Our love and prayers can make all the difference. We can add our faith to others who are suffering and ask God to sustain them in their times of need. In this way we become spiritual teammates by supporting those we pray for.

The Savior set the example of remembering the needs of others in his own prayers. He prayed for Peter (Luke 22:32) and for all of us in the Garden of Gethsemane during his great intercessory prayer (John 17), and after his resurrection, Christ knelt amidst the Nephites. We read that "no tongue can speak, neither can there be written by any man, neither can the hearts of men conceive so great and marvelous things as we both saw and heard Jesus speak . . . at the time we heard him pray for us unto the Father" (3 Nephi 17:17).

I hope we remember our earthly "teammates" in our prayers. The Church is the Lord's team here on earth, and we all strive for excellence and all play to win. Occasionally we need help during the game, so let us help each other via prayer, because as James taught, "The effectual prayer of a righteous man availeth much" (James 5:16).

Temporal Needs

As mentioned before, to play in the highest levels of most Olympic sports requires quite a bit of money. On top of exorbitant equipment costs, you have to pay for food, housing, trainers, nutritionists, massage therapists, travel expenses, race fees, coaching, tools, and more. Sometimes you have to get creative to make ends meet, but many competitors survive only because others support their athletic goals. From sponsors to donors, from family members to friends and fans, every little bit paves the way and fills in the financial potholes of an athlete's life.

Similarly, even affording the bare necessities of life can be a challenge at times. Most parents intimately understand the concern of keeping food on the table, providing clothes for their children, and having a roof overhead. When times are tough, humility softens our hearts, and we remember that the Lord is ultimately the source of our blessings—both the ones we have and the ones we need.

When I first started coaching, I found myself in a rather unexpected position. I was instructing athletes who ranged from age sixteen up to nearly sixty, yet all looked up to me. They came to me for guidance, advice, and support. I found myself constantly working to provide what we could call their mortal needs: equipment, funding, and financial backing. While I was not a parent, I began to understand what it meant to care for others in that manner.

We as a people have been taught that God is the source of all our blessings, and Heavenly Father has invited us to seek his help when we stand in need. But in the end we must be "content with the things which the Lord hath allotted unto [us]" (Alma 29:3). This means we have faith in his timing and his method of responding and blessing.

What temporal blessings do you need? Do you want a new job or help paying the bills? Are you worried about food or shelter? Or are you seeking a blessing of physical health? Whether our needs be great or small, desperate or composed, we can always find comfort and strength in the Lord's promise. "Whatsoever ye shall ask the Father in my name, which is right, believing that ye shall receive, behold it shall be given unto you" (3 Nephi 18:20). Ultimately our eternal coach decides what "is right." He knows our needs and invites us to ask. He is not a heartless mystical being without parts or passion. As Latter-day Saints, we understand the true character of God, that he loves all his children to the extent that he gave his only begotten son so we could have every opportunity to eternally succeed (John 3:16). No wonder Paul invites us to let our needs "be known unto God . . . by prayer and supplication with thanksgiving" (Philippians 4:6), thanksgiving for the blessings we have and supplication for the things we need.

How wonderful is the knowledge that we can use prayer to ask the Lord for the necessities of life. While he expects us to do all in our power to solve our own problems, we should not be afraid to seek heaven's help with our temporal needs. As the Lord taught, "Behold the fowls of the air: for they sow not, neither do they reap, nor gather into barns; yet your heavenly Father feedeth them. Are ye not much better than they?" (Matthew 6:28).

We have a powerful and loving coach on high willing to guide us to our ultimate destiny and help us obtain the blessings we need to get there. The throne room of heaven is always open to those who seek its God with faith and humility. We may not have our prayers answered in the way we want, but the Lord will never let us down.

A small word of counsel. As we go for the gold in our everyday lives, the challenges and trials we face will grow as well. The greater your goals and dreams, the larger the obstacles we will have to overcome. This need not cause us fear or discouragement. Rather, let prayer be our strengthening companion, a comforting teammate that will be with us until the end. That we may we draw ever closer to our Father and entrust him with our needs through prayer is my own humble desire.

OUR COACH IS ALWAYS WILLING TO HELP

When I began bobsled, I came from a background of soccer and baseball, two warm-weather sports. Aside from a few ski days, I really had no experience with winter sports (ice skating and I don't get along). But the Lord has a plan for each of us—and a sense of humor—so as a sophomore in high school, I found myself sliding down an icy track a few nights a week. Cold? Yes. Fun? Yes, to the point of addiction. But being a rookie to the sport, I needed to learn from and ask questions of those who knew more. My first coach, Randy, was instrumental in laying the foundation, and I often spoke with veteran athletes to learn what they knew. Sometimes I just learned the hard way.

In 1999, I entered the US Western Regionals race with my friend Adam Revelli. Adam and I were both preparing for our missions, so we were on the same page spiritually. I really enjoyed working with Adam, and in succeeding years I worked with his father and siblings.

Prior to Regionals, our program received some funding from Delta Airlines, so we were excited to see new paint jobs on the sleds (always cheer the small victories). To be honest, Adam and I were just glad to have a sled to use. Neither of us had fifteen thousand dollars lying around to purchase a new bobsled, so we were excited to race with a program sled. It didn't hurt that a local media station was going to televise the event either.

In order to compete in a race like this, teams must participate in official training sessions and complete at least three runs down the track. Adam and I had to take time off school so we could make it to the training sessions, but it was a sacrifice worth making (bobsled versus school—bit of a no-brainer). It was during one of those training runs that we had an experience I will never forget.

It was a beautiful, sunny Park City afternoon when our turn came up in the rotation. Adam and I pulled our sled to the starting line and went through our prerun routine. We then sprinted down the start ramp before loading into the sled. The run went great driving-wise until about a third of the way down the track. Then things got interesting.

I was making a correction in the middle of turn six when suddenly my right driving D-ring became completely loose. I suppressed my panic through turn seven (a left-hand turn) until I could risk a quick glance inside the sled. To my horror, I saw that the rope connecting my D-ring to the axle had come off. With half the track remaining, I could now only steer left. We had five right-hand turns remaining.

I frantically hunted around the nose of the sled for the loose rope with my right hand while trying to maintain control with my left hand. Luckily, we were now in the area of the Park City track called Albert's Alley (after Prince Albert of Monaco), a stretch of turns that are relatively gentle. If I could find the rope, then maybe I could hold on to it with one hand while steering with the other. After several seconds of grasping blindly, I still couldn't find the rope. Our once-smooth run quickly turned into an adventure as the sled bounced off walls and traveled all over the turns. Now powerless, I pulled myself under the protective cowling of the sled and grabbed onto the frame as tightly as I could.

In the outside world, the tower operators saw every wild oscillation during our decent and called over the radios for the track crew and the medical staff to prepare for a crash. Inside the sled I expected the same outcome, so I tried to prepare myself mentally and physically for the sled to turn over. I wasn't afraid, but I remember thinking, "Time for my first crash as the driver."

But it never happened. To my surprise, and to the amazement of the entire crew, we crossed the finish line right-side up. I pulled myself out from under the cowl and sat there dumbfounded. How in the world did we make it through all that without flipping? It was a question I was asked several times over the next few days. It wasn't logical. Running out of control at those speeds, the sled could have tipped over at any number of points on the track. Why didn't it?

Pulling the sled off the track in the finish area, I removed my helmet and immediately felt an overwhelming sense of peace. The Spirit's voice whispered, "You were protected so you could serve your missions." I looked at Adam and then up toward the sky with tears in my eyes. I knew that our

Father in Heaven had watched over us in direct response to our prayers for safety and protection. That day I gained a powerful testimony of the effectiveness of prayer and of God's willingness to answer our heartfelt pleas.

Too often I hear others use excuses for not seeking help through prayer. "I'm not worthy," "I'm not ready," "He's too busy for me," "Why should I bother God about it," or, worst of all, "God doesn't care about me." Such thoughts must sadden our Father in Heaven. As a parent, he has complete love for each and every one of us. He knows we are not perfect, but our fears and insecurities should never prevent us from praying.

Any thought that keeps us from praying comes from the "evil spirit [which] teaches man not to pray" (2 Nephi 32:8). Why do we give so much credence to the adversary's whispers? That's like listening to the other team's coach because you think your own is mad at you. When we understand God's true nature, no fear, doubt, weakness, or mistake will keep us from constantly turning to him. We can turn to he who sees a champion in all of us (Doctrine and Covenants 18:10).

As an athlete, it is crucial to have a coach (or coaches) that you know you can trust. Nothing is worse than trying to train and compete with a leader in whom you have zero faith, whom you doubt has your best interests at heart. Mistrust, apathy, disrespect, and ultimately a breakdown in the athlete-coach relationship are almost a guarantee.

In the game of life, our Father in Heaven is a coach who always wants the best for us. Sometimes we wish for a bronze-level experience, but God has the gold in mind. Our testimony that he will always be there for his "athletes" will grow as we experience his love through prayer. I can see why Satan tries to trick us into believing that God will neither listen to our prayers nor send the blessings we need. He wants to pull us away from the source of light, hope, and peace that we so desperately need in this world. So developing trust and faith in our Heavenly Father's willingness to answer our prayers is one of the most important aspects of our spiritual growth. When we learn to fully entrust our cares and concerns to "he [who] is mighty to save" (Zephaniah 3:17), we will let nothing stop us from turning to him for our "daily bread" (Luke 11:3).

I know with all my heart that our Heavenly Father listens to every prayer and knows the desires of our hearts. Don't let fear or doubt keep you from enjoying this powerful experience every day. And don't slack off or get lazy with it. As a coach, God wants nothing more than to see us happy in mortality and ultimately help us obtain the eternal medal's podium, even exaltation. I have had too many great experiences to include in any book that allow me to bear this witness. He has promised, "Draw near unto me and I will draw unto you; seek me diligently and ye shall find me; ask, and ye shall receive; knock, and it shall be opened unto you" (Doctrine and Covenants 88:63).

I am so grateful that I can talk to my eternal "coach" about my progress in the competitions of life. I encourage you to open your heart in prayer and embrace the love of a listening Father who is your biggest supporter and greatest coach in this life.

THE SECRET TO VICTORY IS OBEDIENCE

When I started bobsled, one of my goals was simply to have fun. To enjoy sliding, make new friends, and win a medal or two was the complete scope of my desires. I was a sophomore whose world revolved around the social scene, dating, a driver's license, and this newfound sport that encouraged me to drive a bobsled as fast as possible (a freedom not allowed when driving my first car).

However, as the seasons ticked by, I came to see that my enjoyment of bobsled could only be found within a slew of rules specific to the sport. The tracks, our national governing body, and the international governing body set some of the rules. I have a rule book written in the three languages of the sport (English, French, and German) that is over 350 pages long. You might be surprised at some of the rules we have to follow, but having been an athlete, a coach, and a race official, I now understand that every rule has a purpose.

Whether it be to protect the athletes or spectators, or just keep the sport pure, every regulation has been carefully defined and laid forth for the good of all those involved. My first experience with explaining those guidelines actually occurred in March 1999 at a race I never would have imagined I'd be in let alone win.

It was called the Utah Governor's Cup (GC) and was a pretty big race for those of us in the Park City program. Utah's governor Michael Leavitt had helped create a program that allowed some of the state's high schools (Mountain View, Roy, Granite, and Wasatch) to build three-quarter-sized two-man bobsleds that were to be used at the initial GC races.

The race itself commenced at 3:00 p.m. on Saturday, March 6, but Governor Leavitt called a press conference about half an hour before our start time. One of the most exhilarating experiences of the day was that my teammate Jared Heaton and I had the opportunity to drive a two-man sled down the track, an event that was timed perfectly so we rushed through the turn just behind the governor during the press conference. That was pretty fun.

After our run, we left our sled in the finish area and jogged to meet the other race participants at what we call "tourist start" by turn eleven. The race would only include turns eleven, twelve, thirteen, fourteen, and a tiny portion of fifteen. The sleds we were using were those built by the high schools, but our "teammates" were celebrity VIPs selected by a race committee that included Governor Leavitt and Mitt Romney, Salt Lake City Organizing Committee CEO and future presidential candidate.

My VIP teammate for the day was Monte Mounga, a Utah-based sponsor of the Tongan bobsled team, so he and I huddled up to talk strategy. I did my best to give him a piloting crash-course (hopefully without the crash), since the VIPs were going to be the drivers and the athlete-coaches were going to be the brakemen. A nearby reporter heard him say, "I want to beat the governor," and I guess I nodded in agreement, a fact that made it into the newspaper.

As luck would have it, we won with a top speed of over forty miles an hour and a downtime of 36.88 seconds. I'm not sure we were supposed to nab the gold. I got the feeling that public relations-wise, the goal was to let the governor win, but Mr. Mounga and I felt differently. Sorry, Governor Leavitt. We came to win, and because we played by the rules and because Mr. Mounga did such a superb job of obeying the winning guidelines, we went home with a nice big gold medal. On a side note, when the medals were presented on the podium, the person handing them out whispered, "You guys better appreciate these; they were expensive."

Of course I appreciated the medal. I still do. But every time I look at it, I can't help but think that the reason we won was because Mr. Mounga was obedient to the rules and principles of bobsled. He could have chosen to drive the sled according to his own desires, but he didn't. He listened to my counsel and the "dos and don'ts." Because of Mr. Mounga's willingness to obey, we won the first ever Utah's Governor's Cup.

For me, this experience was a lasting lesson on the power of obedience. When I first got a copy of the rule book that governs our sport, I knew that to succeed I needed to become familiar with the information it contained. In addition, I needed to learn as much as I could from my coaches. They also taught me that the bobsled rules also included protocols, attitudes, efforts given, theories, push techniques, and more. The parameters that we live by in our sport can mean the difference between winning and losing.

But let me ask you this: Why do we have so many rules? Why are we restricted by complicated regulations and ordinances when all we want to do is go out there and do our best, and just maybe have a fun time doing it?

We could ask those same questions about mortality. Life's rules—at least those based on morals, high-standards, and the Lord's commandments—may feel restrictive, overbearing, and old-fashioned at times. The temptation to cheat and bend the rules by living as the physical man wants is everywhere. In life and sport, the desire to cut corners and win regardless of the cost is a temptation we can face in any moment. It can tempt us at work to adjust our monthly reports to make ourselves look better, cheat on a test so we can get that 4.0, or break the Word of Wisdom at a party simply to be popular.

So I ask again: why do we have so many governing guidelines that appear to curb our freedom and restrict us from having fun? Don't our parents, Church and civic leaders, coaches, and even God want us to have a good time on this earth? After all, life is short!

Coming back to our victory at the Utah's Governor's Cup, the reason we won was that my teammate chose to follow winning principles. And when it comes to life, the way we win, or enjoy true happiness and greater blessings, is through adopting a similar attitude. God knows which "gold medals" in life are pure and bring lasting happiness and which ones are the cheap pieces of tin that leave us feeling empty and lost.

Because God loves us, he wants to teach us his guidelines—the commandments—so we can avoid painful setbacks and heartbreaking guilt during the game of life. If we obey, we will find greater peace, more blessings, and a stronger connection to the Spirit. That does not mean life will be without trials, but I know of no individual who has ever become lost through obedience. If we truly desire to be happy, to feel spiritually safe, and to enjoy the lasting peace the Savior promised, obedience is the key to opening those doors.

If you want to achieve great things, obedience is a price you'll have to pay. This principle holds true in all aspects of life, especially sports. Obedience is a guiding philosophy that I strive to teach all the athletes I work with. If you want to win, adopt a winning attitude that includes a desire to be 100 percent obedient to the rules of the game. Avoid the temptation to cut corners to victory; there are no easy ways to get the things that matter most.

Understanding this principle can help us make better choices that lead us to happier lives. If you make good choices, you can expect good things (you'll notice I did not say *easy* things). If you choose the ways of the world (wickedness), well, you probably know how that will turn out. Think of athletes who chose to cheat and have to face the consequences of suspension or banishment from their sport. Because they decided to disobey the rules, they were actually limiting themselves.

In the end, anyone who disobeys a law, whether it is civic, spiritual, or athletic, will find that there is no substitute for obedience. Disobedience will never pay off in the long run. As the scriptures state, "Wickedness never was happiness" (Alma 41:10). The reverse, however, is equally true: obedience always brings happiness and progress.

In the world of sports, discipline and adherence to winning principles like hard work, intelligent thinking, integrity on and off the field, and obedience are the secrets to success. The athletes who thrive are the ones who obey their coaches, trainers, dieticians, sports psychologists, and so on. They stick to their training plans, they practice their techniques, and they act correctly during competitions. One thing bobsled has taught me is that if I want to succeed at anything, I must search out winning principles and stick to them. Find people who have succeeded in your field of pursuit, ask them what they did to win, and then obediently do it.

Thankfully, when it comes to "winning" in life, we have a Father in Heaven who freely gives the saving knowledge, guiding commandments, priesthood power, and sacred ordinances that will help us "get the gold." The rest is up to us.

As a coach, I find it fascinating to study the differences between athletes who progress and those who do not. To me the main variance between the two groups really comes down to obedience. The athletes who want to learn are willing to work, and desire to excel are those who listen to what I say, do what I ask, and practice what I preach. I would even say that the athletes who obey enjoy a progression rate that is almost double that of their fellow sliders who are unwilling to exercise some faith in their coach and put aside their pride or laziness. In the end, athletes who are not willing to obey only hurt themselves by claiming a desire to progress. When it comes to race day, the athletes who embrace winning principles and guidelines are confident, while the athletes who did not are disappointed.

As much as Satan wants us to believe we can do whatever we want ("eat, drink and be merry"), he knows that path only leads to sorrow, pain, and ultimately a broken heart. But he doesn't care. He just wants us to see the temporary pleasures of the easy and immoral paths that are contrary to God's commandments.

Let's get one thing straight: Satan is a gold medalist at deception. He can make sin look attractive and can make choosing the right appear difficult. How many times have you been in a situation where the group wants to do one thing that you know is wrong, and they want you to join? Or maybe the temptation to disobey comes when you are alone and Satan whispers, "No one will know." No matter what he lies about, we will always know when we do wrong. And the Lord will know too.

During the long drive to the Calgary, Canada, track on one occasion, we passed a restaurant known for the physical appearance of its waitresses. Teenage athletes need a lot of food (just ask their parents), and since it was dinner time, the teenage hormones, mixed with hunger pains and the other athletes and the assistant coach, announced that they wanted to eat there.

Now, I knew I wouldn't feel comfortable there, but at the same time, I didn't want to offend my teammates. As I sat there thinking about it, I knew what was right, but I worried that they would point their finger and mock me for not wanting to go. Despite the fear, however, I knew what God wanted me to do.

I told them I couldn't go to the restaurant for personal reasons. They did give me a hard time about it (mostly good naturedly), but in the end, we didn't go. We ended up going to a steakhouse, where one of my teammates was completely shut down by the hostess. I remember feeling so relieved. I slept peacefully that night knowing I had done what Heavenly Father expected of me and what I expected of myself.

I was able to make the right choice, because I knew that gospel principles and regulations keep me safe and happy and allow me to feel inner peace. I don't care what people say; you're never a loser when you allow God to coach you in life. After all, he gives us far more than a medal or trophy. He has a heavenly crown and kingdom waiting for those who choose to obey his rules and commandments. Embrace a winning attitude and humbly build your life, thoughts, and actions around the eternal principles found in the gospel of Jesus Christ. It is, after all, the only strategy that saves.

But let's be honest: we can only play by God's game plan if we study it first.

LEARN, LIVE, AND WIN BY THE RULES

In sports, or in any pursuit, to achieve success you must first learn the parameters of the game. So naturally a coach is responsible for helping athletes understand their sport's governing guidelines and for explaining the players' roles within the rules. For example, a new athlete needs to understand what equipment is proper to use. You can't win in bobsled by wearing bicycle shoes just like you can't win in soccer by using a baseball bat.

Knowledge really is power in sports, and when you mix correct knowledge with proper actions, you achieve the power to succeed. And to survive.

I worked at the Park City track for years in what we call the Passenger Ride Program. Customers who want to experience the thrill of hurling themselves down the course at near-competition speeds can purchase a ticket to ride in a four-man bobsled with a qualified driver piloting (for a hefty fee, of course).

But bobsled is bobsled, and the risks are not that different from competitive sliding, so before passengers get in the sleds, we run them through a thirty-minute safety orientation and explain the rules of the ride. We tell them what to expect, what they could and could not do, and so on. After that, we open it up for questions (which often involve jokes about life insurance) and then pass out helmets. We do this because we want people to know the rules of the ride and explain how they can have the best experience possible.

I always smile when people groan about the procedures. Some customers dislike the rule about not carrying a camera on the way down the track, at which point I would explain that the G-forces would probably rip said camera out of their hands and turn it into a few dozen tiny, expensive pieces.

Another sticking point was the way some people with neck or back problems balk at being told they probably shouldn't ride. Maybe they don't realize that five times the force of gravity (more than astronauts feel on take-off) was about to drive down on their injured neck or spine. We always had fun with pregnant women who arrived to ride, a definite no-no since no one wanted the baby to come early due to the G-forces Mom would feel. We're bobsledders, Jim, not doctors.

Every rule we explained was designed to protect the passengers, the drivers, and the track. Rules were never put in place to impede the customers from having fun. On the contrary, they allowed riders to have more fun. Just imagine how bad it would have been if they had hurt themselves on the ride. I can see how people unfamiliar with our sport may not understand the dangers involved or the reasoning behind some policies. However, those of us who live on the ice understand the risk all too well.

In the years since those hardworking (no sarcasm there) days of employment at the track, I have thought about the role we played in preparing those people for the ride of their lives. So let's step back and compare this whole example to our mortal probation and how the commandments prepare us for the bobsled ride we call life.

We know we were taught the gospel in the premortality and that we were allowed to accept or reject God's plan. And I imagine we went through a safety orientation of sorts before we embarked on our mortal journey. Our Heavenly Father, who understood the dangers associated with this ride/world, instructed and prepared us just as I instructed and prepared those customers who were about to ride down the track. And like those customers, maybe we didn't fully understand what we were getting ourselves into. We had to take the instructions on faith.

Thankfully, unlike the fifty-four-second passenger bobsled ride, mortality takes a bit longer, which allows us time to study and implement the rules. After their bobsled ride, people usually smile and say something like "By the time I remembered what you said about shrugging my shoulders, the ride was over!" Your first time down the bobsled track really is a blur, so I recommend going twice.

Similarly, we have forgotten the instruction we received in premortality. Because of the veil placed over our minds, we are now required to walk by faith, but there is good news! Our eternal coach, our loving Heavenly Father, has provided numerous ways for us to be instructed in the commandments/rules of this life. He knows that by learning the regulations, the eternal principles of the gospel, we will better enjoy the ride of mortality and stay safe until we cross that final finish line of physical death.

When I work with new athletes, or serve as a life coach for others, I stick to a simple rule: to better achieve success, find true sources of information and guidance that will lead to victory. Instead of trying to conjure solutions out of thin air, build on the solid foundations that others have discovered or taught. And that works spiritually too.

We all have gospel-directed goals for this life and the next. We all desire the comfort and guidance of the Spirit in our lives, plus an increase in faith and Christlike attributes. We all want to return to our Father's presence and live with our family for eternity. How do we make those goals a reality? We follow the "rules" that God has laid out to help us "win" our goals. So let's look at the sources of spiritual truths—the "rule books" if you will—that we have been given to help us win the competition of life.

The Scriptures

We have been commanded to search the scriptures daily and let their words of peace and counsel sink deep into our souls. I mentioned the big rule book we have in bobsled that instructs us on the "dos and don'ts" of the sport. The scriptures are our rule books and have been revealed and recorded for our benefit and safety. We have a playbook to help us better enjoy our lives and win the game so we can return to God's presence. I would also encourage each of us to take advantage of the Church Educational System, BYU's Education Week, Sunday School, and the countless other outlets of scriptural education. Spiritual champions continually draw upon the words of truth found in the scriptures. How can we expect to win a game if we never read the instructions?

Church Leaders

While a team's head coach is indeed "the boss," let's not discount the value of assistant coaches for the supportive role they play. Additionally, as an athlete you rely on your trainers, nutritionists, sports psychologists, sponsors, teammates, administrators, and so forth. All these people contribute to your chances for victory by sharing their knowledge and skills. If you try to do it on your own, you may win, but then again, you may come in dead last because you never learned winning principles and correct techniques. We are blessed with great assistant coaches and trainers on the field of life in the form of prophets, apostles, bishops, stake and Relief Society presidents, and so on, who lead the Church under the direction of our head coach, the Savior. The Lord, like a team's head coach, often sends instruction through his assistant coaches, and we can be greatly blessed through obedience to their words.

Digital Resources

As athletes, we are constantly working to improve our knowledge of health and fitness, and there are countless electronic programs that help us track our diet and training sessions. As Latter-day Saints, we have at our fingertips thousands of talks and doctrinal sources available through the Church website and other online sources that can teach us how to better our lives through obeying the rules of the Lord. We also have incredible electronic devices to help us listen to the voice of his servants or inspiring music and firesides. There are countless apps for our mobile devices that can help enrich our studies of the gospel and bring the Spirit more fully into our lives.

Coach's question: what's your excuse for not delving into the resources available to better learn how to live as a spiritual champion? The resources for learning the winning rules and principles of life are everywhere, but there are things we can do to improve our receptiveness of and obedience to the Lord's word.

As any athlete knows, winning starts with craving victory, so step one to learning the saving guidelines of the gospel is desire. Athletes who are hungry for success are the ones who usually achieve it. They put forth the required effort to succeed and are humble enough to accept counsel from their coaches, trainers, teammates, and other advisors. If we hunger and thirst after righteousness, the Lord promises that we will be filled (Matthew 5:6). Desire means that we want to learn and grow and are willing to work for it. If we have low spiritual desire, our level of commitment and effort will be just as low.

Another principle that increases our receptivity to obedience is fasting. As bobsled athletes, especially sled pilots, we are constantly working to keep our minds clear and focused when we are getting ready to push off the top of the track. There is a special union of mind and body in those moments that is hard to describe. Scientists would say it is based on adrenaline, which increases our senses, but I think there's something more to it. I think it's our spirits becoming fully awake and alive in that moment as we prepare to push the sled, jump in, and drive down the course. In a similar fashion, fasting is an activity that helps us put aside the natural man and become more alive—more awake—spiritually speaking.

The third habit that helps us improve our levels of disciplined obedience is prayer. Remember, as sled pilots we converse with coaches before, during, and after our on-ice sessions. This communication allows us to learn from their experience and knowledge. Why do we fail to take advantage of a similar avenue of conversing with God? We can try to make it on our own, even resist the natural man with our own limited strength, but if we desire to open our hearts to the Spirit, prayer is the key that opens the door.

I've heard occasional grumbling that Church lessons feel repetitive. "Conference talks cover the same topic," "We reviewed this last month," or "Do we have to read that chapter again?" Why do we need such repetition when it comes to the gospel rules and regulations? We study in class, as families, and by ourselves. What gives?

No matter what sport, every athlete has experienced that wonderful joy we call practice, and, as the saying goes, practice makes perfect. No one comes to the field knowing everything; you may have incredible natural talent, but without practice you'll never grow and develop enough to reach your highest potential.

Like the great coach he is, our Heavenly Father understands that we need the repetition of constant reminders and prodding to reach exaltation. Instead of complaining about hearing the same topic over and over again, we should embrace the opportunity to "practice" and then master the doctrines and rules that God is trying to teach us.

Obedience is the only way to victory. Sport requires obedience to the rules of the game, as well as to coaches, officials, team owners, trainers, and so on. Spiritually speaking, obedience to the commandments is the precursor to the blessings that help us move forward toward the joys of the gospel.

Midway through the 2010–2011 season, I realized I needed to add a step to the program regimes of the athletes I was coaching. Most of them were progressing well, so after a few months, it was time to take things to the next level.

I wanted to create personalized guidebooks to help each athlete grow into the powerful competitors I believed they could be. I asked my athletes to give me a report of what they did the night before, the morning of, and the day of a training session or competition, and I asked for a report on what they did from the time they got to the track to the moment they began their run. Armed with that information, I developed structured proposals based on what I knew of the specific athlete's abilities, personalities, quirks, likes and dislikes, and habits.

By taking what I knew as a sled pilot and what I had been taught from my coaches, I outlined the ways each athlete could better prepare mentally and physically for a session and what to do after the session to better learn from the day's ice time. I also made multiple suggestions on ways to better prepare as a team and gave specific assignments to hone the skills they already had. One thing I universally suggested was purchasing a notebook in which the athletes could keep daily notes of things they did right and things they needed to correct.

In many ways, these guiding documents were like the scriptures for them. By following these guiding principles and practices, the athletes could improve their chances for success on the ice. I say "could" because like mankind and the gospel, not everyone was open to my suggestions. Interestingly, those who chose to follow the outlined counsel noticed a distinctly powerful change in the way they approached an on-ice session. They found their minds and bodies in a better position to perform when called upon. But those who acted halfheartedly or chose not to obey my advisements were "left unto themselves." Some athletes even continued habits that were detrimental, or damning, to their progress.

Any practice we pursue that is contrary to the guidelines of God will ultimately impede our progress. Our Heavenly Father knows this; he knows what will keep us safe and bring us joy or what will bring pain and heartache. I think back to all my coaches over the years, and while some may have been tough at times, they all wanted us to do our best. Similarly, God wants us to do our best, to achieve our potential and be happy in this life and in the eternities. When we feel that gospel instruction gets repetitive or "harsh," we should remember that God is continually coaching from the sidelines, reminding us that the rules are for our eternal benefit. The guidelines may come from the prophet, a bishop, or just a quiet whisper of the Spirit, but the instructions of the gospel should be cherished as pearls of great price, worth far more than any earthly medal, trophy, or award.

We need repetition because the gospel is designed around forward progression, but we are mortal beings who occasionally pause along the way. In sports it can be tempting to slack off following a victory because the thrill of a win brings a natural high that can have detrimental effects if athletes let it lull them into a sense of carnal security. "I won this race, and I can do it again next time without really trying."

The Lord knows there are competitions yet to be faced in our lives that will require every ounce of resolve, faith, and pure effort we possess. Plus, the earthly lines dividing good and evil are being blurred every day. If we do not continue to "practice" and "train" by strengthening our spiritual foundations, how can we hope to stand against the tide of wickedness flooding the earth? The only way to stay safe and ultimately achieve victory is to first diligently study the word of God, then obediently apply the word. It's a concept I am familiar with since I learned about bobsled by studying the lines of other pilots. I would sit in turns (or lie on top of them) and watch sleds go down the track so I could see how they were driving and thereby better understand how to pilot my sled. I also rode with other drivers to learn what taking more aggressive lines felt like. And yes, some drivers are better than others, and I had the bruises to prove it. Although, I'm sure some of my first brakemen received bruises of their own.

As I applied the guiding principles I learned from coaches and through watching other sled pilots, I noticed immediate progress. Ultimately I reached a point where new brakemen were directed my way since I would give them such a smooth ride down the track.

Obtaining knowledge of the guiding principles of the gospel comes in a similar manner. We learn by studying the lives of the prophets, the Savior, our parents, and so on, but eventually we will have to apply what we learn. We have to decide if we are going to follow the teachings of the Savior or not. In bobsled there is only one driver in control of the sled. Similarly, because of our God-given agency, no one can choose obedience for us. We are in control of our lives, and we choose which playbook we will follow. God can invite us, parents can teach us, spouses can love us, and prophets can implore us, but in the end the decision to follow the rules of the gospel lies squarely on our own shoulders.

As champions of the Lord, when we live by God's regulations we thrive under his care and will find ourselves on a path that leads to eternal life, the greatest victory of all.

LEAPS OF OBEDIENT FAITH ALWAYS LAND THE GOLD

Fun fact: I can't ice skate, but I can push a several-hundred-pound metal and fiberglass missile on ice and then jump in it while sprinting on a downhill slope. It's kind of a leap of faith the first few times you do it, and I love the sound our spiked bobsled shoes make when we step onto the ice. The melodious crunch is music to my ears!

So why do I say it's a leap of faith? As a brakeman or a side pusher, you have faith that your pilot will get you down the track in one piece (or leave as few pieces of you on the track as possible). Second, you have to exercise faith in what your coaches have told you about loading into the sled. And last, you must have faith in your own ability to make it into your seat. Even if you've practiced it a hundred times on push tracks, some faith is always required to jump in an aerodynamic sled that costs as much as a car.

Obedience to the instructions of God is a bit like pushing and jumping into a sled for the first time. To follow a certain law or principle, we must first develop faith in the one giving the directions—the coach. Without that trust, we will never take the leap of faith required to act on their words. When my coach(es) taught me a new technique, I had to put my trust in their knowledge and believe that what they were teaching would help me become a better athlete. And that didn't always come easy.

When I first learned to drive sleds, we began pretty low on the Park City track. Out of fifteen curves, we only drove through turns eleven, twelve, thirteen, fourteen, and part of fifteen, so our speeds were not exactly heart-stopping, but it was a big deal to us. As the first youth drivers on the track, in some ways, we were guinea pigs. As time went on, we moved higher up the track and graduated to bigger sleds, until one day we found ourselves at junior start, which meant we drove turns six through fifteen with mind-blowing speeds of about fifty-five miles per hour.

Then the moment we all had been waiting for came: the day we started driving from the top of the track, which a few years later would host the competitors of the 2002 Winter Olympic Games. Calling it an eye-opening experience would be an understatement. I had been down the track from the top countless times in sleds driven by other pilots, but now I was the one behind the steering ropes. It was like going from the driver's education course at your high school to flying down Germany's Autobahn.

It's embarrassing, but when I started driving from the top, I struggled with overdriving. Overdriving is when a sled's pilot drives too long in the turns or holds too much pressure on the steering rings. This pressure causes the sled to slow down. Every time you steer, you turn the runners on the sled, and that creates a minute amount of friction and burns off speed. It doesn't sound like much, but in a sport where you can lose the race by one one-hundredth of a second, speed is everything.

I was getting frustrated with myself because I knew better, but I didn't want to give up my control of the sled. I knew, and my coaches knew, that I needed to steer less and let physics guide the sled in the turns, but I wanted to do it my way, which wasn't working. Then one day I got so fed up that I told myself, "Your way isn't cutting it. It's time to listen to your coaches and do it their way. They've been doing this a lot longer than you, so just do it!"

I remember the first time I let the sled run through the middle of turn six on the Park City track—a big horseshoe curve. I was nervous, but once I let it go, I could feel the increased speed and pressure from the G forces. It felt like flying, and at the finish area I got out of the sled with a shout. I was able to improve in and enjoy my sport even more because I finally put my faith in and obeyed the teachings and guidance of my coaches.

This kind of trust is a big thing between athletes and coaches, but I see it in our society as well. An individual who trusts his or her coach/boss/teacher/parent will do what he or she says, when he or she says it, and how he or she says it. Kind of like the two thousand stripling warriors.

When the Nephites were faced with war, these two thousand youth took up their swords in defense of liberty, their families, and their people (Alma 56:47) and chose to march under the command of the prophet Helaman, who in a real sense became their coach. And even in the face of danger, these sons of Helaman stood firm in their faith in God and in the words of their coach. During their pregame meeting when Helaman asked if they were prepared for battle, they responded, "Father, behold our God is with us, and he will not suffer that we should fall; . . . let us go forth" (Alma 56:46).

Let us go forth. Because of their faith, these mighty young men sought to obey every commandment of God and to do everything their coach asked of them. Helaman later told Captain Moroni, "Yea, and they did obey and observe to perform every word of command with exactness; yea, and even according to their faith it was done unto them" (Alma 57:21). The stripling warriors obeyed Helaman "with exactness," and it is this level of trust that we must develop toward the commandments of God. It may require a leap of faith to obey, but the Lord wants what is best for us, and his counsel will always be for our benefit. After I sought to perform what my coaches were asking of me about driving, I came to understand why we find greater joy in life when we decide to be 100 percent obedient to the commandments. A peace fills our hearts, our testimonies grow, and, like the stripling warriors, we enjoy divine blessings.

I have been blessed in my life to associate with some of the most incredible children of God—gold medalists, authors, musicians, actors, journalists, company CEOs, race car drivers, Church leaders, and so on. But I've always wondered what it would be like to serve alongside those two thousand brothers. Would I obey Helaman's commands with exactness and fight for freedom?

Here's the catch: there are Helamans—or coaches—all around us. How many of us faithfully follow the men and women whom God has called to be our leaders today? How many of us hold true to the scriptures and the teachings of Christ? So many are willing to do great deeds in the name of the Lord, but oftentimes all he asks is that we live a normal life of obedience to the teachings of the gospel, and that obedience takes faith.

Obedience often requires that we submit our will and desires to those of the Lord. We were never promised that faithful discipleship would be easy or that it would be in line with our own limited perspective. We do, however, have assurance that those who are obedient will enjoy the blessings of heaven (Isaiah 1:19) and find themselves lifted up. And let's be honest: we all want to reach greater heights.

On December 7, 1999, I was invited to participate in a team-building night with athletes from various sports within Salt Lake City's Community Olympic Development Program (CODP). We met downtown and were divided up into small groups, which gave us an opportunity to enjoy new teammates for the evening.

One of the activities was an exercise I have since used to help promote communication and cooperation within a team or company. Each group received rolls of clear office tape and several bags of balloons. The instructions were simple: each team would build a freestanding balloon tower during a certain period of time. Whichever team had the highest tower when the buzzer went off would win.

As you can imagine, when the word "win" is involved with a group of athletes the competition gets fierce, though good-natured. My team realized after twenty seconds that we needed an actual strategy and organizational plan. We decided to assign each athlete a task such as blowing up balloons, making small rolls of tape to hold the balloons together, or actually building our tower. When we took the game's rules and decided to accept a guiding plan, we found our tower growing so high that we had to stand on a chair to push aside the ceiling tiles. The last few balloons put our edifice up into the building's overhead conduit spaces. We won, but as I look back on this activity, I know we achieved victory because we chose to obey the guidelines and humbly embrace a winning strategy.

Choosing to submit our will and desires to the commandments of God will help us spiritually grow "above the ceiling" as it were. We will find deeper joys, achieve greater successes, and discover a higher vision of life. The question is how do we do it?

We can develop trust in the commandments of God by strengthening our testimonies through study and prayer. We can seek a more humble heart through service to our fellow man and by attending to our Church responsibilities. But perhaps the best way to develop trust in God's commandments is simply by living them (John 7:17).

Isn't it interesting that often we all just want to be the gods of our own lives? To do our own thing, to ignore those annoying rules our parents set, or to forget about what our bishop asks? I know people who believe that anything they do during the game of life is okay in God's eyes. If we pursue that mentality, then the balloon tower of our life will come crashing down. Obedience takes faith that the god of our lives is really he who rightfully claims that title. It also requires humility to let him fulfill that role.

Listening to our eternal coach and choosing the right is not always the popular thing to do. As the world continues its downward spiral into wickedness, those who stand for righteousness will be few in numbers. But that's all right; champions are used to that. It is always better to stand tall because then we will find ourselves standing with the hosts of heaven. It really comes down to is this: are we going to follow the world's opinion, or are we gong to follow the voice of revealed truth? Are we going to trust in God's counsel or our own? God's counsel requires faith and humility; our counsel requires ego and pride.

Every time my coaches, trainers, or advisors taught me something new, I had to consciously say, "Trust their guidance and do it." Like Nephi, I had to choose to "go and do" (1 Nephi 4:7). I occasionally had to remind myself that I didn't know everything and that maybe the ones giving me direction were right.

It is like that with the commandments of God, the policies of the Church, the directions of the Spirit, and so on. When we soften our hearts and realize that God does know better and wants what is best for us, we will choose to obey. And we don't always need to know why God gives us a specific task or rule. Coaches all over the world ask their athletes to do things they don't understand at first. That is where faith comes in. We can, however, be sure that blessings will come from every act of obedience (Moses 5:5–6), no matter how small.

If you are struggling to obey a certain commandment that our eternal coach has given, ponder this: when we talk about covenants, we usually talk about how we covenant to do something. What about the Lord? We forget that when we make a covenant, it is with him and that he makes promises as well. When we wonder if obedience is worth it, let us remember, "Who am I, saith the Lord, that have promised and have not fulfilled?" (Doctrine and Covenants 58:31). He will never let us down. What could disobedience possibly bring to your life that God can't bring and bring better? It does take faith, and it does take humility, but when we put our trust in God and serve him with all of our hearts, there is no end to the blessings and the peace that will flow into our lives.

Sometimes we feel like a new bobsled athlete stepping onto the ice for the first time. We may ask if obedience to our eternal coach's words is really the best route to follow. But I testify that the end result will always be better when we choose to obey. New athletes who take that leap of faith into the sled always get out at the bottom of the track and say something like, "That was awesome."

If you want to stand atop the medals podiums in life, put the commandments of God first. Spiritual champions know that doing right will never feel wrong.

THE CHAMPION'S WAY IS NOT THE EASY WAY

Even though I started bobsled at age sixteen, I didn't really pay attention to the Olympics for years. I caught glimpses of the 1998 Nagano Japan Games and the 2000 Sydney Australia Games, and I even remember bits and pieces of the 1996 Atlanta Georgia Olympics. Nothing really stuck with me until the 2002 Winter Olympic Games held right in my hometown of Salt Lake City, Utah, . . . and I didn't see any of them.

During the 2002 Winter Olympics, I was finishing the last month of my mission in Belize. The world came to Salt Lake City, and I was on the other side of the equator. Talk about a trial of faith!

Our mission president, President Shumway, gave us permission to watch a recording of the opening ceremonies, so about twenty missionaries crammed around the TV in the senior couple's living room in Belize City. We watched in awe at the incredible performances put on by all the talented performers. The costumes, the music, and the pageantry were astounding. During the Parade of Nations, I had fun watching for familiar faces in the crowd.

One thing that struck me with great force was an important component of the opening ceremonies called the "athlete's oath." This tradition began at the 1920 summer Olympics held in Antwerp, Belgium, when decathlete Victor Boin repeated the original, and slightly different, oath. Today, the oath reads, "In the name of all the competitors I promise that we shall take part in these Olympic Games, respecting and abiding by the rules which govern them, committing ourselves to a sport without doping and without drugs, in the true spirit of sportsmanship, for the glory of sport and the honor of our teams."

Representing all the athletes present, American skeleton athlete Jim

Shea, Jr. recited those words, and I realized that the athlete's oath is a covenant. In fact, the athlete oath sounds a bit like the oath we take at baptism.

As Elder Robert D. Hales taught,

> At baptism we make a covenant with our Heavenly Father that we are willing to come into His kingdom and keep His commandments from that time forward, even though we still live in the world . . . Our baptism is a covenant to "stand as witnesses of God [and His kingdom] at all times and in all things, and in all places that ye may be in, even until death, that ye may be redeemed of God, and be numbered with those of the first resurrection, that ye may have eternal life." (Mosiah 18:9)[15]

As an athlete, when you involve yourself in a sporting event, your participation is a sign or covenant that you are willing to abide by the rules of the competition. You have a duty to honor your team, country, sponsors, family, friends, and—most of all—yourself. And it cannot be a halfway effort; you can't obey half the rules and disobey the others. A judge isn't going to say, "Well, he broke five rules but obeyed five others. Let him keep his medal." One hundred percent obedience is required.

The gospel is no different. Just as an athlete commits to follow each of the regulations of the game, the Lord requires us to commit to obey all of the commandments, not just our favorites. We cannot have one foot in the world and one foot in the gospel because "No man can serve two masters" (3 Nephi 13:24). An athlete cannot promise to obey the rules and then break them with the hopes of becoming a champion. Similarly, we cannot serve both God and the ways of the world. You cannot compromise the principles of righteousness and still be obedient at the same time.

We must always choose the high line.

When you're piloting a bobsled through larger turns, there is a line you want to drive that will give you more speed. This line usually requires you to let the sled get more height in the turn, meaning you are closer to the top than you are the middle or belly. But when you take this line, you have to commit to it! You can't do it halfway. However, if you do it right, you can expect acceleration out of the turn, which helps you maintain a faster time down the course.

Those who commit to following Christ must always choose a higher moral line in life. But this level of commitment requires courage because taking a stand for what is right can bring ridicule and persecution. And sometimes doing what God asks can be hard, especially when it contradicts what we think we want. That's the test of our commitment.

As an athlete, you can find yourself in situations where gospel standards appear antiquated or out of place to others. They may not understand why you do not use foul language, why you attend church every Sunday, why you have scriptures in your luggage, or why you do not drink or participate in immoral activities. In those moments I try to remember that even though we are only in church three hours a week, we are in the Church every hour of our lives. Thinking of my covenants, my spiritual athlete's oath and my commitment to the Savior makes it easier to choose the high line.

It isn't always easy, but it is always the right thing to do. In those moments, when the eyes are all on me, I remember that I have told God that I will obey all the commandments and principles of the gospel of Jesus Christ. Doing anything less would break my promise to he who has given me all I have.

And you know what? Usually when I turn down a chance to do something I don't agree with, the other person understands. I'm not perfect; you're not perfect, but our commitment to being spiritually courageous gives others the courage to have commitment as well. And more often than not, when we do the right thing, we gain more respect than we would have if we had just gone with the flow.

I first met bobsledder Barbara "Babs" Isak at the Park City track in the winter of 1997–1998. When we ran into each other during a trip to Lake Placid, New York, she asked if I could be her brakeman for some runs down the track and from then on we were friends. What I love about Babs is that she has come to respect that I don't drink, smoke, or swear. She would even let other people know that I don't do those things. What's even more fun is that if she accidently let a swear word slip out, she'd turn to me and say, "I'm sorry, Jeremy." She calls me her "little Mormon friend."

Not everyone will react to our decisions to stand firm in the faith as Babs did, but if we ever choose to do wrong then Satan wins. And if we don't choose to stand against evil, we are not being the "peculiar people" that God expects us to be. It can take all the courage we have to "just say no" like I have taught so many elementary school students to do, but courage and commitment are the keys that unlock the doors to righteousness and the windows of heaven.

So how do we develop this courageous level of commitment? I have found that it is pretty similar to the courage and commitment we must develop as athletes. Just as it can be a challenge to do what is right, it can be a struggle to get to the gym every time or resist the temptation to cut corners in your training schedule. An athlete's ability to commit to doing the hard things is what makes a champion. Think of the greatest athletes in sport history. What made them so extraordinary? They played the same game by the same rules as the other players, but I would argue that great athletes commit themselves to doing what is right on the field, in the gym, or wherever they may be. And once they make that vow, they fiercely stick to their commitment. They know what they want and courageously and obediently pay the price to obtain their goals.

Like any habit, we can learn to commit ourselves to the gospel by constantly seeking to live it. It sounds simple, but we learn obedience by being obedient. We learn commitment by being committed. We learn courage by living courageously. It takes effort and faith, but like any good workout, resisting temptation brings strength and growth. If we stumble we need to pick ourselves up, brush off the dust, repent, and get back on our way. Perfection is a journey and a destination, and the Lord deserves our best along the way.

Committing ourselves to following Christ brings peace, joy, and progress. By covenanting to choose the high line, we commit ourselves to happiness and blessings. But the reverse is also true.

Lehi told his son Laman, "O that thou mightest be like unto this valley, firm and steadfast, and immovable in keeping the commandments of the Lord!" (1 Nephi 2:10). Laman had many of the same experiences that Nephi had. Both saw an angel, heard Lehi's prophecies, witnessed the miracle of obtaining the brass plates from Laban, and built the ship that brought them to the promised land. What made Nephi so committed to the Lord's game plan while Laman wanted to play by his own rules?

The answer lies in verse sixteen of the same chapter, in which Nephi chose to "cry unto the Lord," and the Lord softened his heart so that he "did believe all the words which had been spoken by [his] father." Nephi committed to the Lord because he had a testimony that the commandments come from God and because he knew that God would make it possible for him to obey.

Now, consider Lehi's words: "Laman, look at this valley. It is strong, immoveable, firm, and steadfast. That is how you need to be when it comes to the commandments of the Lord. Don't budge from the paths of righteousness!" Shouldn't we all be strong, immoveable, firm, and steadfast in keeping the commandments of God? I call this level of commitment the

"No Return" policy. In bobsled, we have a "point of no return" that exists at the top of the track. Once that sled gets past the crest of the start ramp, we must go with it. When we enter the sled we are fully committed to finishing the course. There is no going back, no hesitation, and no time for second thoughts. Likewise, we must see the gospel course through to the finish line.

I considered Nephi's commitment to the Lord during a training session in Park City while I looked at the track's foundations. The Utah course is different than other courses because the turns are up on pillars. The engineers who designed the Park City track built the course like this so that if an earthquake shook the course then it would move with the pillars instead of breaking apart. In other words, it has a "firm and steadfast" foundation. The thought struck me that Nephi always chose the high line because he had strong spiritual pillars. Because he committed to being courageously obedient, everything was all right in the end.

Nephi pled with us to "press forward with a steadfastness in Christ, having a perfect brightness of hope and a love of God and of all men." This great champion of God promises that if we "press forward, feasting upon the word of Christ, and endure to the end, behold, thus saith the Father: Ye shall have eternal life" (2 Nephi 31:20).

Every athlete has a goal in mind for his or her sport, whether it is the Olympics, winning the next competition, or setting a world record. Each of us has eternal life as our goal. And like the Olympics, our goal of eternal life takes real commitment and deep courage if we are going to pursue it. Sometimes that means we need to reevaluate our commitment.

A few years into my bobsled career, I decided to more fully blend the spiritual with my athletic dreams because I felt I could not be fully committed to the sport if I was not committed to the Lord first. As a visual representation of my desire, I chose to add a personal touch to the paint job of my first bobsled. Just inside the sled, above my right shoulder, I added an inscription from Deuteronomy 31:6, which reads, "Be strong and of good courage, fear not, nor be afraid of them: for the Lord thy God, he it is that doth go with thee; he will not fail thee, nor forsake thee." I chose this scripture because champions in any field must have courage, strength, and faith to stand alone when they choose the high line. By its definition, a champion is someone who stands out, who excels. The Lord desires us to be individuals who stand for their commitment to the gospel, who courageously excel in their obedience.

When mortal voices ridicule and mock us for our faith and obedience, I hope we remember that the Lord is on our side. Learning to live with a deep desire to do what is right requires a champion's courage. But as the Lord reminded the prophet Joshua, "Have not I commanded thee? Be strong and of good courage; be not afraid, neither be thou dismayed; for the Lord thy God is with thee whithersoever thou goest" (Joshua 1:9).

As champions of the Lord we must remember the sacred promises of our eternal coach, our sacred covenants, our athlete's oaths, and our commitment to obedience.

STAY SAFE BY COMPETING WITHIN THE GUIDELINES

The written rules of bobsled are pretty specific, but you may not know that the unwritten rules are just as important. One of the most imperative unwritten guidelines is that you always protect your teammates and never do something to endanger them.

I participated in a special four-man bobsled driver's course at the Park City track in November 2002, nine months after the Olympics concluded. Having driven sleds before my mission, I knew what to expect, but some of the other participants were new to the sport. They muddled through the two-man driving, so when we switched to four-man sleds, I was understandably concerned because I had to sit in the back of their sleds. But to be a good sport, I kept my concerns to myself. So yes, I did a lot of praying while tucked down in my seat, hoping that each bump I felt was not a harbinger of bad news—in other words, a crash.

This continued for several weeks until some bad news did come. It was discovered that a few of the program drivers partook of illegal substances (drugs), possibly while piloting sleds. Think about that. They drove expensive four-man bobsleds down a twenty-five-million-dollar track with three helpless, trusting people in the back. How would you feel?

I was mad. They carelessly jeopardized my safety by taking illegal drugs that have been proven to affect mental capacity and reaction times—two crucial faculties a bobsled driver must have full control over. These drivers threw away a future in the sport and their employment at the track. I expect better from sled pilots because, again, you never do anything to endanger your teammates.

Now think back to a time when someone, maybe a parent or church leader, gave you a rule and you thought, "That's dumb." Did you keep it anyway? If not, what were the results? Was there a suspension, a fine, a job loss, a missed opportunity, or perhaps the loss of gospel privileges? Then again, maybe nothing bad happened. Maybe you got off scot-free. Or at least you thought you did. I'm sure those sled pilots who took drugs during our driving program thought they could get away with their acts. They were wrong, and if you think you can get away with living disobediently, you need to remember that cheaters never win. Disobedience will always catch up to us—in this life or the next.

As Latter-day Saints, we believe that obedience to eternal rules and regulations is a matter of spiritual worthiness and progression (twelfth article of faith). No matter how silly the rule appears, there will always be one result of obedience to gospel principles: safety. Sometimes we don't recognize how good we have it because we never find out how bad it could have been. When it comes to the gospel, all of the rules are given to keep us safe from some danger the Lord wants us to avoid. I like to compare the commandments to specific points on the bobsled track that I use while driving to make small corrections to the sled's steering system. If I ignore these points, the sled can go too high and hit the top of the turn (very hard) or flip over in the exit (ouch).

God knows where the dangerous "points" are in mortality, the ones that can flip our lives upside down or lead to painful "crashes" that result in sorrow and heartache. Just as our coaches walk us through the track and point out the areas that we need to steer in, God reveals to the prophets guidelines that we can follow in order to make it through this life in safety and peace (Amos 3:9). Do we trust God enough to stay within those navigational points and let them guide us safely home to the medal's podium of exaltation? Remember, Satan has no reward for his "champions," so why bother playing for his team?

While God gives commandments to keep us safe, they only work to our advantage if we follow them. The more diligent we are, the safer we will be. But when we ignore the Lord's rules, the promise of protection is removed. And, like a bobsled driver who pilots his or her sled outside the safe areas on a turn, the results are probably going to hurt.

And hurt is something bobsledders try to avoid. Participating in a sport where you hurl yourself down an icy track at over eighty miles per hour comes with a lengthy list of potential injuries. Bruises, scrapes, ice burns, concussions, broken bones, and yes, even death. Sometimes I stand at the top of the track and think, "What am I doing?" But then I get out on the ice because I know that the precautions I have taken will keep me safe.

What precautions? Paul mentions putting on the whole armor of God (Ephesians 6:11), and while there are entire volumes that discuss spiritual armor, I want to explain the armor of bobsled because there is more to our safety methods than meets the eye.

The most important article of protection is the helmet. You will never see a bobsled athlete, no matter how talented, attempt a run without one. They protect our heads from serious injuries that can result in memory loss, reduced physical mobility, paralysis, or perhaps even death.

The next part of our "armor" is called a burn vest. Burn vests look like thermal underwear and fit underneath our spandex uniforms to protect us from the intense heat generated from rubbing on the ice in the event of a crash. Think of them as a friction shield. Hardly fashionable, but effective.

Many sliders also wear athletic gloves to protect their hands from the cold and ice. Gloves provide a better grip for pushing and holding the frame handles.

We also wear distinctive shoes called Bobspikes that are specially made in Germany. Bobspikes look like track shoes on top but underneath have several hundred four-millimeter spikes that allow us to run on the ice. Imagine a couple hundred pushpins pointing sharp end down.

No safety precaution completely eliminates the risk of danger, but this gear lessens our chances of getting hurt on the ice. As athletes we follow these standards of safety because we know they protect us and allow us to fully enjoy our pursuit.

We could say the same for the commandments. Just as wearing our bobsled "armor" protects us from injury, spiritual obedience provides shelter from the dangers of this world. God loves us and trusts us, but he is completely aware of all the pitfalls that exist and the painful consequences—eternal and immediate—if we sin during the entire game of life.

I mentioned that sometimes I stand at the top of the track and wonder if I'm crazy to drive sleds. I wonder if in the premortal existence we ever stood looking down at the earth and pondered the long list of potential spiritual, mental, and physical injuries we could experience.

But, like in bobsled, we have a winning system to protect ourselves from the dangers of sin. By clothing ourselves with the armor of obedience, we can drive through life and remain in the safe areas that will take us home to spiritual gold.

While cameras capture sliding events spectacularly, people rarely notice what we call "the short wall." The short wall is the short cement barrier that lines the straightaways and the base of all the turns. If you watch sliding on TV, the short wall is what the sled bounces off if we mess up. Short walls are thinly iced over because sleds never ride on them, but they play an important safety role. Let's say a driver crashes; their two-man sled becomes an out-of-control, 860-pound ballistic missile traveling close to ninety miles per hour. Using Newton's Second Law of Motion (force = mass x acceleration), the sled's mass (860 pounds) multiplied by the sled's acceleration (90 mph) equals 77,400 pounds of force. Imagine the damage that sled would cause if it flew into the crowd. Thank goodness for the short wall. Flipped sleds hit the short wall and stay inside the track, and that is far safer for the spectators and the athletes.

God provides similar short walls for the course of life in the form of commandments. These spiritual barriers allow us to move through mortality without experiencing the dangers that exist on the other side of the short wall. As long as we stay in the track of the Lord's commandments, we will be safe, but the minute we cross over the wall, we find ourselves in perilous situations. If you ever feel tempted to shed the gold-medal practice of obedience, remember the following story.

My four-man team and I crashed before a race one season, which left a deep impression on my brakeman Brad and me. Brad chose not to wear a protective layer underneath his uniform that day. Granted, his reasoning was, "Jeremy, you don't crash. Why do I need it?" But once we flipped over, gravity pulled Brad against the ice, which instantly burned his skin. Rather than wait for the ride to end, Brad kicked out of the sled and slid through turn twelve on his back.

When he pulled his spandex speedsuit off, scrapes, ice burns, and blood covered his back. Our experience is a firsthand example of how bobsled clothing, like God's commandments, can provide safety only if we stay inside their protective limits. Cross beyond those limits and we remove our spiritual armor and that only leads to the burning pain of guilt, sorrow, and heartache.

We need to keep our protective armor of obedience at full strength and stay away from the painful burns of sin. Compete in life within the short walls of the commandments to find greater peace, strength, and fulfillment. There is no other way to find safety and the gold-medal "joy of the Saints" (Enos 1:3) than obedience.

TEMPTATION'S FOG, SPIRITUAL BLINDNESS, AND SORROW LIKE ICE

I learned a valuable lesson the hard way during an official competition heat at the 1998 Western Regionals held at the Park City, Utah, track.

The adrenaline levels ran pretty high that evening because of the good-sized crowd and the news cameras on-site to record the race. For some of us, it was the biggest competition we had ever participated in, and I know I wasn't the only athlete walking around with butterflies in his stomach. It was a beneficial trial by fire.

We went through the start list, and soon my teammate Adam Revelli pulled our sled to the starting line. My mother took a great shot of us, which you can see in the photos pages. We look professional, calm, and ready to go. I was actually nervous. I was about to drive a bobsled down the track after all; I needed to clear my mind of distractions. Notice I said needed to, not successfully did. I still had a lot to learn.

The buzzer sounded and the sixty-second start clock began to count down, indicating how much time we had to cross the first timing laser. Adam and I called our cadence and pushed off the start block. After loading in, I hit the latch to drop my push bar. As I looked down into the first turn I thought, "Hey, it feels awfully cold and drafty tonight." Then it hit me. In all the excitement at the start, I forgot to close my helmet's face shield! It was wide open, and my eyes began to tear from the breeze. I was quickly losing vision clarity. What a rookie mistake.

I released the steering ring with my right hand and reached up to pull my visor down. Unfortunately, at that time I didn't know to hold both steering rings with my left hand, so the sled quickly drifted left and bounced off the wall, thus fouling my entrance into turn one. Another rookie mistake that cost us crucial speed and time.

And I psychologically carried the mistakes I made at the start all the way to the finish, and it showed in our downtime. That initial error kept us from being able to do our best. Because I left my helmet's visor open, I was momentarily blinded and found myself deviating from the path I desired to follow.

And if that doesn't sound like sin, I don't know what does.

People often describe mortal life as "a wild ride," one full of wonders and experiences beyond imagination. Each day is a beautiful gift from our Heavenly Father, and we should embrace it with faith and enthusiasm. That being said, mortality has its fair share of lows mixed in with all the highs. And as much as we would like to believe that the bad things we experience are the result of fate and the Lord's will, too often we are the greatest source of our own suffering. Not because we are lacking in righteous desires or even spiritual capacity. No, the trouble is the Lord's champions often find themselves tempted and misled by their mortal, or rather immortal, opponent. Satan deceives, and we listen, which leaves us headed for the wrong finish line time and time again.

Here's the problem. We have a God-given game plan that clearly indicates how obedience brings victory through safety, increased blessings, and peace. But just as obedience brings these treasures, disobedience provides sorrow and missed opportunities. As Nephi taught, we are "free to choose liberty and eternal life, through the great Mediator of all men, or to choose captivity and death, according to the captivity and power of the devil" (2 Nephi 2:27). When we choose to disobey, we leave our spiritual "visors" open to having our hearts and souls blinded by sin. Whether we stay safe or venture out into the danger zone is up to us.

The Lord could make every decision for us during the competition of life, but he knows we would never learn that way. For real education to occur, every instructor knows that pupils must digest and then apply the instruction. As a coach, I could tell an athlete what to do all the time, but that kind of teaching leaves no room for growth, which is exactly what we're on earth for. To progress we need agency, the ability to learn from our good choices and from our mistakes. To truly be able to decide for ourselves, we need to understand the sorrowful and damaging consequences of throwing the Lord's counsel out the window.

In athletic terms, the opposing team is there to compete with you—to challenge you during the game. Spiritually speaking, we have an opposing team that wants to win far more than trophies or medals. Led by Satan, this rival team inflicts pain and destroys us spiritually. These talented players will confuse us at every opportunity during the game of life. Their seductive temptations cause us to open our spiritual visors, leaving us blind to the paths that lead to true victory: eternal life.

How does that happen? How do we go from being gold-medal, obedient disciples of Christ to doing something we know is wrong? There is a process to sin, and it all starts with what I call "the fog of temptation."

Like the dishonorable competitor that he is, Satan tries to "take us out of the game" and to spiritually injure us as bad as possible. He will stop at nothing to cheap shot those who are on the Lord's team, and Satan's cheap shots leave us full of guilt and sorrow if we violate God's commandments. Satan wins through our disobedience.

Like the wind coming through my open helmet caused my vision to blur, the fog of temptation can blur our spiritual vision. Every temptation is a lie, a smoke and mirrors deception designed to pull our focus away from the dangers of sin and to trick us into letting our guard down. Satan can then use his silky voice to call today, just as in millennia past, "All is well in Zion; yea, Zion prospereth . . . I am no devil, for there is none" (2 Nephi 28:21–22).

Around bobsled tracks you'll see posted signs that discourage the use of flash photography. Visitors may wonder why, but for sled pilots the rule is a blessing. Imagine coming around a turn and then a bright flash momentarily blinds you. Your instinct would be to look toward the flash, which means you're no longer focused on your path. You may bounce off a wall, power slide in a straightaway, or even crash, all because a momentary distraction stole your focus.

We may be strong, but if Satan can distract and trick us into cracking open our armor just a hair, he will work on that crack until all our spiritual protection is removed. And like my face was exposed when I failed to close my helmet visor, opening temptation's door leaves us exposed to the blinding winds of sin. As the prophet Esias said, "He hath blinded their eyes, and hardened their heart; that they should not see with their eyes, nor understand with their heart" (John 12:20).

I know something about trying to progress while partially blind. On some bitterly cold nights during training sessions, we huddle by the heaters in the start areas before dashing outside to take our run down the track. Our helmets work great most of the time, but occasionally those really cold outside temperatures and the heat and humidity from our breath don't mix well. Even with the helmets' air vents and anti-fog treatments, I've had moments in which portions of my visor have clouded over with condensation. You can still see the track, though it is distorted, and maintain an idea of where you are based on the sensations, pressures, and timing. I share all this because Satan's temptations work in a comparable fashion.

When this clouding over begins, I can watch the condensation form on the outer edge of my visor and move toward the center of my visor, to the most important area I see with. Temptation, like condensation on my visor, starts as a faint whisper, one that is barely within our range of attention or recognition. Satan isn't dumb. He won't throw a huge enticement our way because he knows we'll reject it. Instead he starts small, but if we heed those faint whispers, then Satan's lures will eventually become a spiritual fog. No wonder Lehi says so many people get lost in the mists of darkness before they can reach the tree of life. (1 Nephi 8:23). The fog of sin caused them to lose track of their path.

I have driven down a good portion of a track with a clouded visor, and I can tell you there is little chance of getting a race-winning time. So I use a small piece of tape to create a break between my helmet's visor and seal to avoid driving blind. If the visor begins to fog over, I can tilt my head back a bit to increase the airflow, which immediately clears up my range of vision. We must do something similar when temptation begins to fog over our hearts. Whether it is praying, studying the scriptures, singing a hymn, or talking to a good friend, we need to take action the moment temptation begins to cloud our spiritual vision. It's interesting that to clear my fogged visor, I tilt my head back, thus allowing me to look up more easily.

My open visor left my eyes and face exposed to the elements during the Western Regionals, but sin leaves our souls open to sorrow and guilt. My "sin of omission" at Regionals pushed me from my path, and we lost precious time. Disobedience leaves us struggling to progress because every sin has its consequences and effect on our eternal progression.

We all make mistakes during the game of life. I know it, you know it, and Heavenly Father knows it. So while it is important to discuss the destructive nature of sin, it is equally crucial that we remember that because of Christ's sacrifice we can do more than overcome our slipups—we can be washed clean and be forgiven.

After all, the best athletes aren't necessarily those who get everything right the first time. True champions, the ones who excel in their field of play, are those who keep trying until they get it right. Obedience is the only way to keep your sight clear and clean so you can best navigate the bobsled track of life.

CHOOSE THE HIGHER PATH BECAUSE CHEATERS NEVER PROSPER

I mentioned choosing the high line in life, but during an America's Cup race in 2007, I witnessed the results of one athlete's lower-line choice.

My teammate Mark and I entered the two-man competition, but because I was not piloting a sled in the four-man race, my friend Lars asked if he could borrow Mark as a brakeman to which we both agreed. Given the tight scheduling between training and race sessions, some of the athletes, like Mark, who were pulling double-duty had a pretty active week. That is fairly common in our sport since the two- and four-man races are sometimes held within a day, if not hours of each other.

But this particular race did not end as well for Lars as it could or should have. While Lars sat in the pilot's seat, Mark sat in the back of the sled in the brakeman's position. On the first day of the four-man competition (there were two heats a day for two days) the third guy in the sled showed up hungover from all the alcohol he had drunk the night before. You could see it in his bloodshot eyes and in the way he had trouble moving his body around the start area. In a moment of stark admission, he asked Mark to pull him into the sled if he was unable to do so himself.

I was stunned. This athlete's poor choices went against everything that common sense would dictate for competition. Here he was working with three teammates to win an international race and instead of showing up ready to give his best, this athlete chose to arrive in bad shape. Lars was understandably upset when he found out, and he recruited a replacement for the next day's race, but to my knowledge that athlete who chose so poorly was never invited to slide with any other team again.

I don't know why this athlete got drunk the night before a big race, but at some point he chose to move from "that would be fun" to "I think I'll have another." Not only is this a classic lesson on why the Lord gave us the Word of Wisdom, but it is also an example on the difference between a temptation and actually sinning. When this athlete chose to cross the line into acting on his desires he became 100 percent responsible for the consequences.

By its simplest definition, sin is using our agency to think, act, or speak in a manner that is contrary to God's commandments. We call these "sins of commission" (Doctrine and Covenants 88:35), but James also teaches that to know the way we should act and then not do so is called a "sin of omission" (James 4:17).

Why do champions of the Lord need to know this? Well, sometimes as a coach you have to dish out "tough love," so to paraphrase the words of Alma to his son Corianton, "I would not dwell upon [sin], to harrow up [our] soul[s], if it were not for [our] good" (Alma 39:7). I look back at this athlete who decided to get drunk the night before the America's Cup race and I wonder how differently things would have turned out if someone had helped him make a better choice. I hope his poor performance and that being labeled an irresponsible athlete led to changes in the way he approached future athletic endeavors.

I often hear people say, "It's my life; I can do what I want with it." That's true. God controls the game of life, but he has given us agency that allows us to decide for ourselves between the high and low lines in life. The problem is too many misunderstand the true meaning of agency. In their minds they are free to choose what they do, say, or believe (true), and they can choose the effects of their choices and actions (not true). To them agency is truly free: free from consequences or governing influence. Phrases like "I want to live a little" or "I'm not hurting anyone" appear as justifications. I bet that athlete who went out drinking before the America's Cup race told himself the same thing.

The lie that our choices are free of consequences bombards our lives every day, but as Latter-day Saints, we know better. We know that "do whatever you want and don't worry about the cost" is a trick of the adversary. He is the original author of the phrase, "Eat, drink and be merry" (2 Nephi 28:7). And like so many in our world, Satan inspired Korihor to preach that "whatsoever a man did was no crime" (Alma 30:17). He taught people that once they died, there would be no judgment, no consequences. Since there was nothing after this world, it didn't matter what they did while living in it.

And if that doesn't work, Satan would have us falsely believe that freedom from God's commandments is better than freedom through them.

Remember what I said about temptation's ability to fog over our spiritual sight and affect our choices? Satan wants to blind us to the fact that while we can choose what we say, do, or think, we cannot choose the consequences. However, this devilishly designed game plan has a catch. We may enjoy the fleeting "pleasures of sin for a season" (Hebrews 11:25) but afterward will come the pain, heartache, and sorrow that results from leaving the divine path of safety and peace. To know right and then do wrong is to ignore right and then end up feeling wrong. For champions of the Lord, it is never wrong to do right and never right to do wrong.

Any thought, act, or speech that undermines our character is contrary to the teachings of Christ, and any thought, act, or speech that is selfish and prideful in nature cheats us out of potential blessings, the companionship of the Holy Ghost, and joy. Sin can never bring victory because every disobedient act brings a spiritual loss that we will have to rectify someday.

I'll never forget a local race we had during the 2008 season where I saw a team cheat to win . . . at least on paper. As my teammate Matt and I got our two-man sled ready, we watched another team flip their sled over to make a few small adjustments. As we and the other participating teams began to bolt our runners onto our sleds, we wondered when these athletes would do the same. Normally a team must have their sled to the top of the track one hour before the race's start and have their runners on the sled thirty minutes later. On this day, however, about five minutes before the first sled was going to leave the starting line, this team's pilot walked over to his truck, pulled his runners out of the front seat, and made a beeline for his sled.

This athlete's truck was parked nearby with its engine running. When he opened the door, we could hear the heater going full blast, which meant that for twenty minutes those runners were getting warmed up. During sanctioned races the officials test the temperature of the runners to make sure they aren't heated. In principle warm runners melt the ice beneath them, creating a thin layer of water that reduces friction on the way down the track—meaning the sled goes faster. Because there were no officials at this race, this team got away with what they did. I could just see the steam coming off the runners as they hit the outside colder air.

They won the race. I won't say it was only because of the warmer runners, but I can't say the warm runners didn't help. My teammate and I medaled as well that day, but I honestly can't remember if it was silver or bronze. All I remember is thinking how cheap and hollow that winning team's "victory" was. It wasn't real; it wasn't honest. In the end, they lost what really matters: integrity. In the words of Albert Einstein, "Relativity applies to physics, not ethics."

Satan cheers when we give in to our carnal natures and do whatever we desire. However, the scriptures remind us that the adversary and his teammates are well aware that the more we sin, the more negative consequences we bring upon ourselves (2 Nephi 2:18). Does he care if we get injured in the game of life? Of course not. Satan just wants us to keep sinning because then he'll gain more power "to deceive and to blind men, and to lead them captive at his will, even as many as [do] not hearken unto [the Lord's] voice" (Moses 4:4).

But let's be honest. Sometimes his attempts to blind and lead us captive seem difficult to reject. A gold medal is enough for some to do what they know is wrong. For others it may be popularity, a bigger paycheck, or satisfying an addiction. Whatever the motive, Satan knows what buttons to push to make his temptations seem more attractive. Thank goodness we can "choose the right when a choice is placed before [us]"[16]

I had an experience with this principle during the summer of 2005 when I worked at the Park City track as a tour guide. It was fun to work in that beautiful environment, and I was blessed to meet some incredible people there.

One day, a couple came up to me to ask more about bobsled and my future in it. With a smile, the wife asked me about sponsorships. Keep in mind that as athletes we live or die by support and contributions. Without sponsors most of us could never pay all the expenditures of our sport. This guest went on to explain that she had connections with one of the largest alcoholic beverage companies in the world and that she could possibly get me a sponsorship with them. I'll be honest; I imagined new sleds, uniforms, helmets, and money to travel. I felt Satan whisper all the reasons I should accept the offer.

But then I began thinking about the consequences of accepting such a sponsorship. I would have to promote this company in everything I did. I would be seen on television and in photos in their apparel, and I would have to promote their product. I would have their logo on my sled when I went to schools for assemblies, hospitals for visits, churches to speak, and out in public at expos or parades.

The consequences of accepting the offer were clear in my mind. In the end it didn't matter how much the money would have helped; I didn't agree with the products, and I would be losing power to be a good representative of Christ. I graciously thanked this wonderful couple for their kindness and willingness to help and explained the reasoning behind my declining their offer. They completely understood and wished me the best of luck before they left to continue their vacation.

There is no reward Satan can offer that is worth more than the blessings that come from obedience. He will tempt, bargain, and whisper that we can do whatever we want, but nothing, absolutely nothing, he promises is what it seems. The price of doing wrong when we know what is right is always too high. As Paul testified, "the wages of sin is death" (Romans 6:23).

So as champions of the Lord, we need to be smart about our choices. We must choose the high line in life because sin is a choice we can never afford to make. God desires and expects better things of us!

THE PAIN OF SPIRITUALLY LOSING

The rules that govern bobsled are meant to provide for our safety and help us enjoy fair play during competition. But there are also natural edicts we must abide by because, well, we have yet to figure out how to break the laws of physics.

Physics was never my strong suit in school. I'm just glad I passed the class, but life is full of irony, and now I find myself engaged in a sport that relies on it. Bobsled has taught me quite a bit about the natural laws that govern our universe, especially the law of gravity.

Gravity is the main power behind our sport. Bobsleds have no engines, paddles, or other forms of external propulsion that move us forward after we load into the sled at the start. Instead we rely on the incredible power of gravity to "pull" us down the track (mixed with centripetal force that "whips" us around the turns). We use gravity to increase our speed, but using gravity takes skill. Driving a bobsled requires a heavy mix of concentration, quick reflexes, mental agility, and hand-eye coordination. To put all this together in a race-winning run requires a pilot to follow crucial "lines" in the curves.

A turn's drive lines determine when you steer, how long you hold the correction, and where you enter and exit the turn. The drive lines aren't visible, but when you understand the principles and physics of the sport you know where they are and pilot the sled accordingly. If done right, you can reduce overall time on the course and increase speed.

For example, when you first enter a larger turn, you do a slight "check" with the steering so the sled will follow the contours of the curve instead of driving up to hit the top of the track (which kind of hurts). Then, depending on the length of the turn, you might let the sled glide around the middle before you drive out and head into the next curve. Think of it as an elaborate game of connect the dots; what you do here affects where you will go there and so on. Now those "dots" are partially based on what we call pressure points that are determined by the design of the curve. How much you steer is determined by your speed, the curve's shape, and how high or low on the track you are.

When I first learned to drive sleds I realized that guiding ourselves through life works in a similar fashion. A loving Heavenly Father gave us "steering points" and natural laws that help us make it safely down the course of mortality and have as smooth a ride as possible if we follow them. Sure, we will have trials and hard times, but they are a natural part of this life, just as there are bumps and jostles in a bobsled ride.

When it comes to following the lines on a track, I learned quickly that if I don't correct my driving mistakes, I could hit the top of the turn, or worse, the sled can stay on a troublesome course and we can be too high at the end of the turn. If you have ever watched bobsled, you know that this only leads to one possible outcome: a crash.

My first crash occurred back in 1998 while riding as brakeman in a two-man bobsled with my friend Alex on the Park City, Utah track. I actually knew from the first turn that it was going to be a rough ride because Alex's driving was way off that afternoon. I tucked as low in the sled as I could and death-gripped the handles, expecting the worst. I was about to get a personal lesson on the law of consequences.

The law of consequences means, to paraphrase Isaac Newton's third law of motion, that for every action, thought, or spoken word there is always an equal and opposite reaction, or consequence. The law of consequences holds true for righteous living, which results in blessings (Doctrine and Covenants 82:10), and for disobedience to God's commandments, which results in pain..

As Alex and I entered turn eleven, we shot up pretty high and then came down low in the middle. Because turn eleven's curvature comes down in the middle, sleds usually shoot high at the exit. It's all because of physics, or more specifically Newton's first law of motion: an object in motion will stay in motion (like a moving bobsled) with the same speed and in the same direction (toward the top of the turn) unless acted upon by an unbalanced force (a driver who is in control). Got that? There will be a quiz later.

Alex managed to pull the sled down in time and change the direction of the sled before we hit the top of turn eleven, but his drastic steering had a consequence: we came out of the turn and hit the side of the track pretty hard. Another consequence: we bounced off the wall, which caused us to go late into turn twelve. The same thing that happened in turn eleven happened in turn twelve: we went up high, then low, and then up again in a big "W." Alex pulled the sled sharply out of the turn, but this threw off our entrance into turn thirteen. Turn thirteen is notorious on the Park City track for crashes, so it is appropriately numbered. As we rode high in the curve, I knew that Unlucky Thirteen was about to claim two more victims.

During a crash there is a moment of silence when the sled starts to tip over. As the bobsled goes from riding on four runners down to two, the noise diminishes significantly. I noticed it as I felt my world turn upside down after turn thirteen's exit. Although I had mentally prepared for a crash since my first time on the ice, the real thing is an adventure. When a sled flips over, gravity pulls you against the ice, so you tuck inside the sled to stay safe. I tried to pull into the sled as low as possible before uttering a quick prayer and hoping for the best.

As the sled scrapes and thunders down the ice, the control tower operator calls over the radio to the medical staff and track crew using the code "10-81" to indicate a crash. It can be "all hands on deck" as everyone rushes to where the sled comes to rest after its wild ride.

Alex and I walked away without any burns, and the sled and track were in good shape, but as the medical staff checked us over, I thought, "This was the result of mistakes made." If Alex had driven better, the outcome would have been more positive, but because he did not follow the right drive lines, we crashed. This experience taught me a valuable lesson.

When it comes to sin, the law of consequences always has an less than ideal outcome. Just as you cannot improperly drive a bobsled in a turn and expect to do well, you cannot use your agency to sin and expect to feel good or be blessed. Bobsled crashes may hurt, but sin will always hurt. Period.

In a loving call to repentance issued to his son Corianton, Alma reminded his wayward son (and us) that unrepentant sinners can find themselves in "the gall of bitterness and in the bonds of iniquity . . . they have gone contrary to the nature of God; therefore, they are in a state contrary to the nature of happiness" (Alma 41:11).

For me, bobsled is a state of happiness. It's hard to describe the sensations that come from flying down an ice-covered track at speeds you'd get a ticket for on the freeway. Throw in team camaraderie, the thrill of victory, and the confidence that comes with self-discipline, and you have one of the greatest pastimes in the world . . . unless you crash. If riding down the track right-side up is fun, then crashing is, as Alma said, "a state contrary to the nature of happiness." I know of no athlete who gets excited about crashing, and we should approach sin with the same attitude.

Would you want to ride in the back of a sled with a driver who told you they love crashing and who planned to flip the sled on your run? No-brainer, right? So why do we allow Satan to lure us into spiritually crashing? We know the results are not going to be pleasant. Sin, like a lost competition, will always send us home empty-handed, not to mention spiritually empty-hearted. There are no successful sinners, just as there are no real successful cheaters in sport. You may be able to hide your sins for a while, but eventually the truth will come out (Luke 8:17). The question is how long do you want to carry the burden on your back?

I find it ironic that when a team crashes on the Park City track, they always end up in the lowest point on the course between turns fourteen and fifteen, which is appropriately called "low point." Sin causes us to crash, and if we don't repent, it can lead to the lowest points of our mortal probation. Sin can leave our hearts broken, our spirits in pain, and like a heavy bobsled on top of us, it can weigh us down into the valley of anguish.

Alma described the experience of remembering his wicked life to his son Helaman as "eternal torment, for my soul was harrowed up to the greatest degree and racked with all my sins" (Alma 36:12). I find the word "harrowed" particularly meaningful because bobsleds use a harrow-type brake. How do you stop a bobsled? Well, once we cross the finish line, the brakeman pulls up on metal handles that pivot a row of metal teeth (a harrow) down into the ice. This harrow-type brake digs into the ice and slows the sled down, but I can tell you from experience that it rips the ice up in the braking stretch, the area we slow down in. After a few days of bobsled training, the braking stretch is pretty chewed up, so I have a vivid image of what "harrowed up" means to our souls when I think of what our brakes do to the ice.

While this "harrowing up" is good because it leads to repentance, calling it a good way to progress would be like saying a bobsled crash is good because it teaches the driver. Both statements are true, but willfully sinning while planning later remorse is never a spiritual gold-medal winning strategy.

And the pain that comes from sinful living isn't limited to our own lives. Just as a bobsled pilot's mistake can potentially hurt his teammates in the back of the sled, oftentimes our disobedience hurts those around us. Like the athletes in a crashed sled, these victims are helpless to avoid the consequences of our mistakes. We are the pilots of our lives and it is completely up to us to avoid choices that lead to pain in our lives and heartache and suffering in others' lives.

One season, some of the athletes I coached got to forerun (hill-test) the track before a World Cup race. We worked hard to get the sleds ready, and one thing that I knew would throw off a particular driver was the arrival of the television cameras and crew who were on-site to film the race. When you're accustomed to driving through a turn and seeing only ice, the sudden appearance of a camera platform and its operator can distract you if you're not ready for it.

I made sure to warn this driver about the new additions to the track's scenery and review the mental focusing techniques he should use to ignore them. After a successful run down the track, he energetically expressed that while the cameras did surprise him, knowing about them beforehand allowed him to focus on driving instead of letting them distract him. This time The law of consequences brought good results because this athlete made choices that kept him and his teammate safe.

Because I cared about this pilot and his brakeman, I warned him about the track's new and potentially dangerous distractions. Should we really be surprised that God has clearly warned us of the potential dangers of sin? He loves us more than we can possibly imagine, so he wants us to avoid the "Low Points."

We cannot hope to win the race of life by cheating spiritually. When temptations come, drive by them like the pointless distractions they are. I told that driver before he drove down the track with all those new cameras to "Focus on the track; focus on where you're going. Nothing else." So focus on your spiritual progression and keep your eyes firmly fixed on the Savior and your ultimate finish line—eternal life. As James taught, "Blessed is the man that endureth temptation: for when he is tried, he shall receive the crown of life, which the Lord hath promised to them that love him" (James 1:12).

SIDELINED BY SIN

News flash: bobsled is a cold sport, so if you decide to participate, you can either accept the cold and love it, or hate the cold and be miserable. Growing up in Edmond, Oklahoma, which sees an average of eight inches of snow a year, I had to adjust when we moved to Utah, which can receive eight inches of snow in one hour. Eventually the cold and I learned to get along as the bobsled years progressed.

Training in the ski town of Park City, Utah (elevation 7,000 feet), has led to some firsthand experiences with cold and snow. One of my most memorable experiences with snow occurred during the 2007–2008 season in January. Utah endured a winter storm that lasted several days and that provided an abundance of snow across the northern part of the state. The organization running the bobsled Park City track had to cancel all activities for a week. To cancel events for a day because of weather is a bit of a deal so canceling events for a week can tell you how bad the situation was.

Some parts of the track were basically buried. The track workers tried to clear the snow, but after a few days they needed more help so they called on us as athletes, coaches, officials, and administrators to grab a shovel and lend a hand. If you have ever shoveled a driveway you have a sense of the effort required. But take your driveway's length and multiply that by about thousand and you get a better idea of how many pathways, roads, and track entrances and exits that had to be cleared. And I'm not talking inches of snow: it was feet.

I spent hours around the lower portion of the track trying to clear snow away from the sides and covers of the curves. During breaks I imagined driving through the turn I was working on and visualized what I would do in the entrance and exit. It struck me that because of the snowfall we could never get those missed training sessions back. Although we could work hard to get the track open as soon as possible, we could not change the past. We could fix what was wrong and move forward, but we were powerless to gain the missed opportunities—a stark lesson about the effects of sin.

You've probably heard the saying that cheaters never prosper, which reminds us that cutting corners or performing illegal or immoral acts gets us nowhere. But some athletes do make fortunes by cheating, and they get away with it for years, sometimes for their entire lives. Even so, their victories are tarnished by an eroded sense of sportsmanship and morality. Even if no one finds out about it, a victory gained through deceit or cheating is no victory at all. As the Savior taught, "For what shall it profit a main, if he shall gain the whole world, and lose his own soul?" (Mark 8:36) So why do people seek benefit through acts they know are wrong, especially if someday they might lose it all once the truth comes out? Perhaps the world of sports can answer that too.

While most of the athletes I have trained alongside are extremely disciplined and intelligent, they are still human and possess their own inherent weaknesses. We all do. I know athletes whose outward self-confidence is a mixture of the bravado needed to compete and the forced game face they mastered in order to conquer their own private fears and personal insecurities. That some of the world's greatest champions live with some of the deepest pains should not come as any big surprise. It is often these hidden demons that drive them to excel.

That being said, those same flaws can become the seeds of their undoing. The need to be the best and to find validation by winning can drive competitors to cheat or take unwise risks. Athletes who are desperate to win (instead of determined to win) may decide to bend the rules or let their self-control go in the short-term, thinking that it will benefit them in the long run. It never does. We see this all the time in professional sports. Coaches are ejected from games for throwing tantrums on the field or court. Players are sidelined for illegal plays or actions. Some athletes are fined as punishment for cheating and must sit on the sidelines as their teammates compete without them. The pressure to win can be overwhelming, especially since, as an athlete, you only have a few "prime" years to make it happen. As with nearly every temptation, the thoughts of "now" can blind a consideration for the future.

Apart from the consequences that come from getting caught, in my opinion, the greatest danger to such athletes is the way they have allowed their competitive spirit to become corrupted by a willingness to cheat. As they try to unbury themselves from the "winter storm" of their mistakes, they will have to face the reality that the missed chances may never come again. They may lose sponsors, their position within a program, and the respect and trust of their teammates and coaches. On top of all that, if an athlete on a team is caught cheating, then their teammates may also suffer by losing their own medals or records.

When it comes to sin, disobedience to God's commandments can bring a loss of blessings and opportunities we might have enjoyed had we been wiser. As Jeremiah taught, "Your iniquities have turned away these things, and your sins have withholden good things from you" (Jeremiah 5:25). Sin buries us in the "snow" of unrighteousness and some blessings are "canceled" like the events were on the track.

Let me put it another way. When I am piloting a sled down the track, I can choose from several different drive lines in a turn. Depending on my speed, the curvature of the turn, and the angle I need to best enter the next curve, one of those lines will be better than the others. So let's say I should go high in a turn in order to get the fastest time. If I choose to hold a lower line and therefore burn off speed, once I exit the curve my opportunity is gone. I cannot go back and change what I did; all I can do is affect the rest of our run down the track. My choice squandered an opening to pick up extra speed and nothing I do after the fact can change that missed opportunity.

The blessings we miss out on because of disobedience are often, at least in mortality, lost opportunities. We can repent of our sins and positively affect our future, but we cannot go back and change the past. While the atonement has infinite restorative and healing powers, one aspect that cannot be returned is the opportunities we lost through walking disobedient paths. Time marches on, and while we may gaze longingly at the past, we cannot get it back.

There may also be long-term consequences of our sins that affect our future prospects. For example, I once knew a young man who through the use of illegal drugs lost a great portion of his mental faculties. His mind and body will be restored to their perfect state through the resurrection, but the chances he missed to progress mentally, physically, socially, spiritually, and emotionally due to the damage to his brain and physique are too complex to calculate. It reminded me of a story my coach once told me regarding the deadly outcome of one athlete's decision to cheat.

During an official training session one evening in the late 1970s, the coaches of a two-man team pulled a sled to the starting line. Everyone watched in shock as a new brakeman, who was bigger than anyone they had ever seen, walked out to the start area and stood by his driver. When the green light lit up, they flipped the sled down and this brakeman went through his personal routine of shouting and slapping his thighs to get the adrenaline flowing . . . and then he stopped and fell over. The start area was silent as the team's coaches and staff rushed to the listless athlete's side. After several minutes of frantic activity, the sled was pulled from the line and the athlete was carried away. It wasn't until years later that everyone discovered that the monstrous athlete's heart had suddenly stopped due to all the steroids he had been injected with. His attempt to win at all costs killed him.

I deduced that the story was fictional (I have yet to find evidence of such an event), but the lesson remained stuck in my mind. Sinful choices may not lead to physical death like in this story, but in the end cheaters never prosper. But here's the problem. Satan "snows us in" a little bit at a time. A fine layer of powder is no big deal, but as we continue to sin, that layer builds until we find our spirits and hearts buried in wickedness, just as the track was. And if that happens, our hearts may "stop," or give up, as this fictional athlete's did.

That our sins cause us to miss out on potential blessings should not come as any surprise. It is not because our Father in Heaven desires to withhold his blessings; rather, the Lord reminds us that when we receive a blessing, it is because we were obedient to the laws and ordinances upon which that blessing is predicated (Doctrine and Covenants 82:10). When we choose to walk in foolish paths, we "have no promise" [*sic*] and can anticipate missed windows of opportunity along the way, much like the prodigal son (Luke 15).

This young man squandered his inheritance, and while he was out living it up, his father, his brother, and their household back home were enjoying relative comfort. Eventually the young man suffered for his poor choices. And his wicked ways led him away from his father's house. Because of his poor choices, he found himself envying the pigs his father owned. But how different would his life had been if he had not wandered in forbidden paths and become lost (1 Nephi 8:23)? This man could have enjoyed all the blessings that his father desired to provide, but because of his adventures in the ways of the world he missed out on those opportunities.

Our disobedience results in lost blessings and opportunities for several reasons. Through spiritual waywardness we become buried in sin and lose the influence of the Holy Ghost. Without his guidance we may not make the decisions that lead to good opportunities. Also, by choosing actions that move us away from the Lord, we inject wicked "steroids" into our hearts and diminish our sensitivity to the ways of righteousness. Disobedience by its nature means we have chosen to act, speak, or think in a manner contrary to the laws upon which a blessing is predicated (Doctrine and Covenants 82:10), which negates the blessings we could have enjoyed had we chosen differently.

Spiritually speaking you can never cheat the commandments and win. If you try Satan's fake "steroids" of happiness you will only end up miserable and buried in sorrow. Let us live within the bounds the Lord has set for the game of mortality. Let us live each day like spiritual champions who follow the rules that God has given to protect and help us win the greatest "medal" of all, even exaltation. By so living we can enjoy all the blessings that the Lord desires to give us and as Paul reminded the people of Corinth, "Eye hath not seen, nor ear heard, neither have entered into the heart of man, the things which God hath prepared for them that love him" (1 Corinthians 2:9). And if we love him and keep his commandments, the blessings of Heaven can be ours so much that "there shall not be room enough to receive it" (3 Nephi 24:10).

DISOBEDIENCE LEAVES US TO COMPETE ALONE

When you mentally prepare for a run down the track, you imagine that everything will turn out perfectly. Your team is going to have a great push, your sled is going to react ideally and your driving is going to be precise. While you formulate "What if?" plans for the unexpected (a crash or a brakeman who does not make it in the sled), you run through the experience from start to finish as if it was going to be your best run ever.

But reality doesn't always go as smoothly as we'd like, as many athletes can attest. I saw this several years ago while studying drive lines during a session at what we call the old Lake Placid track in New York (they revamped the track in 2000). On this particular day, I was standing near a famous pair of turns named Zig and Zag, a ninety-degree left-hand then ninety-degree right-hand combination. Zig and Zag were sled eaters; areas of the track notorious for flipping bobsleds, because at high speeds you would zig left then zag right so quickly that some pilots were too slow to react. To aggravate the problem, prior to Zig and Zag, pilots would face Little S, a nasty little blip of ice that could throw off your entrance to Zig. Next to the push start, Zig and Zag were key to winning on the old Lake Placid track, so I wanted to study what the local pilots were doing so I could better understand how to handle it.

I later walked up the track to watch lines in turn fourteen, a fourteen foot high "wall" that curved 170 degrees to the right, known affectionately as Shady. Teams pulled over four G's while traversing Shady at speeds of over seventy miles per hour. As I sat there, I heard a name announced over the loudspeakers that I recognized. I had seen the veteran pilot, whom I'll call Charlie, train on the Park City track before, and as they flew past, I admired the way Charlie guided his sled through Shady. I imagine he spent plenty of time at the start mentally practicing his drive down the track, and from what I saw it was probably going according to his hopes. But Zig and Zag were about to change that.

I didn't see all this because I was up in Shady, but Charlie must have done something wrong in Little S that threw off his entrance into Zig, which really messed up his entrance into Zag. The next thing I heard was the loud grinding sound of a sled upside down on the track. Turns out Charlie had flipped out of Zag, and by the time the sled came to a stop, he had a broken collarbone to remind him of the experience.

This experience got me thinking. I believe every one of us came to earth with the hope that we would do everything right, that everything would be great, and that we wouldn't have any problems. The thing is, mortal life is a journey, and sometimes we don't make the best choices during the game. Like the old Lake Placid track, sometimes we get caught up in the Little S-turns, or Little Sins, that throw us off course, and then we find ourselves Zigging and Zagging under the burden of iniquity and then—crash! We find ourselves exposed to the unforgiving surface of the ice—the results of our poor decisions—but instead of a broken collarbone like Charlie got, we end up with broken hearts or broken lives and the loss of the Holy Ghost's guidance.

One of the gravest dangers of sin is that our disobedient acts, thoughts, and words offend the Holy Ghost and cause us to lose his protective guidance and companionship for a time. King Benjamin taught his people, "after ye have known and have been taught all these things, if ye should transgress and go contrary to that which has been spoken, that ye do withdraw yourselves from the Spirit of the Lord, that it may have no place in you to guide you in wisdom's paths that ye may be blessed, prospered, and preserved . . ." (Mosiah 2:36). If you are looking to go off course in life, losing the Spirit's companionship is a sure way to do it.

The Spirit guides us in wisdom's paths so we can progress (Doctrine and Covenants 8:2–3), find deeper joys (Doctrine and Covenants 11:13), and be secured against the things of this mortal world (Doctrine and Covenants 18:18). Like the protective burn vests that we wear underneath our spandex racings suits, the Holy Ghost can be a shield that protects us from Satan's temptations and the potentially painful outcome of a wrong decision (2 Nephi 32:5). The Spirit can also strengthen us in times of need, direct us in important decisions, and increase our faith. No wonder we have been commanded to remain worthy of his presence in our lives and to "deny not the spirit of revelation, nor the spirit of prophecy" (Doctrine and Covenants 11:25).

I say this to point out that before we choose to disobey God's commandments, we should ask ourselves if we will be better off without the companionship of the Holy Ghost. Do we want him as a teammate in life or not? Making choices that will offend the Spirit and cause us to lose his guidance for a time will only bring similar results to what an athlete experiences when they choose to not wear protective layers under their racing suit. The only difference is that instead of ice burns, we will suffer the stinging ache and pain of sin in addition to the loneliness of losing the Spirit's companionship.

In Helaman 4:23 we read that "the Spirit of the Lord doth not dwell in unholy temples." As a member of the Godhead the Holy Ghost cannot abide sin nor can he reside in spiritually polluted places. As champions of the Lord, we have been counseled to "stand . . . in holy places" (Doctrine and Covenants 45:32) since those are the only settings where the Spirit can accompany us.

I had an experience while driving up to the track in Calgary, Canada, in 1998 that taught me about this. We had four athletes and one coach tucked into a spacious fifteen-passenger van, which made the fourteen-hour trip a little more bearable. After stopping for food and gas, another athlete hopped back into the van with a tape in his hand that he wanted to play right away. I took one look at the tape's case and knew it was going to be full of lewd jokes and immoral stories. It was a recording of a popular comedian, but I had a sinking feeling I was going to be doing anything but laughing.

Although I objected, I was outnumbered, and the van soon filled with the sound of verbal filth. I lay down in the back seat and tried to get my Walkman to work (yes, I said Walkman). No luck; dead batteries. I tried to block the tape's content out of my ears, but found this to be impossible because of the loud volume. I had to listen to the garbage, and the longer it played, the sicker I felt. As the audible smut filtered in, I knew the Spirit was offended, and I found it harder to feel good and positive. I didn't have complete control over that situation, but another experience I had can help illustrate the importance of keeping our lives pure so that we may "always have his Spirit to be with [us]" (Doctrine and Covenants 20:77).

One cold Park City night in 1999 after a training session, my friend Joe and I were down in the finish area. I had already put my sled away for the night, but Joe was finishing up some final work on his. I was getting ready to leave when he asked if I could help him put the scabbards on his sled and pull it into his car. "Of course," I replied. I made the regretful decision to leave my gloves in my car as I walked over to help. When I reached down to grab the steel handles on Joe's scabbards, my skin immediately felt a shock of sharp pain. Remember when your siblings dared you to stick your tongue to the metal pole during winter? Well, at the glacial temperatures we sometimes train in, metal gets very cold. When my bare skin touched the steel handle on the scabbards, the cold metal actually flash-froze the surface layers of my skin. Ouch.

I learned a painful lesson that day about the importance of wearing protective layers when handling cold metal, but it was a lesson that applies to the gift of the Holy Ghost. Without my gloves on, I burned my skin and suffered pain. Without the protective layer of the Holy Ghost, we become weaker and lose the protective guidance and uplifting influence of the Spirit, and that will leave us exposed to the cold pain of sin.

If we really got the meaning of the gift of the Holy Ghost into our minds, we would be less apt to commit sin. Those living their lives in a righteous manner can, as Alma taught, "[be] sanctified by the Holy Ghost, having their garments made white, being pure and spotless before God, [so that they] could not look upon sin save it were with abhorrence" (Alma 13:3). As we draw closer to the Lord and the Spirit, our desire to sin fades. Like a swinging pendulum, we will move away from the things of this world and closer to the things of God. However, the reverse can be equally true so be careful.

I pray that as champions of the Lord we can find the strength to resist evil so we can have the protective influence of the Holy Spirit each and every day. I've lived long enough to know that if we want to win eternal gold, we need his help to do so.

EYES ON THE WRONG PRIZE

One of the most unique experiences I have had in the world of bobsled was to act as a Drug Control Escort (DCE) for the 1998 US Olympic Trials.

Held in Park City, Utah, from December 30, 1997, to January 5, 1998, this competition was exciting and dramatic. The best of the best in the United States were out in force to compete for their shot at Olympic glory in the upcoming Nagano Japan Games. I was thrilled to watch sleds driven by American-greats like Jim Herberich, Bruce Roselli, and Todd Hayes. The US's top pilot, Brian Shimer, received a pass on the trials and would go on to miss a bronze medal in Japan by two-hundredths of a second (the human eye takes about three-tenths of a second to blink). So two other drivers still needed to be selected, one to race and one to act as an alternate, which made for some fierce competition since the nine push-athlete berths were still open as well.

After a big race like the Trials, certain athletes (usually selected from the medaling teams) are assigned a Drug Control Escort like me. As DCEs our job was to watch our assigned athlete like a hawk. If memory serves, my charge was two- and four-man pilot Jim Herberich, who went on to place seventh in Nagano's two-man bobsled competition. While our role was serious, the task was simple: meet the athlete in the finish area and watch everything they do until we passed them over to representatives who would perform the official doping tests.

What is doping? In the world of sport, *doping* is another word for cheating through the use of performance enhancing substances such as steroids. Unfortunately, even the best athletes can fall to the tempting promise of, "Take this and you're sure to win." Our task at the 1998 Olympic Trials was to make sure our assigned athletes made it to the official testing area without doing anything that might change the results of their blood or urine tests. You'd be surprised what athletes have attempted so they could hide their illegal activities.

At the top levels of sport the pressure to win can be overwhelming, and gaining an edge on the competition has led contestants to make dumb choices from the beginning of time. The interesting thing about many of the banned substances is that they also have side effects, some of which are not pretty. The temporary effects on the athlete's body can indeed enhance their performance, but the long-term results can do serious damage. While modern science is improving these substances and reducing their side effects, the risks remain.

From a logical standpoint, the question begs to be asked, "Why take the risks?" Why jeopardize an Olympic medal if you test positive for steroids? Why increase the possibility of damaging your body or mind, the same body and mind you've worked so hard to cultivate into a perfect biological machine? All athletes who dope will have to answer that question for themselves, but as I have thought about the dangers of using banned substances, I believe there are similarities between doping and disobedience to God's commandments.

No matter the technique or chemical used, doping breaks the rules set down by the governing body of a sport. When athletes participate in events organized by these administrations, they agree to abide by those rules as if they were law. Willfully breaking these regulations can lead to serious consequences, not the least of which could be damage to their own bodies. Athletes caught doping can be banned from their sport for the rest of their lives, and they may lose records they have set and be ordered to return medals or trophies they won. Some even have to pay back sponsors for money they received while lying about their performance and cannot coach future athletes themselves. And in some countries athletes caught doping may even serve jail time.

Doping can be compared to sin in so many ways. Not only do we damage our bodies and minds, but we also may find ourselves unable to participate in "the game" when we cannot partake of the sacrament, attend the temple, and, in the most severe of cases, we may lose our membership in the Church for a time. Yes, sin is cheating—cheating ourselves, cheating those who love us, and cheating the Lord.

In his vision of the tree of life, Lehi watched various groups of people make their way toward the tree (1 Nephi 8:21–22), but as some commenced forward on the path, the mists of darkness (temptation) arose and they soon found themselves lost (verse 23). Similarly, many good athletes start their path to Olympic glory with a real intent to compete honestly. But the temptation to put things into their bodies can leave them wandering in cheating paths that lead everywhere but toward the goal they want to achieve. Their goal may be the Olympics, but as Latter-day Saints our ultimate goal is returning to our Father's kingdom, and no sinful decision will lead us there.

Just as the decision to dope ultimately moves athletes away from their sport-related goals, so too will sin drive us away from what matters most in this world: obedience to the commandments, activity in the Church, and gospel progression. If you're moving away from heaven, the isolation you feel is the bitter reward of sin.

Perhaps the most painful effect of spiritual "doping" is that lonely feeling that comes from drifting away our Father in Heaven. The scriptures remind us that God does not change (Malachi 3:6), so if we feel like he is far from us we are the ones who moved. No wonder the gospel is so full of invitations to turn away from sin (Ezekiel 33:14–16), to return (3 Nephi 9:13), and to come home again (Luke 15).

During the 2005–2006 season, I went through a long list of unexpected trials, struggles, and setbacks. I freely admit that I allowed my reliance on the Lord to slip as my focus became more directed toward bobsled and the social aspects of life. I was trying to use the ways of the world to increase my happiness instead of relying on faith. I found myself becoming complacent in my prayers and scripture study. I began to work more and train harder, and as a result, I found less time for friends and family.

I was unhappy and stressed, and the ironic thing was the more I tried to enhance my performance in life with the things of this world, the less enthused I was about bobsled. I felt myself gently drifting. While I still attended my Church meetings and activities, my spirit was slowly losing its strength.

After a few months I knew I needed to get back with the program. I was holding on to the iron rod by a fingertip or two instead of grasping it with all my strength. I realized that I was witnessing the contrast between a separation from God's influence and the blessings that come from staying close to him.

I decided to kick it in gear and bring the Lord back into my life through consistent prayer and scripture study. I focused on my gospel responsibilities, and I tried to be more Christlike every day. Soon I began to feel closer to my Heavenly Father, and I noticed his guiding hand to a greater degree in my life. Most of all, I felt a deepened sense of his love for me, that he was welcoming me back with open arms (Luke 15:20). I learned that just as doping can lead good athletes away from their ultimate goals and the guiding influences of their sport, disobedience only leads us away from the Lord.

I doubt any of us consciously want to move away from our Father in Heaven and lose his proffered blessings, protection, and guidance. That would be like an athlete walking away from the certifiably best coach in the universe. Don't sell eternal victory with God for a mess of temporal pottage. When temptations come, ask yourself if you would rather deny your cross or deny the Christ? Love and respect yourself enough to avoid spiritual "prohibited substances" and, instead, fight for the gold medals that matter.

In July 1998, I was invited along with athletes from other sports to a Park City ski resort to help unveil their new development. The event was an open house for potential investors, and it proved to be an exciting experience for a seventeen-year-old kid. Upon arrival, I was led to an upper floor in a lodge to sit and wait with all the other athletes until the time came for the unveiling when they would announce our names and sports as we walked down the stairs. Easy enough, right?

As we sat conversing I remember watching one athlete grow a bit louder and obnoxious as the alcoholic drinks appeared. As the clock ticked by, this athlete's inebriation increased and their actions became a bit more, shall we say, slurred. How they planned to make it down the stairs or converse with the crowd, I have no idea. But I remember thinking, "Our invitation to come was a gift. This isn't what we are here for."

This isn't what we are here for. Can you think of a better rebuttal to Satan's temptations? "That's not what we are here for. I will not lose the gift of the gospel. I am here to prepare to return to my father. I will stand strong as a champion of the Lord."

We are here on this earth for great things, and the Lord expects us to live up to that potential. He knows what we are capable of, what great accomplishments, acts of service, and joyful memories we can experience. Do not toss away those gifts! Do not be like the athlete who lost every Olympic medal because of steroids.

At this point perhaps you have made some mistakes and maybe you feel like the race is lost and you can never feel our Heavenly Father's love again.

That's a lie. We all slip up. We have all sinned and fallen short (Romans 3:24). In bobsled we make mistakes. We crash, we hit walls, we slack on our technique, and we do things in practice and competition that need correcting. But we must always remember that our Father in Heaven is just that—a father. Your eternal coach loves you and is anxiously waiting to help you change, repent, and come back.

FORGIVENESS WITH A SIDE ORDER OF HOPE

The path to excellence, especially eternal excellence, is fraught with challenges, but the desire to achieve can push competitors far beyond their limits as they reach for the stars. I have seen athletes sacrifice everything in order to stand on the medals podium. Are we willing to do the same so we can stand clean before God?

Although we know the gospel game plan for spiritual victory, we are still mortal beings subject to temptations, weaknesses, appetites, habits, and confusion. While playing for the Lord's team, when we experience those errors in judgment it takes a deep level of maturity to look in the mirror and say, "I fell short." Quite often our natural inclination is to hide our sins away.

Athletes often have similar reactions to physical injuries. No true competitor enjoys sitting on the sidelines, and that mind-set can easily outweigh any fear of aggravating the wound further. Athletes tend to think of the here and now and not about the damage playing with an injury may cause later in life.

To make matters worse, some coaches overlook injured players and focus solely on those who can still compete. This leads to several psychological, social, and emotional problems for the sidelined athlete. They may feel vulnerable (they are obviously no longer invincible), isolated (the team can practice and play, they cannot), and less valuable (they cannot contribute to the final score). Throw in the fear of losing a contract or scholarship, and it's no wonder injured athletes are tempted to hide a problem.

Satan labors to instill those same feelings in us when we become spiritually injured. He whispers that our eternal coach, God, is going to focus on those who can "still play" (those we think are more righteous) and ignore injured us. The adversary works to isolate us from our teammates in the

Church and get us to hide on the spiritual sideline, which, ironically, makes it easier for him to recruit us for his diabolical team.

Satan is far more successful at this than God prefers. Our secret mistakes can quickly develop into anchors that slow our progress because we plant chains of discouragement in the ground and sit there on an ever-growing pile of hell-inspired hopelessness. Like an athlete who can see no future beyond his or her current injury, we may view our sins as the referee's final whistle. We may even believe that our mistakes are so grave that the spiritual game is over and we should give up hope.

At first, Satan's logic appears solid. Unlike an unexpected injury received during the chaos of the game, for a sin to be a sin it must result from our choice. As the guilty party why shouldn't we feel depressed, of low self-worth and isolate ourselves from God, the Savior and the society of the Church? Don't we deserve it? Absolutely not.

In a previous chapter I described what it feels like to be in a bobsled crash. It's loud, it's intense, and sometimes it's scary. All you can do is hold on, try to "think small" (pull as tightly into the sled as possible), and wait until the sled comes to a stop.

My four-man team and I experienced this while forerunning for the 2008–2009 Park City World Cup. We spent hours getting the sled ready for the big day and were stoked to participate in such a fun event. The positive energy transferred over to our start as we pushed the fastest we ever had together. I could tell we were going fast on the super-clean World Cup ice, and everything was going flawlessly until we hit turn eleven, when we exited the turn a hair late. Many bobsled crashes are the result of going for extra speed. In some turns you want to keep the sled on the curve and then drive it off to let the exit of the turn accelerate you. The problem with this is that if you hang on just a bit too long, you crash.

As my team exited turn eleven, I was looking straight into the entrance of turn twelve when my gaze suddenly pivoted sideways before going dark. The next thing I knew my shoulder was starting to tingle then burn, and I realized we were on our sides. We rolled out of turn eleven and were now passing through turn twelve upside down.

I quickly pushed myself away from the ice's surface. Incidentally I found out later that by moving my shoulder below the protection of the sled's body, the G-forces pulled my body against my number-two athlete, Don Osmond, and he ended up breaking a small bone in his hand. Sorry, Don. That makes up for falling on my helmet when you loaded in at the start of the track.

Needless to say, I was disappointed with myself. Physically I was fine, but as the driver I took full responsibility for what happened. We had been tasked with forerunning, or testing the ice and timing/camera systems for the World Cup. So while the best of the best were waiting at the top of the track, we were lying upside down at the bottom. To make matters worse a large crowd gathered when we came to a stop, and their digital cameras caught it all. Not my best on-ice moment.

When we came to a stop after our crash, I breathed a sigh of relief and mentally checked every part of my body to make sure nothing was broken. After a few seconds of post-crash silence, someone grabbed the sled, and I heard, "We've got you! Are you guys okay?" I sensed my team getting out, and then a voice called for me to exit. I tried to pull myself out of the nose, but with the way the sled was wedged against the wall I could barely move. I couldn't get any leverage to move. I remember sticking my hand in the air and immediately another strong hand grasped mine and pulled. I don't know who it was, but I was so grateful he helped me get out of the mess I caused.

As soon as we stepped off the track, people surrounded us to make sure we were safe. The medical professionals, along with the track workers, did everything in their power to put us back together and get us back on our feet.

Despite their concern, frustration was my dominating emotion. Prideful, I know, but I had thoughts that many of us have when we sin: "I should have known better." "I can't believe I did that." "I'm so ashamed." "What will others think of me?" I hadn't had a Park City crash all season. My runs had been clean, our pushes and loads accurate, and the sled had been performing superbly for months. It wasn't until later that the whole experience got me thinking: if sin is like a bobsled crash, then repentance is what happens after you come to a stop.

Satan tempts us to "hold on the turn," a bit too long with whispers of alluring results. He wants us to believe that sin will make us happier, increase our popularity, maybe make us wealthier, more beautiful. He whispers for us to push the limits, push the limits, push the limits until—*bam*! We are spiritually upside down and feel like our souls have crashed. If we continue in the path of sin, we will find ourselves at the lowest points of the track of life. Soon depression, loneliness, spiritual darkness, and an internal hunger will set in. As Nephi warned, " . . . and thus the devil cheateth their souls, and leadeth them away carefully down to hell. (2 Nephi 28:21).

But if bobsled has taught me anything, it's that there is always hope. The invitation to cross the eternal finish line is still open. There really is a light at the end of the tunnel, or bobsled track in this case. You can learn from your mistakes, improve, and come back to win. I know this can be challenging at times, when, like a bobsled pilot, you know the "crash" resulted from your choices. As a driver this can be difficult to swallow, especially when a wreck costs you a medal.

The weight of disobedience can be compared to being inside a flipped sled. You may hurt, feel stuck, and can't wait to be done with it. The thing about sin is that the sorrow can end if we seek forgiveness and healing through the Atonement of Christ.

And just like with a bobsled crash, helping hands are all around us to lift the burden and get us back on our feet. I find it interesting that the people who help athletes after their mistake-inflicted injuries are medics who wear red coats with white crosses on them.

No spiritual crash in life is too great, no burden of sin too heavy for he who endured the crushing weight of Gethsemane. When our sins come roaring down like an overturned bobsled, we need to remember there is hope in Christ, we can be comforted, and our tears can be wiped away. No matter how big our problems may seem, there is always "good news."

This good news was taught to Joseph Smith and Sidney Rigdon in Doctrine and Covenants 76:40–41: "And this is the gospel . . . That he came into the world, even Jesus, to be crucified for the world, and to bear the sins of the world, and to sanctify the world, and to cleanse it from all unrighteousness."

According to Thayer's *Greek-English Lexicon*, "The word gospel itself means 'good story' and comes from the Greek word, 'evangelion', which means 'good or glad tidings.' " In the New Testament, the verb meaning "to preach or bear witness of the gospel" is evangelidzo, literally, "to bring good news, to announce glad tidings."[17]

These translations cause me to reflect on the angel's announcement to the shepherds on the night of our Savior's birth in Luke 2:10–11: "Fear not: for, behold, I bring you good tidings of great joy, which shall be unto all people. For unto you is born this day in the city of David a Saviour, which is Christ the Lord." The angelic message is a message to all of us, especially to the champions of the Lord who are struggling under the weight of sin: Fear not, Christ was born and therefore there is always hope.

Why was Christ's birth an *evangelion*, or a good tiding of "great joy?" Our elder brother was chosen to be the Redeemer of Mankind (Abraham 3:27, 1 Peter 1:20, Mosiah 18:13, Ether 3:14) and to come and rescue us from our fallen state. Since he has paid the price for our spiritual "crashes," we have hope because through repentance "the blood of Jesus Christ . . . cleanseth us from all sin" (1 John 1:7).

Just as helping hands rush to our aid if we crash in bobsled, I know loving hands will always be there to lift the burden of sin from our shoulders if we repent. You're not alone. You are never alone. Our Heavenly Father loves us no matter what shape we are in. He knows we are going to make mistakes and that our spiritual sleds are going to crash time and time again. Don't we all have a few scrapes, dings, gouges, and cracks by now?

Like the father of the prodigal son, God anxiously awaits our return (Luke 15:20). True repentance isn't necessarily easy, but the things most worth having rarely are. But I testify that when we turn to God with full-purpose of heart, we will find a coach who has been waiting for us with love, mercy, and compassion. He will not berate us for the crashes of this life; rather, we will find ourselves overwhelmed by his care, concern, and continued faith in our potential. Like that strong person who helped pull me from my crashed sled, God's hand can lift us from the "wrecks" of our sins.

As one of my favorite hymns teaches us:

> Fear not, I am with thee; oh be not dismayed,
> For I am thy God and will still give thee aid.
> I'll strengthen thee, help thee, and cause thee to stand,
> Upheld by my righteous, omnipotent hand.[18]

Instead of being disappointed or angry that we had crashed, our coach was only concerned about our welfare. He could see I was frustrated about it and was sure to remind me that crashes are a part of the sport, that it happens to all of us, and that the important thing is to get back on the ice and move forward. His words and reaction to my mistake were an illustration of our Father in Heaven's response when we "come to ourselves" and desire to repent. Even if you find yourself upside down in life there is hope and help ahead. When we find ourselves at the lowest points in our lives (like a flipped bobsled resting at the lowest point of the track), we logically have nowhere else to go (or look) but up.

Up is the best direction to go after all.

HOPE AND INTERNATIONAL MISTAKES: CONDITIONS OF REPENTANCE

Right before the 2004–2005 season, I was able to purchase my own two-man bobsled with the help of a local company. To understand how big of a deal this was, imagine what you felt when you got your first car, only about a hundred times better. It wasn't a new sled, nor was it the fastest, but it was mine.

When the shipping company dropped off the moving pallet, I ripped the packaging off as the employees of this business gathered to join in. As we stood back to admire the cherry-red paint job, I decided she looked like a sports car—yes, like a fighter aircraft or naval vessel, a sled is a "she." For the next half-hour we examined the sled as if it held the secrets of the universe, and as I've thought back on that moment I realized that getting this new sled is a personal metaphor for the Atonement.

When I returned home from my mission in 2002, the Park City track no longer had a large number of two-man sleds available, and the few that were around had hefty rental fees for a several-months-long season, not to mention a deposit for any damages. I was able to make it through the 2002–2003 season, but the next season was only seven months away with another round of costs. Remember, I was also paying for my college tuition, car payments, health insurance, and all the other general expenses a returned missionary has (dating).

There were a couple solutions to my equipment problem. One option was to try and find some sponsors to pay for my sled rentals and training fees. Another was to raise enough money to purchase a sled, which is what I really wanted. Having your own sled is more convenient, and training/racing with your own gear makes a big difference.

After months of searching, the Lord opened some doors with a Salt

Lake City-based company, and shortly thereafter the new sled was sitting outside their shop. So how does this situation remind me of the Atonement? In purchasing an expensive new bobsled for me, that company did what I could not do for myself. With my own limited resources I couldn't pay the bill.

Man by himself can indeed do great things and cause much good in the world, but powers and constraints exist far beyond us. Because of the Fall and our sins, we could never overcome physical death (2 Nephi 9:6–11), nor could we meet the demands of justice to overcome spiritual death (Alma 42:12, 14) and return to God's presence. Sin leaves us with an infinite bill that we can never pay with our own finite assets. And justice always comes to collect. Although God loves us unconditionally and wants us to come home, he cannot deny the conditions of justice. If he did, he would "would cease to be God" (Alma 42:22).

To get the new bobsled, justice had to be met, and rightly so. I couldn't just steal the sled; I needed to meet the terms set down by the sled's owner, which was a price that that I couldn't pay on my own. However, justice/the bill could be met by the intervention of a third party, or a mediator. A mediator is someone who works to bring together two (or more) estranged parties and help them come to a reconciliation or agreement. In the spiritual sense, the two parties are us and our Father in Heaven.

Because of his infinite sacrifice, Christ may act as a mediator and pay the debt with his infinite resources. In this way the Atonement truly is the "at-one-ment," or bringing together of these two parties. As Amulek taught, "this being the intent of this last sacrifice, to bring about the bowels of mercy, which overpowereth justice . . . And thus mercy can satisfy the demands of justice, and encircles them in the arms of safety, while he that exercises no faith unto repentance is exposed to the whole law of the demands of justice" (Alma 34:15–16).

So the Savior has already purchased our "sled," our opportunity to return to our Father's kingdom. But just as I had to accept the conditions offered by this company before they would buy me the new bobsled, so too must we accept the stipulations that Christ has set forth so the debt of our personal sins can be paid. Amulek called those conditions of forgiveness repentance. As Aaron taught King Lamoni's father, "since man had fallen he could not merit anything of himself; but the sufferings and death of Christ atone for their sins, through faith and repentance" (Alma 22:14). Without these conditions, we would be like athletes who blame their equipment for a loss; there will be neither acceptance of responsibility nor change of behavior.

What athletic contract is going to be signed by either party if the conditions are not clearly agreed upon? What bank is going to give a loan without concrete parameters about payment and interest rates? Even a marriage certificate has legal requirements set on both parties. It should not surprise us that justice has specific conditions that must be satisfied before forgiveness and mercy can be given.

Repentance itself is the condition that must be met in order for our sins to be washed away in the blood of the Lamb. The Atonement of Jesus Christ makes it possible for us to exercise our faith through obedience and repentance when we fall short. But that is the Lord's half of the contract.

What, then, are the conditions of repentance that we must meet? True repentance is a deeply emotional and spiritual process that requires godly sorrow for our sins (2 Corinthians 7:10) and a change of heart that effects a desire to leave all evil behind (Alma 19:33). Worldly sorrow is based on pain from getting caught or suffering the consequences of our mistakes, like an athlete who is ejected from a game for an illegal move. Godly sorrow is a pain of the soul because we have broken our covenants, but this grief can turn us from our transgressions and "make . . . a new heart and a new spirit (Ezekiel 18:31).

The word "make" indicates some work has to be done. After a bobsled crash on the track we work to get the sled ready to use again. These repairs can be intensive and can require many long hours. We work to replace the weakened section of the fiberglass body and strengthen any parts of the sled that need reinforcement. Repentance is like the repair work that goes into fixing a broken bobsled. It is spiritually and emotionally intensive, it can require long hours of prayer, and it can only succeed when we remove the damaging aspects of our lives and humbly reinforce our spirits with faith and obedience.

As a coach, I try to apply this principle of conditional forgiveness when it comes to helping my athletes learn from their mistakes. For example, one of our pilots hurt his hand playing another sport off the ice, but when he returned to the track for a training session, he did his best to hide the injury. I knew something was off but chalked it up to nerves.

But this pilot had a rough day on the ice. His runs down the track were all over the place, and his brakeman ended up pretty sore. After the session I reminded this pilot that we all have off days and suggested he go home and relax and refresh his mind with some mental imagery the next day. I thought he just needed to get his head back in the game, but when I found out about his secret injury, it all made sense.

At first I was angry. As a sled pilot myself I believe that as a driver you never put your teammates at risk in such a manner. I asked this athlete how he could betray his brakeman's and my trust and put himself, his team, the sled, and our program in jeopardy in such a way. This athlete felt pretty bad. I knew that while he had suffered a serious lapse in judgment, I was facing a choice myself: give free forgiveness without consequence, punish the athlete judiciously, or consider some conditions and use the opportunity to teach. A few options crossed my mind: suspension, a public chastening in front of the group, perhaps even removal from the program. None of those options felt right. I needed to come up with the conditions for this athlete's "repentance."

First, I required the pilot to tell his brakeman what he had done, a requirement that terrified him, but he needed to make amends with the person whose trust he had broken (a good analogy for repentance when we break trust with the Lord and the Church). Second, the pilot needed to be cleared by a medical professional before I could allow him on the ice again. He had lost physical strength in his hand because of the injury, and I wanted to be sure that he had healed before restoring him to full activity with the team. Looking back, I realize that this is exactly what a good bishop or stake president does: he helps make sure we have regained the strength necessary to enjoy full membership on the Lord's team.

I am happy to report that things worked out for all parties. The brakeman involved was understandably upset about having his safety jeopardized, but he forgave the offender. Once the conditions were met, this athlete was able to come back and enjoy all the benefits of our program.

Repentance and forgiveness do not come without conditions, but because of the Savior's sacrifice we can be healed and cleansed if we meet the required conditions. While our sins may cause us to die spiritually, through Christ we can be made alive again. As the father of the prodigal son said, "For this my son was dead, and is alive again; he was lost, and is found" (Luke 15:24). And while forgiveness may not come without prerequisites, we can rest faithfully assured that as we seek mercy so shall we find. I found this out for myself in December 2005.

My teammate Mark and I entered an international race held on the Park City track, a race that would be our first with that new sled I mentioned earlier. When a bobsled team enters a race, they promise, or covenant, to follow all the rules of the sport. One of the rules is that a team must have its sled up to the top of the track one hour before the race. Half an hour later, the team flips the sled over with the runners pointing up in the air so the officials can come perform inspections.

With minutes to spare, Mark and I got our sled to the top and turned it over on the stand. We took our gear to the US athlete room inside the start building and proceeded to go through our ritual warm-ups before changing into our racing uniforms. A few minutes later, one of the officials told me to go out to my sled. Concerned, Mark and I walked outside and noticed the race director (the head honcho for the competition) standing over our sled with a gruff look on his face. Then again, he always has a gruff look on his face. He pointed to our sled and said, "Your runners are too thin, Jeremy." I stopped in my tracks. "What?"

In bobsled, the officials check our runners before the race to make sure their sides have not been shaved down. Thinner runners will have less contact with the ice, which means less friction. Since thin runners will help you go faster, the rules designate a minimum width in order to maintain consistency. I watched the race director place the tool he uses to measure the curvature of the runner's bottom surface (remember, it is supposed to be round, not sharp) on the polished metal. I clearly saw light shining through the sides of the gauge, which indicated that my brand new runners were too thin. I shook my head as he repeated the same test on the other runners. One passed, but three runners were not race-legal. The person who owned the runners before me had sanded the sides thin, a major no-no.

I had assumed the runners would be okay since I bought them with the sled, but I still should have tested them before the race. In the end it was my fault. As I sat there while the race director lectured me, I tried to remain calm. We had worked hard to get to the race, had completed all the required training sessions, and now we were standing at the start area where all the other teams could see us getting "caught" for something we did not mean to do. Ours was a sin of omission, not commission.

I expected to be kicked out of the race. I had broken the rules because I hadn't been careful, and I waited for the race director to tell us to pack up and go home. But he didn't. Instead he pulled me off to the side so we could talk in private. Folding his arms, he gave me a half-smile and said something like, "Jeremy, those runners are illegal, but I know it was a mistake, not intentional. I'm not going to punish you today, but you will have to get new runners for the race tomorrow. Okay?"

I nodded emphatically. Because of mercy we dodged a bullet. By all rights the race director could have removed us from the race. It really didn't matter that the runner width infraction was an inadvertent mistake; I still broke the rules. But in this case, the mercy of the race director outweighed the demands of justice. At first it may sound like we were given free forgiveness, but that was not the case. Conditions were set and requirements agreed upon. The race director gave us time to correct our mistake and continue on with the competition as long as we would "repent" and have race-legal runners for the next day's competition. In spiritual terms, we had sinned and therefore justice had the right to kick us out of the race, but one who had the power to assuage justice allowed us to stay in the game after we met his "conditions of repentance."

The same thing happens in our lives. Our main goal is to return to the presence of our Father in Heaven, but even one sin, just one, can get us "removed from the race" (Doctrine and Covenants 1:31). And just as we couldn't trick the race director when it came to illegal runners on the sled, there is no way we can slip one past justice. A transgressed law has a price attached and that debt must be paid. As Alma taught his son Corianton, "there is a law given, and a punishment affixed, and a repentance granted; which repentance, mercy claimeth; otherwise, justice claimeth the creature, and executeth the law, and the law inflicteth punishment; if not so, the works of justice would be destroyed, and God would cease to be God" (Alma 42:22).

Because we were willing to meet the conditions of our agreement, the race director acted as a mediator and allowed me to race. We continued on our way, and since mercy satisfied justice, we were able to have a good race. And because a company was willing to help pay what I could not, we were able to race in a new sled. Christ is our "race director" who lovingly invites us to accept his terms of repentance and forgiveness and covenants that his atoning blood can be applied so that our sins may be washed away (2 Nephi 2:7).

Whether you are a youth who is struggling to find your way in the world, a young single adult who has lost their way, or an elderly individual who just desires to improve, God believes in second chances. And third chances. And seventy times seven chances (Matthew 18:22). Because of the Atonement, the demands of justice can be met and we can repent. As renewed champions of the Lord we can still go on to win the "spiritual competition" and return to God's presence.

THE HURT BEFORE THE HEALING

Coach Holm logic: to fix a problem, you must acknowledge that one exists, and in my experience, sport is a pretty blunt acknowledger of things that need fixing. In order to excel as an athlete, you must embrace a healthy attitude toward having your weaknesses pointed out so you can correct them. Whether it comes from a coach, a teammate, or even the stark reality of a performance, sometimes you receive a clear indicator that something needs to change so you can succeed.

But for the majority of life this correction comes from within. We have all been blessed with a guiding light, from which our conscience emanates, that can help us identify the areas of our lives that need changing. As Mormon taught, "The Spirit of Christ is given to every man, that he may know good from evil" (Moroni 7:16).

Like a coach who constantly works to help their athletes improve, the Light of Christ can be one of our greatest sources of growth. It can be a guiding influence that leads us closer to God (John 8:12) by increasing our desire for righteous living and quickening our understanding (Doctrine and Covenants 88:11). That being said, like in an athlete-coach relationship, an open heart and a willing spirit are crucial components of maintaining a healthy learning environment. The power of influence a coach, or the Light of Christ, can have is dependent upon the recipient's willingness to receive instruction. If we turn a deaf ear to this assistance, eventually we will find ourselves with a hardened heart that casts aside the things of God (2 Nephi 33:2, Mosiah 3:7). A willingness to accept and apply correction is critical for salvation.

My first bobsled coach, a three-time Olympian named Randy Will, became a friend and confidant during my first seasons in the sport. Because of his experience, Randy was able to pass along crucial principles and techniques used in the sport. He taught me how to drive sleds, how to prepare for a race, and how to perform physical and mental exercises to get my mind and body in shape. He provided a base upon which I was able to build my bobsled future.

That doesn't mean the progress was all consistently forward, however. I made plenty of mistakes along the way, but Randy was a great coach. He knew what would help me reach my full potential and that often required correcting my ineffective actions or habits. Randy had a humorous way of dealing with our mistakes. You have to remember that we were all new to the sport so we started lower on the Park City track, on the "bunny hill" you could say. The sleds we used were smaller than what you see on TV and our speeds were slower. Mistakes made at those levels probably wouldn't put anyone in danger, but Randy focused on helping us learn the basics of the sport nonetheless. It was up to us to be open to what he was trying to teach.

Randy never wrote anything down; he just made mental notes of any mistakes we made. Once we crossed the finish line we would jog to where he was standing and review our run together (we didn't use radios at the time). If we made an error, Randy would say, "Stick out your hand." Then, like some Old West schoolmaster, he would playfully slap our hand before walking us through our mistake(s) and patiently explaining how overcoming the slipup would help us become a better sled pilot. He would issue a call to change and it was up to us to accept it or not.

Through Randy's long-suffering I came to better understand the Lord's invitation to "become as little children" (Matthew 18:3). Kids have a natural openness to coaching and place a lot of trust in what adults say because anyone "older" must have a great deal of knowledge. Are we that humble when it comes to accepting the guidance of the Light of Christ, the Holy Ghost, and our priesthood leaders? Or, in the pride of our hearts, do we run from the invitations of the Spirit (or our leaders, family, or friends) to repent? The scriptures warn us repeatedly that we should not procrastinate the day of our repentance (Alma 34:32–33) lest our hearts become hardened. In our hardened state we become like the athlete who refuses to listen to his coach's wisdom, and that is a dangerous state for any player to be in.

As a coach, I've seen the contrast between a childlike attitude and a mind focused on the ways of the world. When I initiated small challenges or changes to the program to help the athletes grow, I was always fascinated to see how quickly the competitors who really wanted to become their best embraced and implemented the new factors. The athletes who resented my calls to grow and change, however, often put in little effort. I guess they believed there was nothing wrong with what they were doing, but when I saw the errors in their technique or routines I wanted to paraphrase the Apostle John, who said, "If [you] say that [you] have no sin, [you] deceive [yourself]" (1 John 1:7). Ironically, by believing they were doing everything right and that there was nothing to correct, they were damning their progression as athletes. I felt sorry for them.

Spiritually speaking, we have a similar choice to make. The Light of Christ and the Holy Ghost can help us improve and grow, but this requires humility and a trust that our coach, the Savior, will never lead us astray, even when what he asks us to change seem difficult or "unfair" to our mortal minds. This invitation may range from a twinge of guilt to an overwhelming racking of the soul (Alma 36:18). In these moments, we would do well to remember that like a good coach, the Savior is giving us an opportunity to change and correct our wrongs through the Atonement. The hurt, that sickening pit in the bottom of our stomach, is something we should welcome. Like Alma's love-driven chastisement of his son Corianton, our guilt can work for our good if it produces true sorrow for sin (Alma 39:7).

That the Light of Christ softens our hearts toward our sins should come as no surprise. There is an old Latin saying, mens sana in corpore sano, which translates to "a sound mind in a sound body." The ancient Greeks who pioneered the Olympic Games (they held the first Games around 1200 BC), were fascinated with the refining of the body, mind, and spirit. To their way of thinking, perfection could only be gained by bringing their passions, energies, and thoughts in line with worthy pursuits and goals. If one of these key areas was off balance, then the whole being could falter.

The Greeks were not that far off. The gospel teaches us that the soul of man comprises the physical body and the spirit (Doctrine and Covenants 88:15) and just like the ancient Greeks, we are trying to refine and balance our physical bodies with our minds and spirits. If that balance is thrown off through sin we will feel pain because pain is the greatest indicator that something needs correcting. And as we experience true godly sorrow, our spirit and our body both will let us know, like a good coach, that it is time to change.

When you are working out or training as an athlete and you feel a sharp pain or pop, you're probably going to do something about it such as talk to a physical trainer or physical therapist. So rather than ignore the spiritual pain of sin, we should take courage in Paul's counsel that "godly sorrow worketh repentance to salvation" (2 Corinthians 7:10). Our sorrow can be the catalyst we need to change and receive healing through the Atonement. In the New Testament the original Greek word for repentance was *metaneoeo*, which means to change one's mind, thoughts, or spirit. Guilt is a calling from the Light of Christ to do just that.

As an athlete, a frustrating loss can ignite a determination to train harder. Similarly, godly sorrow can motivate us to bring forth the "fruits meet for repentance" (Matthew 3:8), which is more than regret over "getting caught." When the Holy Ghost indicates we have done wrong, there must be a true desire to change and make it right.

True repentance means digging deep, beyond the superficial. Good coaches know the difference between athletes who say they will change just so they can play next time and those who will change so they can play better every time. Like a "brutal" rehabilitation routine, true repentance won't be easy, but the only way through is through. True sorrow, the "broken heart and a contrite spirit" (3 Nephi 12:19) kind, indicates a desire to make everything right with God, no matter the cost. It is an attitude that leads us to accept whatever our coach, even Jesus Christ, asks of us.

When we feel godly sorrow working in our hearts, let us be cautious not to let it become fear. The Savior is a coach, a friend who wants to help us improve. Without that firm testimony, we will never exercise faith unto repentance, and unless we have an honest desire and work to make things right, he cannot intercede in our behalf (Doctrine and Covenants 19:16–17). Anything less than this will not bring the desired healing results.

When I previously told the story of our crash on the Park City track, I failed to mention that our borrowed sled ended up in pretty bad shape. Not that we can take full credit for the damage; the crash revealed several areas on the sled that had been repaired with cosmetic fixes only. These weakened sections either broke off or fell to pieces when we flipped. Additionally, the crash revealed several joints and welds that were structurally weak on the metal frame. In a nutshell, whoever had crashed the sled in the past had done the bare minimum to fix the results of their mistakes and errors. To the naked eye, the sled looked fine before the wreck, but afterward all the hidden weaknesses were laid bare.

To really fix those problems my teammates and I, alongside my ever-skilled engineering father, had to do the work that should have been done in the first place. We spent several days grinding away the weakened sections of metal and replacing them with newer, stronger pieces. Countless hours were spent cutting and sanding down the previously damaged areas of the body that had been smoothed over with weak adhesives. With this completed, we were able to strengthen the body with layer upon layer of fresh fiberglass, which led a more uniformly strong shell.

Now I suppose that if the sled could talk it would say that the repairs were difficult and painful, but in the end she was stronger and more structurally sound for use in further competitions and training. In regards to repentance, we may be tempted to follow the example of our sled's previous users and apply superficial fixes that "hide" our sins and dull our conscience. We may act like those athletes I coached who never wanted to correct their mistakes and wouldn't admit something was wrong. However, just as those superficial repairs on our sled came apart during the crash, any attempt to cover a sin will fall apart at some point. When we are brought before the judgment seat of Christ, all our excuses, denials, justifications, and half-hearted attempts to repent will crumble to dust.

Like athletes trying to hide an injury so they can still play, we may try to hide from the pain of our sins and ignore godly sorrow, but eventually the truth of what we have done will wash over us. Our spirits will feel the pain of knowing that we have gone against the commandments of God. That being said, I repeat Alma's words spoken to his son Corianton, the same Corianton who left his mission "area" to go consort with the harlot Isabel. Of all the things a loving father could say to his wayward son, Alma chose to give uplifting instruction along with an invitation to repent. Not once does Alma berate his son for his mistakes, a practice of a good coach. He does, however, give a clear rationale for bringing up Corianton's transgressions: "I would not dwell upon your crimes, to harrow up your soul, if it were not for your good" (Alma 39:7).

If it were not for your good. Alma knew the true reason for godly sorrow and the benefit of allowing those feelings to bring about changes within our souls. As he described to his son Helaman, "Oh, what joy, and what marvelous light I did behold; yea, my soul was filled with joy as exceeding as was my pain!" (Alma 36:20).

When you feel a stirring of conscience due to transgressions, I invite you to let those feelings lead you to repentance. Be like successful athletes who embrace correction and strive to do better next time. Yes, we may miss some opportunities because of time wasted in sinful ways, but we can come back and face the future with pure hearts and clean hands. And like that bobsled my team so painstakingly repaired, repenting of our sins "with unshaken faith in [Christ], relying wholly upon the merits of him who is mighty to save" (2 Nephi 31:19) will allow us to become stronger. Similarly, godly sorrow helps us repair those parts of our lives and spirits that have become damaged through sin. It is part of the price we pay to be washed clean by Jesus's atoning sacrifice. It is the cost of the Balm of Gilead and as such I would invite you to embrace Amulek's powerful invitation, "come forth and harden not your hearts any longer; for behold, now is the time and the day of your salvation . . . if ye will repent and harden not your hearts, immediately shall the great plan of redemption be brought about unto you"(Alma 33:31).

In the grand scheme of things, the quiet invitations to repent are challenges from our Heavenly Coach to change, to improve, and to do better. Godly sorrow means we are ready to accept those summons with full purpose of (a changed) heart. Champions always accept such a call.

MERCY AND GRACE: SOME ASSEMBLY REQUIRED

Sports are all about continual improvement. What worked yesterday may not be enough for today, so you have to keep a healthy attitude toward learning and growing. Bobsled is a culmination of dozens of minute techniques that can make or break a team's competition run. It's the little things that matter, like how you push off the block or when the driver pilots out of a turn. While every action may have only small effects, they add up to crucial differences in a sport where you win or lose by one one-hundredth of a second. It doesn't take much to drop out of the medal hunt in bobsled. To give you an idea, in the two-man men's event at the 2010 Vancouver Olympics, the difference between the combined times of the gold medal team and the sixth place team was 1.29 seconds . . . after four runs.

The goal is to do everything correctly at the right time in order to win, which is why bobsled athletes practice so much. The best competitors in the world know they must continually push themselves to perform better. Somewhere out there is an opponent who may be working harder than you are, and that means they are obtaining an advantage through good old-fashioned hard work. To succeed you must practice hard and work harder; that is how victory is achieved.

Some aspects of bobsled are relatively easy to learn. Others require more time and practice to perfect. Either way, it takes patience, discipline, and consistent effort to learn and grow. Those same characteristics apply to the gospel. Changing and progressing through hard work can be challenging for athletes and disciples of Christ.

I see legendary coach Vince Lombardi misquoted a lot as saying, "Winning isn't everything; it's the only thing." But in the golden years of his life, Coach Lombardi constantly claimed to have actually said, "Winning isn't everything—but making the effort to win is." Repentance, like training as an elite athlete, can take time to get where you want to be. The key is to remember how important every effort is on the journey.

As mortal beings (even though some athletes think they are gods), we tend to want results right now, and when you're struggling to get something right, it can be easy to become frustrated. Ever feel that way about a gospel principle or a commandment? Whether as an Olympic athlete or a rank-and-file member of the Church, it is much easier to stick with a habit instead of exerting the effort necessary to improve. Change can be scary. Imagine being a gymnast preparing for your floor routine when your coach says, "Make up your routine instead. Good luck!" Good luck? Coach, I practiced this routine a hundred times and you want me to change right now?

Repentance is often described as a turning back to God. While half of this process means returning to the doctrines and habits we know are good and true, the other half can mean learning new ways of living in order to be obedient to the commandments. Basically we must stop the old and (re)start the new. Repentance is a change from bad to good, but when we are trying to correct a tough habit, we're probably not going to get things right the first time. It can be easy to lose patience, which only makes our mental state less optimal for attempting these gospel-inspired changes. Whether as athletes or as Latter-day Saints, when we set our sights on a new habit or obedience to a certain rule/commandment, we should apply Christlike love to ourselves if we stumble at first.

During the 2008–2009 season, my four-man team and I planned to attend an evening training session, but unfortunately one athlete was called away at the last minute. So I asked another athlete friend named Abby to stand in for the day. Now, Abby was a skeleton athlete (they go headfirst down the track on a sled the size of a lunch tray), so she was no stranger to the track. We found her a helmet and walked to the sled to practice loading in before the session started.

In all honesty, pushing and loading into a four-man bobsled takes a bit of practice, more than we could give Abby before it was our turn to take the ice. But she was still game to try, so we pulled the sled up to the line and got ready. After being given the green light, we called our cadence and off we went. A few steps into the push the sled went over the crest and began its downhill decent. I loaded in, hit the latch that dropped my push bar, and a few moments later I heard a shout of "I can't!" We were almost to the first turn, so I had to focus and put the shout out of my mind.

The rest of the run was perfect, and after we crossed the finish line my brakeman Brad brought the sled to a stop. After a few seconds I exited the driver's seat and stepped onto the ice. Pulling my helmet off, my eyes did a double take. One, two . . . only two teammates? "Uh, guys, where's Abby?" Brad and Don traded a look and explained that she hadn't made it into her seat. Abby had pushed right up until the end, looked over at the sled, and decided that leaping over the side was too challenging. She simply shouted, "I can't!" and let go of the push bar while we continued down the track. Our coach made sure to give us a hard time about it when I called him on the radio.

After loading the sled onto one of the sled trucks, we piled into the back for the drive to the top. Upon arriving at the start, we saw Abby standing there with a sheepish look on her face. She apologized profusely, and we assured her that it was okay. It happens, and she was not the first push athlete to miss loading into the sled. And to her credit, Abby pulled her helmet back on for our second run, pushed again, and this time she loaded in to make the ride with us. Fear may have scuttled the first attempt, but courage gave her the confidence to try again.

Repentance isn't easy. I have seen how difficult some addictions and weaknesses are to get over. But as athletes and members of the Church, we must remember that effort is the key. What matters most when you are trying to get your life in order is that you are trying. When I'm attempting to perfect a new technique in bobsled, I have to work on it bit by bit. I also have to remember that it's okay (and sometimes necessary) to reach out for that additional help from the coach so I can nail what I'm trying to learn.

If you are struggling with a weakness, with that "favorite sin," try to keep in mind that you are pursuing two worthy goals: quitting and changing. You are not a failure for stumbling along the way because you are still moving forward. That's what repentance is all about: getting back up when we fall. Satan will do his best to feed our emotions of guilt and shame because he knows that the worse we feel, the easier it will be for him to tempt us with falling back into sinful ways. The Holy Ghost beckons us upward, but Satan's deceptive voice seeks to pull us down: "You are worthless." "You're a spiritual failure." "It's too late for you. Just give up." What horrible lies.

Are you weighed down with sin or an addiction? Are you crying out in agony because the entanglements of transgression keep you from enjoying the light and joy that you desire and, by heaven's decree, rightfully deserve? I fear you might even believe that devilish voice that calls out, "Unclean,

unclean!" What I find most troubling is that these feelings can become mental accusers similar to the Pharisees and Sadducees who judged the woman taken in adultery (John 8). We condemn and are ready to cast the first stone at ourselves because we feel guilty.

The problem with thinking like this is it usually leaves us standing still. When discouragement and doubt win, we will probably cease making any efforts to progress, to keep moving forward. We stop trying to change, we stop trying to draw closer to the Lord, and we stop trying to repent. We forget that repentance denotes progress, a change that brings improvement. Shouldn't we allow ourselves room to repent while repenting?

Don't give up. You're a champion of the Lord, and champions never run away because Satan and his minions are encircling them with their jeers and laughter. Don't take direction from the other team; rather, listen to your coach on high, who always calls out for you to get back up and try again. We never lose our worth, only our worthiness, and the best part is that we can always get our worthiness back through repentance.

When I first started coaching adaptive bobsled athletes, I wasn't sure it was the right thing to do. During all my years in the sport I had made plenty of errors along the way. Dozens of athletes had more experience and success than I did. I kept looking back, and all I could see were my mistakes and weaknesses, not the strengths or achievements I have. I'll admit that coaching the adaptive athletes and trying to help organize the group into a professional unit took a lot of work, but the hard work paid off. The athletes, at least those who were willing to listen, improved so much, and they came to be respected as serious, professional competitors. If I had only focused on my past mistakes, I never would have had all the joyous experiences that came as one of the first adaptive bobsled coaches in the world.

So what about you? What great things are waiting in your future? What blessings does the Lord have in store. No good things come without effort, and repentance is no different. As Nephi taught, "For we know that it is by grace that we are saved, after all we can do" (2 Nephi 25:23). Repentance may require throwing out all your packages of cigarettes or attending a weekly meeting for those struggling with addiction. It might mean apologizing to your spouse or telling the truth to your business partner. Whatever the required labors may be, do as our pioneer ancestors did and "put your shoulder to the wheel and push along" (although I prefer the analogy of putting your shoulder to the sled).

I know of no athlete who regretted the hard work required to win the gold medal. The same can be said of those who experience the sweet, peaceful healing that comes through repentance. No task is too great, no sacrifice too heavy when it comes to obtaining forgiveness of sin and strengthening our relationship with deity. And never fear that you don't have the strength required to change and repent. In heaven there is enough power to create universes. There is enough hope for the blind to see, the lame to walk, and the deaf to hear. There is enough charity to forgive the sinking, doubting Peter. There is enough mercy to welcome home the prodigal son and enough grace to heal a woman who suffered from a condition, as many of us do spiritually, for years. Never doubt that there is enough compassion in heaven to help you overcome a weakness. As the Lord said to Moroni in Ether 12:27, "I give unto men weakness that they may be humble; and my grace is sufficient for all men that humble themselves before me; for if they humble themselves before me, and have faith in me, then will I make weak things become strong unto them."

Our efforts to change and improve, when combined with the help of the Lord, are what make us stronger spiritually, emotionally, and mentally. Repentance can take time, but the length of the process should not discourage us. It is worth it in the end. That's what repentance is about after all: moving forward.

SECOND CHANCES: IT AIN'T OVER 'TIL IT'S OVER

Some of us may feel like it is "too late." I have seen those whose flame of faith has been blown out by the winds of sin. They may wear a brave face, but deep down they worry that their spirit is too weak, their life too broken, and their sins too great. We must ignore these feelings because they are devilish lies.

As an athlete, you are constantly battling the fear that you've missed your chance. So many factors play into your career that it can be mindboggling to keep track of them all. You have your pre-competition dynamics such as nutrition, physical and mental training, and then you have game-day performance as well. Was your first of two runs down the track clean and fast? Did you do well in the semifinals?

Yes, athletes are intimately familiar with gut reality check of the "first half." I had such a moment during a two-man race one Saturday morning in January 2009 when my teammate Don and I had a less-than-perfect first run. My team and I had been focusing on four-man training for about two weeks, and we didn't even know about the race until Thursday evening. Let me just say that my "first half" was not my best, and I spent the truck ride back to the start area wondering if it was indeed too late (to medal, that is). We arrived at the top and found ourselves in fourth place.

And when I discovered the reason for our messy first run, I wanted to kick myself. Don and I had done quick maintenance on the sled's steering system to prepare for the race, and I—my responsibility being to double-check the equipment—failed to tighten a crucial center pivot point that the steering system hinged around. I remember looking at the loosened connection with disgust (at this race we could work on the sled between heats without needing permission from the nonexistent race jury). We had already completed one of two runs, and that first one was not good. Should we bother trying to make our second run? Don never had any question in his mind. He took one look at the now-ready sled and boldly declared that we could still win. And you know what? We walked away with a bronze medal. Was it too late? Only if we had decided it was.

We all love watching an underdog come back from seeming defeat to gain a hard-fought victory. It is inspiring to watch athletes stand toe-to-toe with a "Goliath" adversary who, at least on paper, outmatches them in every conceivable way. Even if they lose the game, an athlete or team who refuses to admit defeat wins admiration in the eyes of their teammates, their opponents, and the fans.

That being said, the problem with feeling like it is too late is (a) it's a lie, and (b) it steals the hope we need to rise up as underdogs. Satan knows that fear paralyzes and that discouragement drains energy. When an athlete hesitates because of fear, he or she is said to have "choked" in a critical moment. Instead of acting upon the principles that could help athletes win, distress takes over, and the athletes find it difficult to perform even the most routine technique. Whether you are an athlete or a Latter-day Saint, a perceived fear of failure can lead to self-sabotage when chances for success were initially fairly high. No wonder Satan wants so badly for us to believe that it's too late.

Have you ever seen a team go to a game or competition they truly believed they couldn't win? It isn't pretty, and the downcast looks on their faces say it all. They have little hope for victory; therefore, motivation is low. They look miserable out there, and you can't help but feel their pain. The reaction in which an athlete feels incapable of affecting the outcome is called learned helplessness. People who succumb to learned helplessness are prone to giving a poor performance even though they really had a good chance at victory.

From a gospel standpoint, we all have a great chance at victory because of the plan of salvation and because of the Atonement of Jesus Christ. Champions cannot afford to sit on the bench, and neither can we. No matter our mistakes, we need to get into the game.

But that's the trick, isn't it? We must believe that our efforts to repent are going to be successful and help us "win" spiritually. If Satan can get us to give up faith for fear and despondency, our level of spiritual activity and hope will suffer. The "underdog" will roll over and give up. But Satan is a liar. While he dances around the playing field of our lives like a victor and continually whispers in our ears that he won, the truth is that when we sin, it is only halftime. And every coach knows that the second half can be where everything turns around.

I know of no teaching in the gospel that says you can't turn your life around right now. Will it be difficult? Maybe. Will it require true effort and humble repentance? Yes. But is it too late? Never. Your seat at the "victory" feast of the Lord is not open for the taking; it is reserved for you by the host himself. God will always be there waiting. No matter how far we travel from the gospel's warmth, the sign above the door will always read, "WELCOME HOME" upon our return. What matters most are the things we do and the decisions we make when we must choose between "It's too late" and "I will try again."

People always ask how to get into bobsled, and I usually quip, "First, you fail a psychiatric evaluation." Joking aside, there are a couple of different ways, but the most common method involves a tryout. During these evaluations, athletes participate in various physical tests that examine their strength, speed, and overall agility. Depending on the country you're trying out for, you may be tested in exercises such as the bench press, power cleans, squats, underhanded shot put toss, sprints, and jumping. These tests are difficult for some because they forcefully bring reality into their Olympic dreams, and they must decide to quit or work harder and try again. I would know.

During the summer of 1998, my coach held one of these tryouts at Skyline High School. Wanting to see what my seventeen-year-old body could do, I attended the event just to run through the various assessments. Since I was in the youth program, I wasn't required to take the test, but I wanted to give it a shot. Looking back, I had no idea what I was doing. I had zero real training as a sprinter and even less physical preparation as a bobsled athlete. Our youth program focused more on driving technique than on training our bodies for competition. I was so unprepared.

While trying not to roast on the black surface of Skyline's old running track, I watched over a dozen incredible athletes run through their various warm-up drills. One thing quickly became clear to me: I was out of my league. Most of the hopefuls were retired college or professional athletes who were bigger, faster, and far more disciplined than I was. There were previous bobsled World Cup participants, football players, track and field athletes, and more. I took one look at the field, and a part of me wanted to get back in the car and drive home.

But I couldn't. Call it courage or stupidity, but I chose to stay. Maybe it came from watching too many sports movies, but I had an unrelenting habit of putting put myself in the underdog position in life.

When it was my turn for the sixty-meter sprint, I tightened the laces on my new track shoes and stood on the starting line, trying to look calm and collected. After a deep breath, I floored it right out of the chute, sprinting as hard as I could down the track. I had terrible form. There was no transition, no drive phase, no extending as I picked up speed. I knew I was running at a fraction of the speed the other sprinters were, and as I walked back to the start, I focused way too much on that fact.

On my second sprint, I got halfway down the lane before I felt pain shoot through the front of my leg in my quads. Foolishly I kept pushing until I crossed the finish line, and only then did I reach down to grab my thigh. I could tell it wasn't bad, but I could not deny the mild burning in the muscles. I debated the dangers of taking a third sprint and decided I would go for it. I was lucky I didn't do more damage, but my leg was starting to really ache, so my time was terrible.

A veteran driver, Joe McDonald, wisely advised me to play it cautious, so I decided to pass on the one-hundred-meter sprints for safety sake. At least that's what I told myself and the other athletes. To this day I can't decide which won out more: the desire to protect my body or my ego.

After a small break it came time for a few other tests that I felt I could do as long as I was careful. Let's just say they didn't turn out so well, but even as my performance decreased, I found myself unable to walk away. Call it pride, call it embarrassment, but I just couldn't do it. I had to finish. Now before you cheer me on as an underdog, I should point out my own learned helplessness here. With each test, as I compared my results to those of the other athletes, I believed less and less in my ability to perform well. In my mind I couldn't run as fast, jump as high, or throw as far as they could. This damaged my attitude.

After receiving my test results, I dejectedly gathered my gear and threw it in the back of my jeep. I was pretty numb at this point from the heat, the exertion of the testing, and from my failure. Leaving Skyline's parking lot, I drove to the Mount Olympus trailhead on the east side of the Salt Lake Valley. After parking, I gingerly walked up the trail until I came to a large rock formation. Climbing out to the edge, I plopped down in disgust. I don't know how long I sat there, but as the bright summer sun bore down, the reflections of my own personal feelings of failure seemed to push down on my discouraged heart. I wondered if the test was a message that I should give up the sport less than two years after starting it. Was it a wake-up call that I would never experience anything big or great on the ice? I had two bobsled medals then, but were they going to be the last?

I wish I could go back and sit next to that disappointed youth, put my arm around him, and tell him about all the amazing things he has yet to discover in life. I want to show him the medals he will win, tell him about the trips he will take, and describe all the incredible experiences that are yet to come all because he decided to keep going. I want to tell him about the friends he will make and the lives he will touch. Most of all, I want him to know that I understand and that he shouldn't give up because there are breathtakingly beautiful things just over the horizon, things he can't even fathom.

Life and repentance are hard. Just as Shadrach, Meshach, and Abednego were protected in Nebuchadnezzar's fiery furnace (Daniel 8), when we are cast into the refining fires of sorrow and repentance, we can stand tall and know there is One who walks with us, One by whose power the earths and universes were created, One who overcame death and sin through his selfless sacrifice, even Jesus of Nazareth, the Savior of Mankind.

We must be cautious not to let Satan turn the healing process, no matter how difficult, into a reason to turn from the Lord. Christ is the only one who can redeem us from our fallen state. Satan wants us to believe that we are failures when we struggle, but what is failure? In the world of sport (and every aspect of life), disappointment is founded on your predetermined perceptions of success. A quarterback and his team can win the game, but he may consider his performance a failure because he threw two interceptions. A gymnast may win a silver medal but consider her competition a failure because she could have given more effort and perhaps won gold. As bobsled athletes, we may set a personal best time on the track during a competition but not win the event, thus giving a good performance in once aspect but not in another.

Failure is perceived. The problem is Satan knows that as Latter-day Saints, we may perceive complete obedience as victory and sin as failure. This cognitive model is faulty in that it contains an unhealthy view of the competition of life. If we follow Satan's whispers, we can never be successful in God's eyes because we all sin every day and therefore live as failures. Embracing this black-and-white perspective of righteousness can make it easier for the adversary to whisper words of discouragement and disappointment. Yes, a sin is a sin, but it's only a failure if we fail to repent and try again.

The cleansing process of repentance is not some test designed to discourage or dissuade. Rather, like the metals used to make the sought-after gold, silver, and bronze medals used in the Olympics, our hearts must undergo a refining process to purify our souls. It takes over 1,300 degrees to purify the gold found in a gold medal, and if you feel weighed down by repentance, remember that it took 1,900 tons of pressure to mold the medals used during the 2010 Olympic Games held in Vancouver, BC, Canada.

Don't give up on yourself, your future, or the Lord's ability to help you succeed. Have the faith to trust that your Father in Heaven will help you get there. The path back isn't always easy, but know that it is often when you feel the lowest that Christ is the nearest. Trust in your bishop, your parents, your spouse, your friends, and your own capacity to change. In the words of Elder Jeffrey R. Holland, "Don't give up. Don't you quit. You keep walking. You keep trying. There is help and happiness ahead—a lot of it—. You keep your chin up. It will be all right in the end. Trust God and believe in good things to come."[19]

Put aside your fears of failure and, as Paul declared, "come boldly unto the throne of grace, that [you] may obtain mercy, and find grace to help in time of need" (Hebrews 4:16). I promise that His grace will always be there in our times of need.

TRIALS ARE TRAINING CAMPS FOR THE ETERNITIES

For most of us, the word "adversity" has a bit of a negative connotation. It means an experience or period of our life is going to be tough and maybe even painful. Even as Latter-day Saints who believe that adversity is ultimately for our good, we would rather enjoy continual blessings, promises and happiness. But champions know that an easy life is not always the best life.

In ancient Greece athletes often sought out the toughest, most disciplined trainers to help them prepare for the demands of competition. These contestants wanted to perfect their bodies, minds, and spirits before presenting themselves before the gods on the field of competition. Any task asked of them was worthy of completion since it would help them prepare for the glory of the Games. As champions of the Lord, can we expect our pursuit of eternal excellence to be any less challenging? Are we not preparing our minds, bodies, and spirits to "compete" before the judgment bar of God?

Adversity brings growth, just like adding a few more pounds to the bar in the weight room builds muscle. When we remember what we are striving for, even exaltation, it becomes easier to understand why our eternal coach, even Jesus Christ, allows us to experience times of growth. If we truly desire to become like him, we must accept the fact that he knows what we need to go through to get there. Like an effective training schedule, trials are designed to push us to our limits so we can become stronger spiritually and further develop Christlike attributes. Champions of the Lord embrace adversity because it helps them become more like the Master.

Like a good trainer, the Lord knows what we can handle today and what we can handle tomorrow and we can rest assured that he never confuses the two (1 Corinthians 10:13). Our trials are customized to meet our needs and current levels of mental, emotional, physical and spiritual strength. Plus, every tribulation falls under the power of the Master in whom we have entrusted with our mortal training program. He may push us, but he will never leave us to face it alone.

Like athletic competition, adversity is a pressure cooker. It will either bring out our best or show us our weaknesses. After all, the word "adversity" comes from the thirteenth-century Anglo-French *averse*, which means "contrary, opposing." So what does adversity oppose? During my own times of difficulty on and off the ice, I've tried to find the purpose behind our trials and here is just one observation.

King Benjamin taught, "For the natural man is an enemy to God . . . and will be, forever and ever, unless he yields to the enticings of the Holy Spirit, and putteth off the natural man and becometh a saint through the atonement of Christ the Lord, and becometh as a child" (Mosiah 3:19). Adversity, then, opposes the natural man: our fears, doubts, weaknesses, temptations, appetites, desires and limitations. Adversity is part of "the refiner's fire" (Malachi 3:2), and I love this analogy because in bobsled we are competing for gold, silver and bronze, three alloys that require high temperatures to become purified. The heat and pressure of adversity can burn off the natural man and make us into something more precious and wonderful.

Yes, adversity is a refining fire, but we're the ones who benefit. Peter taught, "That the trial of your faith, being much more precious than of [Olympic] gold that perisheth, though it be tried with fire, might be found unto praise and honour and glory at the appearing of Jesus Christ" (1 Peter 1:7).

But there is a caveat here: our attitudes toward adversity will determine whether we become better or bitter. Athletic competitions are tests of prowess, skill, and spirit. An athlete can learn what he or she needs to improve based on his or her performance, or he or she can get angry at a loss and never progress. Likewise, adversity can bring our weaknesses to the forefront, at which point we can turn to the Lord and find the strength to endure and change, or we can let our trials discourage us and turns our hearts sour. The choice is ours.

To succeed as an athlete you must learn to deal constructively with the "adversities" of your sport and use them to grow. Players who understand how to use loss, injury, discouragement, and pain will develop more quickly physically and mentally. Champions willingly seek out some hardships such as adding heavier weight to the bar or running another sprint because these mini-challenges refine their bodies and minds. Sport is full of tasks that, like life's trials, can help us advance to reach our potential, but it takes continual (that is, faithful) effort, which requires a heart willing to embrace even the tough times. Attitude in sport, like the gospel, is everything.

When I began bobsled back in high school, I knew there would be challenges waiting for me, but I made up my mind that whenever adversity arose, I would fight it with inspiration from the scriptures and good books. From renowned athletes to Church leaders, motivational speakers to scriptural heroes, I devoured the words of history's greats and found hope and encouragement, two things I really needed at that time in my life.

You see, I know something of adversity. In addition to the normal pressures of high school and later a mission and college, I felt the strain of sport creep into daily life as I came to partially believe that winning was the only thing that mattered and that in some ways it defined my worth as a person. I do not blame anyone for my faulty thinking, but I bring this up because my inner demand to succeed only added to the heavy burdens of my "thorn in the flesh" (2 Corinthians 12:7). Despite my optimistic and outgoing nature, in junior high I began to struggle with depression and anxiety, which felt like great weights on my heart, mind and spirit.

Over the years, friends have expressed surprise when they learn of these struggles, because I was a master actor. I felt that I couldn't allow the world to know about my weakness, since I was "supposed" to be a strong athlete and priesthood holder who could handle any challenge. "That's not realistic," you might say. I agree; it was foolish and prideful to always bottle up my pains and never talk to anyone about them, especially those who loved me most. The stubbornness that served me well in bobsled also kept me from letting others help.

My battles with anxiety and depression led to irrational fears and thoughts that hurt me and impaired my existence in many ways throughout the years including the evening when I almost took my own life.

Yes, I know something of adversity, and yet it was during these times of trial that I followed my decision to find encouragement in the words of history's heroes. Often before a bobsled training session or competition I would open a good book and dive in. One of those whom I studied frequently was England's prime minister Sir Winston Churchill. As I read the words he spoke to his besieged country during the dark days of World War II,

I found strength to face my own troubles, and my faith was rekindled.

Churchill relates the following: "Sure I am of this, that you have only to endure to conquer. You have only to persevere to save yourselves."[20]

"We shall fight on the beaches, we shall fight on the landing grounds, we shall fight in the fields and in the streets, we shall fight in the hills; we shall never surrender."[21]

Reading Churchill's speeches before stepping on the ice helped put my adversities into perspective. His statements became personal invitations to stay strong, and by choosing to faithfully endure, I found myself stronger, happier, and more at peace. While my trials never melted away, I felt less like a victim and more like I could conquer the trial at hand with the Lord's help. I came to understand the Lord's invitation to, "Come unto [him], all ye that labour and are heavy laden, and [he] will give you rest" (Matthew 11:28). Like a spotter in the weight room, the Lord is willing to share the load when the burden becomes too heavy.

Adversity rarely comes at an opportune time, and that's okay. Bobsled has taught me that a period of testing is an invitation for us to draw closer to our eternal coach. Despite all those struggles in my younger life, going up to the bobsled track was a way to draw near to Heavenly Father. I felt he was there with me and that gave me great strength and joy.

Despite natural instinct, as mortal beings we are not always the happiest when times are easy. Like elite athletes, we learn and grow through opposition, enduring the purifying fire, and struggling up the steep hills of life. Trials are necessary for happiness because "if [we] never should have bitter [we] could not know the sweet" (Doctrine and Covenants 29:26). And victory always tastes sweeter to those who have experienced loss.

I discovered more about myself as an athlete and a son of God on the days when my burdens felt great. Some days the anxiety and depression were overwhelming, but as I turned to the Lord, I felt renewed strength and hope. How could I experience that without adversity? If I never experienced a piece of hell, how could the Savior "refine [me] like silver and test [me] like gold" (Zechariah 13:9)? Time and time again Christ has taught me that with his help life's adversities can turn out far better than we could possibly imagine, especially when we allow his loving hand to guide us through them.

During the 1996–1997 season, I worked at the track after school to earn money for training (and dating). I loved being outdoors in beautiful Park City, working alongside fellow athletes and the customers were great, so you could call it a dream job (minus the big paychecks).

One evening in January 1998, Randy, my coach (and the boss), injured his neck, which left us short-staffed for Sunday. Normally I had the Sabbath off, but I was asked to come in due to the situation. My stomach tightened. I believe in honoring the Sabbath, but I also knew that my coworkers really needed help. Feeling like I was the ox stuck in the mire (Luke 14:5), I told Randy that I would volunteer my hours so I could help yet not be working. It made sense in my head, but Coach just gave me a funny look and said he was going to pay me anyway.

I awoke the next day feeling unsettled. I guess a part of me said I should just quit my job and be obedient, but I didn't want to leave my teammates, my coach, and the program in a bind. And in the back of my mind, a small voice told me it would be okay—that there was a purpose in this. I almost didn't listen.

I arrived at the track and tried to make the best of the situation and enjoy the beautiful afternoon, but I felt guilty. Despite the real need for me to be there, I wasn't sure I was doing the right thing. However, a few hours into the day, something interesting happened. One of the passengers started asking me who I was and how I had become involved in bobsled. After a few minutes of conversation, he said: "My name is So-and-So. How would you like to come represent your sport at the annual Utah Winter Games Banquet at the Little America hotel?"

The Spirit whispered that this was the reason I had to be there that day. I heartily agreed to the banquet and offered a silent prayer of thanks. I felt overwhelmed that Heavenly Father had turned my adversity into such a great opportunity. Please understand, I'm not saying that it is okay to bend the guidelines of the gospel, but the Lord can turn trials for our good, and we definitely need the guidance of the Spirit to successfully walk that path.

On the evening of January 22, 1998, I found myself at the Grand America Hotel surrounded by several hundred people whom I had never met before, yet I could not stop smiling. The night's itinerary consisted of a dinner, some speeches, and some videos, and then all of the sudden I heard a list of names being read, and, to my surprise, my name was called. A little stunned, I stood and followed the other athletes to the main stage, and we lined up to face the crowd. Were they going to give us medals or execute us? I had no clue.

We soon found ourselves holding black fleece vests and the announcer said something like, "Here they are, the next generation of top athletes. These are the young men and women who will represent our country in the upcoming 2002 Olympic Winter Games. Let's give them a round of applause!" It turned into a standing ovation. I can only imagine how big the grins on our faces were, but I remember thinking again how God had turned a situation that I felt was awful into something that was truly remarkable.

I know this experience pales in comparison to the difficult adversities many of you have experienced, but I hope it gives some perspective. The dark cliffs of adversity will loom before us at times, and we will face a mental, physical, or spiritual "opponent" who is stronger, faster, and better equipped, and who will tax our limits. The heat of the refiner's fire may feel more like a cruel task master than a training camp for the eternities.

Those are the times that we must make the extra effort to lean on the Lord. The Savior knows how to push us to grow, and that pushing can often seem like more than we can handle. It's like when I was first learning to do squats in the gym and the coach/trainer added more weight to the bar. I didn't think I could do it, but then I was taught the technique of looking up when doing squats (which helps with form), I could do more weight. Isn't that interesting? When I look up, I can handle more weight. In our moments of fear or inadequacy, I hope we remember that as our Coach the Lord knows exactly how much "weight" we can handle. It is up to us to square our shoulders under the bar, look up, and lift.

Challenges will come, so what are we going to do when they show up? How will we react when the seemingly huge wall of adversity looms in our path, when they overwhelming struggles occur within our hearts?

In the next few chapters I want to share some experiences and insight that I pray will be of help and encouragement during times of trial. Most of all, don't give up. Have faith; I promise it will all work out in the end and "shall be for thy good" (Doctrine and Covenants 121:7).

PHOTOS

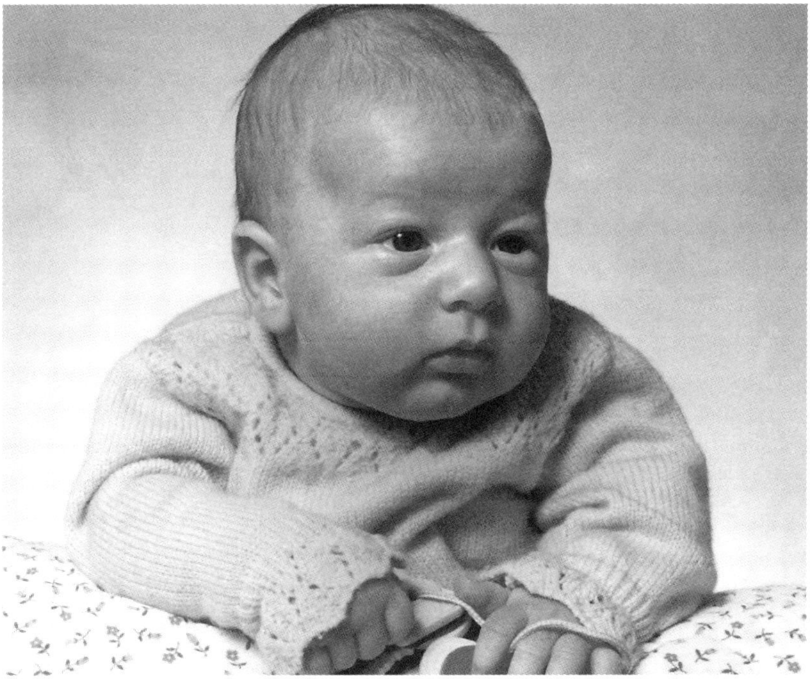

It all began on a stormy Pennsylvania December night. I'm practicing my blue steel here. (Photo: Candy Holm)

Minus the Beatles haircut, growing up in Edmond, Oklahoma, was a dream. Go Sooners! (Photo: Candy Holm)

Dad played, Grandpa played for the Cardinals, might as well play me some baseball. With best friend, Ryan Stansbury. (Photo: Candy Holm)

Broken arms are nothing for soccer players. Game on! (Photo: Candy Holm)

Learning to drive fast while young in Junior Dragsters.
Team Holm beings! (Photo: Jeff Holm))

Nothing would ever be the same after my first bobsled ride on the Park City 2002 Track. (Photo: Candy Holm)

And winning my first gold a few months later sure didn't hurt. Thanks, Bruce! (Photo: Candy Holm)

The friendships I've made through bobsled have made it all worth it. (Photo: Jeremy's collection)

I cannot describe the amazing feeling of standing at the top of a track before a run. (Photo: Candy Holm)

No gold medal can ever take the place of that little black nametag. (Photo: Jeremy's collection)

To all my teammates past and present, thank you for standing and sliding with me. (Photo: Candy Holm)

Sled maintenance, particularly runner work, is a never-ending "joy." (Photo: Candy Holm)

Six Flags on steroids, bobsled is the most exhilarating thing I have ever done. (Photo: Rachel Wickern-Packard)

Preparing to drive four-man for the first time. Me, nervous? Never. (Photo: Candy Holm)

Sprinting downhill, pushing a bobsled on ice before loading in . . . priceless. (Photo: Kristen McMullin-Pack)

Nothing beats a hard four-man push, as long as no one ends up "spiked." (Photo: Candy Holm)

I love moments like this one, feeling the speed and acceleration push you to the floor. (Photo: Getty Images)

Coaching moment caught on camera. Some of my favorite memories were teaching others. (Photo: Lori Blood)

Some of the best and bravest athletes I know were the adaptive athletes I coached. (Photo: Lori Blood)

Few things in life make me happier than sharing my passion with others and helping them find theirs. (Photo: Poonam Kumar)

I could never be where I am today if not for all the coaches and mentors who have helped me along the way. Thank you, all! (Photo: Jeremy's collection)

Me with my dad who has been sled mechanic, supporter, and cheerleader along the way. (Photo: Candy Holm)

Those initial moments after a push-start and you're looking into the first turn . . . love it. (Photo: Rachel Packern-Wickard)

I always thought of this sled as "The Mormon Meteor," like the famous automobile, in honor of all those who have gone before and stayed true to the faith. (Photo: Kristen McMullin Pack)

I will forever be grateful to my Father in Heaven for the experiences he gave me and the lessons he taught me on the ice. (Photo: Rachel Packern-Wickard)

KEEP YOUR EYE ON THE ETERNAL PRIZE

When it comes to enduring adversity, perhaps a technique I learned from piloting sleds can help. While driving, you want to look as far down the track as possible, which means that when you are coming out of one turn you tilt your head to look as far around a bend as we can. When you look at some bobsled pictures you'll see the sled going one way and the pilot seems to be looking in a totally different direction. Why is that? Because, and here's the principle, where you are looking is where you will go.

In bobsled looking even slightly to the left in a straightaway, instead of down the center, can cause a pilot to subconsciously drive the sled left so the team ends up bouncing off the wall, which, as you know, can be disastrous in a race since it will (a) slow you down, and (b) can lead to a crash in extreme cases. To avoid both outcomes, we pick a spot deep inside the turn in front of us and head right for it. We focus intensely on that spot and ignore any outside distractions like cameras, lights, or cheering spectators.

It's all about where our vision is directed, a principle that holds eternally true during trials. Adversity can act as distractions that will, if we let them, pull our focus off of the important things in life. Please understand I'm not saying we should ignore our challenges. Rather, I'm talking about keeping our head up and looking toward heaven, instead of casting our eyes down in defeat. Like a bobsled slowing down after hitting a wall, sometimes adversity can burn off our spiritual steam. We may even wander off course for a bit, wondering "Why me?" If we let them, trials can pull our concentration off that point we are aiming for, even eternal life. If that happens we may find ourselves bouncing off the walls of discouragement, loneliness, and even sin or addiction.

But what if instead of looking down, we chose to look forward in faith? As a sled pilot I have to focus on where I want to go instead of letting outside distractions grab my attention and pull us off course. Through faith we can choose to keep an eternal perspective about trials instead of letting ourselves be drawn into the distractions of discouragement and doubt. As the Book of Mormon teaches, we have the power to decide.

In 57 BC the Nephites achieved victory over the Lamanites, but peace in their land came at great cost. Tens of thousands had been killed during the long wars, and the people had suffered greatly. The Nephite nation as a whole had endured the conflict, but Mormon explains that individuals reacted in two different ways: "But behold . . . many had become hardened, because of the exceedingly great length of the war; and many were softened because of their afflictions, insomuch that they did humble themselves before God, even in the depth of humility" (Alma 62:41).

I have actually seen a similar phenomenon in bobsled. At first I was surprised about how many people start sliding only to quit within a season or two. There has never been a large number of sliders in the United States (or in the world), but the turnover rate at the entry level is interesting. When I started analyzing the people who left and those who stayed, I noticed some fascinating differences between the two groups and how they handled adversity.

Those who quit the sport early perhaps started it for fame, money, or to experience the thrill of the track a few times. But once they found out how expensive the sport is, what it feels like to get hurt in a crash, or how much practice is required they cut out. I'm not faulting these athletes, mind you; they decided the sport wasn't for them and chose to pursue other interests. I just found it interesting that when there was no solid foundation, adversity quickly ended things.

However, those who stayed in bobsled, despite the same adversities, did so because they enjoyed it and had real commitment to their pursuit of gold. Because of this perspective, they found ways to endure and thrive and were determined to be successful in their dreams no matter what. Their foundations were firm and their vision was focused on where they wanted to go.

Whatever comes our way, peace or adversity, we have the power to choose how we let it affect us. Will we keep a positive perspective and, like a winning bobsled pilot, focus on where we want to go? Or will tribulation turn our hearts to bitter ash? To a great extent, our reactions are based on the strength of our faith. Like bobsled drivers, we need to concentrate on the destination we have picked out (that is, exaltation) and keep it firmly in our minds as we "compete" for it. If we choose to focus too much on the obstacles, we will find ourselves crashing into them and not progressing. We, like some athletes do with bobsled, will find gospel living "too hard" and may drift away from the principles of salvation.

Don't focus on "why me." Instead, focus on your progression and the end goal of returning to Heavenly Father's kingdom. Keep your vision firmly fixed on the Savior. When I am driving down the track and have my point picked out in the next turn, I say to myself, "That is where I am going, and nothing will distract me from getting there." Spiritually speaking, we must do the same. I suggest that in your darkest hours you put forth an even greater effort to look to the light of this world (John 8:12) because when we embrace Jesus Christ as a teammate, we can go forward with confidence. Faith is crucial to enduring the trials of life, or of sport, because without hope, we may give up and walk away.

When I'm driving a sled and I focus on a point down the track, I have to believe I can get there. It may not be a conscious thought, but it's there. In life, when adversity comes, we must have faith that we can get through it, no matter how tough. When maintain a winning attitude and remember that trials are meant to help us progress, we will see them not as "problems" but rather teaching experiences sent from our heavenly coach that are designed to help us become like he is.

By determining right now that you won't let anything stop you from reaching the celestial kingdom, you immediately gain power over the events in your life. This eternal perspective puts us in a mental and emotional state capable of handling each obstacle in a faith-determined way. Yes, some trials will wrench our heartstrings, but rather than going to pieces, we can humbly face adversity with conviction, courage, and hope.

However, there is another side to "enduring well." If my hands are not rock-solid in guiding our sled when I'm driving through a turn, then we are going to wave up and down in the curve. If we are flaky in our eternal focus, then any trial or disappointment that arises can throw us off course. That's when Satan whispers, "Heaven doesn't care about your suffering"; he uses adversity to turn us away from the God who wants to help us. Like a bright camera flash outside the bobsled track, his discouragement is meant to distract us from focusing on what is important.

I learned this lesson in a manner after returning to Utah from a trip to the Calgary, Canada, track in the latter part of February 1999. The season was coming to a close, so our coaches decided to have one last race. I faced some difficulties going into this competition, the first being that it was our first on-ice session since coming home from Calgary. The second problem was I had been assigned a sled I was not familiar with (imagine entering a car race with someone else's car). I chose to give the competition my best effort anyway.

On race day, I found myself struggling to get situated in the driver's seat as I drove through the first few turns of the Park City course. Since we were sharing the sled with another team, I could not adjust the backrest, pedals, and steering ropes to my liking. When we entered the first major G-force turn, I felt myself slide in the seat, and my helmet bumped off the side of the sled, thus blocking part of my peripheral vision. I shook the helmet back straight and stared down the track, but the next major G-force turn had the same effect. I couldn't remain solid in my seat and my helmet kept bumping the side of the sled. These problems led to several brushes with the short-wall of the track, which slowed us down.

So let's review. I wasn't stable in my seat (you could say firm and immoveable), my vision kept getting pulled from where I should have been looking, and, as a result, we experienced bumps along the way that slowed down our progress. Let's apply that to life's more challenging competitions. If we are not firm in our seat (faith) with our eyes focused on the goal (the Savior), we may make our adversities more difficult and experience more bumps along the way through poor choices and bad attitudes. No wonder the adversary tries to distract us with self-pity and temptation. When life's challenges arise, we'll be looking everywhere but where we need to!

But Satan is clever and has more than one trick is in his bag to try to throw us off course.

One of the worst things people say during adversity is, "Well, if this trial is happening, maybe I'm not supposed to pursue my goal." They think that just because an obstacle has appeared, they must have chosen the wrong path. Nothing could be further from the truth. When you set out to do good things, especially things like obeying a commandment, going on a mission, or getting married in the temple, you can expect challenges. As any athlete can attest, the best victories are often on the far side of adversity.

Sometimes we must go through hell in order to reach heaven, and to survive the bobsled ride of mortality, we need to keep our eyes focused heavenward and stubbornly remind ourselves that it is all for our eternal good

(Doctrine and Covenants 122:5–8). Like a bobsled pilot ignoring outside distractions, by looking beyond the trial and toward heaven instead, our hearts will find the patience to endure and our spirits the strength to overcome. As we walk through the fires of adversity, may we keep our perspective focused on the loving arms of our coach, Jesus Christ.

THE BEST OF TIMES AND THE WORST OF TIMES

Have you ever found yourself at the gym, sweat pouring down your face, and wondered, "Why does something so good for me have to hurt so bad?" I have. Why can't sitting down to a good movie be as good as a leg day or chocolate be as healthy as a chicken salad?

Answer: the experiences that challenge us the most are often the best things for us. We need opposition in order to grow, to discipline the natural man in us, and to become more like the Savior. Even the best athletes in the world know they must continue to push themselves to stay in top form, and that requires discipline and hard work. Should a people striving to become like the Lord and eventually experience exaltation expect their path to be easier?

A misconception surrounding adversity is found in the question we have all asked: "What did I do to deserve this?" Sometimes the answer is absolutely nothing. We can do our best to keep the commandments and serve the Lord, but, being the great coach that he is, God knows that resistance is an effective teacher.

Resistance training as an athlete involves any exercise that uses an opposing force to cause muscular contraction. This can be done with elastic or hydraulic resistance, weight training, plyometrics, speed drills, and so on. The weight, or resistance, opposes your muscles as you push or pull, and the more weight you use, the stronger you get. Adversely, if we never increase the amount of resistance being used, we plateau and won't progress physically. This also occurs when the same exercises are done over and over again without any variation. Sometimes we need to up the weight or change our workout program to better challenge us to grow.

Adversity works in much the same way, and the Lord knows that. What challenged us last year may not do so today, and that is part of the trial itself: accepting God's timing and understanding. If all we had were blessings and peace, we would never develop. Adam and Eve had to leave the garden in order to grow; should we be surprised when we are nudged toward heaven by the tests of mortality?

God allows trials to come even we are "doing everything right" because he knows the benefits we will receive. We needn't waste time or energy wondering why he is punishing us simply because he isn't. A good coach pushes his or her gold-medal team after the win because another race is coming up and they need to prepare for it. That isn't punishment; rather, it is a sign of the coach's desire to help his or her athletes reach their full potential.

Plus, even the best athletes face defeat. This time spent in practice or prayer is no guarantee that adversity won't still bring disappointment. Even the righteous will have to suffer afflictions during this life (2 Nephi 2:11), because if we didn't, we would plateau spiritually, mentally, and emotionally. While in our limited mortal view what we have now may be good enough, God knows our full potential and desires to help us get there. This explains the unexpected tests of adversity even when we feel like spiritual gold medalists.

When I was seventeen a director for our program pulled me aside after training and told me I had been extended an invitation to a special camp at the Lake Placid, New York, track. Out of all the youth athletes in the Park City program, only my teammate Joe and I were being asked. Needless to say, we were thrilled and I left that night feeling like I was on cloud nine.

My friends and family were excited at the news. They could see what a dream come true this camp was going to be since I was going to stay at the Olympic Training Center and be instructed by national-level coaches on the same track that held the 1980 Games.

Now, you're probably wondering what this story has to do with adversity. You'll see.

Joe and I only had about a week to prepare, which meant packing all our gear, asking our teachers for homework, and, most important, finding the money to go. While we would stay and eat at the Olympic Training Center, we still had to find airline tickets from Salt Lake City to Albany, New York, which proved to be our first obstacle. When we researched last-minute ticket prices, the cheapest we could find were over one thousand dollars. Considering I was a student who made around eight dollars an hour, I could never come up with that much money on my own.

So I turned to my parents for help. I will never forget the heartbroken look on my mom's face when she told me that they just didn't have the money. I could see her mind working, trying to figure out a way to find the funds so I could go. But after a long discussion, she tearfully said she didn't see how it was possible. I hate to say it, but I was crushed. To come so close to such an incredible experience, only to have it taken away. . . . After crunching some numbers and trying to devise a plot to raise money (I had to do my part), I knelt and told Heavenly Father how discouraged I was and that I really wanted to go to New York. I pled with him to somehow make it possible.

I felt like I was doing everything right (sound familiar?) in my sport. I also felt like the special camp invitation was an A+ report card on my performance. Plus, I was working hard at my job and paying my tithing, so the funds should have miraculously appeared, right?

I started to worry. Those same fears we've been talking about came into my mind. I wondered if God was punishing me by not letting me go to the camp. Was I being too prideful about it? Had I committed some grave sin that put me on "the naughty list"? What had I done to bring this trial upon myself? Drawing a blank, I fell asleep from exhaustion.

Well, God answered my adversity-inspired prayer. Later my sister Linnea woke me up with a note in her hand and a smile on her face. Apparently Joe had found a flight to New York that would only cost a few hundred dollars, round trip. I couldn't believe it. Despite my lack of faith, God extended forth his mighty hand in my behalf and did what I could not to overcome the obstacle. While this trial may not have any real significance in the eternal scheme of things, it was important to me, and God knew that. And despite the fears, I know now that I didn't face this setback because of anything I had done. I wasn't being punished; it just happened.

Why does Satan want us to give in to false beliefs during times of adversity? If we fear that God won't help us, that he is angry, or that we deserve to be punished and are therefore unworthy, we will never ask for heaven's help. Can you imagine how tough it would be for an athlete if he or she felt like he or she couldn't turn to their head coach in times of great need?

I understand the desire to know the "why" when we face a specific trial. We want to understand the context of our adversity. Players and coaches analyze race footage to see what went right and wrong, plus the heat of competition can displays habits, movements, and attitudes that were dormant during training. While studying video, you may catch something that you need to improve to increase the chance of future victories, which is why we spend so much time reviewing video of our runs down the track. The danger, however, lies in how we react to what we find. Do we beat ourselves up for a mistake we made in the flash of the moment, or do we see it as an opportunity to change, to grow, and to better ourselves? Champions know they will make mistakes, but their attitude focuses on turning the lessons of a loss into future victories.

My point is that when adversity arises, we can always find fault in ourselves if we look hard enough, some weakness we indulged in or mistake made. Our energies would be better spent turning to the Lord in humility. Don't let your flaws keep you from the strength of a Savior who wants to be your teammate through whatever trial you are facing.

Believing that every bad thing that happens to us is the result of God's anger would be like an athlete blaming every loss on divine displeasure. It may be tempting to do so, but the Lord told us adversities would come and that we should "Be patient in afflictions, for [we] shalt have many; but endure them, for, lo, [he is] with [us], even unto the end of [our] days" (Doctrine and Covenants 24:8). Any coach who fails to push his or her athletes to grow and excel is failing in his or her duty. Even the most naturally gifted players have to work on their trade, and it is a coach's responsibility to help them do so. And yes, this growth requires work and effort and even some pain and sacrifice.

Spiritually speaking, we will face trials and adversity so that we can "prove [ourselves] herewith, to see if [we] will do all things whatsoever the Lord [our] God shall command [us]" (Abraham 3:25). He is a loving coach, but he is still our coach, and he has clearly stated that his "work and [his] glory . . . [is] to bring to pass the immortality and eternal life of man" (Moses 1:39). Should we be surprised in any way that such a lofty goal requires some difficult tests and even some pain and sacrifice?

Remember that Greek athletes who wanted to excel sought out the most skilled and often the strictest trainers. Well, these coaches were called tektons, which is Greek for "builders" or "carpenters." Their task was to build each athlete into a fierce competitor who was worthy of contending before the gods at Olympia.

Now think about that for a second. The Lord has promised that he would help us get ready for "immortality and eternal life" if we accept his help. And if he, like the tektons of old, is dedicated to building us into individuals worthy of presenting ourselves before the gods, even our Eternal

Father and himself, at what point did we think that such a faithful coach would not push us to become our best selves along the way?

Ask any champion, and he or she will tell you that to become your best, some pain is required. So when trials come, it just means that the Lord is helping us get ready for the only competition that really matters in our eternal journey: the big day before the judgment bar (Mormon 3:20), a competition at which he desires we all win gold.

In times of trial, let us ignore Satan's whispers that we have failed or that God must be angry. I challenge all of us to face the storm with heads held high. Instead of being the first to cast a stone at ourselves, we should be the first to offer a drink of water and bind up our own wounds on the side of the road. Satan was the architect of the "great and spacious building" (1 Nephi 8), and he and his "teammates" will mock and point their fingers and do their best to make us feel inadequate and unworthy of God's help. In those moments we should remember the Lord's invitation to the people on the American continent after his resurrection, "Yea, verily I say unto you, if ye will come unto me ye shall have eternal life. Behold, mine arm of mercy is extended toward you, and whosoever will come, him will I receive; and blessed are those who come unto me" (3 Nephi 9:14).

Stay close to the Lord in your times of adversity. He is the best teammate and coach we could ask for and will heal our spirits, strengthen our hearts, and bind up our wounds if we let him. There alone will we find true peace and stand tall as champions of faith. After all, with the Lord as our tekton, we may "be strong and of a good courage . . . for the Lord [our] God is with [us] whithersoever [we] goest" (Joshua 1:9).

The ancient Greeks believed that the gods of Olympia watched them compete. How blessed are we to know that no matter how hard the trial, we can rest assured that the God of Israel is cheering us on from the sidelines, saying, "Get up, get up and finish the race."

KEEP YOUR HEAD UP AND GIVE YOUR BEST EFFORT

A few years ago, we headed up to the Calgary, Canada, track, and on the way back, I had an experience that taught me a lot about handling adversity like a champion.

I found myself driving a minivan that our coach inherited in Calgary while he was out in front in the team van with the other athletes. My teammate and I were doing our best to follow, but a horrible blizzard struck in the middle of nowhere in northern Montana, and traveling down Interstate 15 under those conditions was not fun. The wind was blowing so hard and the snow was so thick that I couldn't see the road, the signposts, or even the foliage next to the freeway. I could barely see the front of our own car, let alone those of our fellow travelers. I had a white-knuckle death grip on the steering wheel; piloting a sled on ice was one thing, but driving a minivan on it was quite another. I had horrifying images of some future policeman finding the wrecked remains of a blue minivan with the frozen bodies of two teenage athletes inside.

So how did I know where I was going? After an eternity (half an hour) of prayer-filled driving, while doing everything in my power to stay on the road, I noticed a small change in the swirling snow ahead of us. Every so often I caught a glimmer of a faint flashing yellow light, and I realized that no more than seventy feet in front of us was a huge snowplow. Although I could only see the flashing light, a quiet peace filled my heart. With a trustworthy guide in front of me, I could now focus on driving safely and calmly. I no longer felt powerless and lost. That little flashing light kept us safe and led us in the right direction through the storm.

When the blizzards of adversity come into our lives, we often need similar guidance, but we must be careful not to diminish our own intelligence and abilities. As Nephi teaches in 2 Nephi 25:23, "we know that it is by grace that we are saved, after all we can do." We are far stronger than we think and our Heavenly Father expects us to act accordingly during times of trial. Could he give us solutions to every problem we face in life? Sure, but he knows the value of letting us stretch our minds, spirits, and bodies to do as much as we can for ourselves. If he fixed everything right away, it would be like a coach stepping in during a weight-training session and lifting the bar for the athlete. The weight may move, but the athlete gets nothing out it.

When the storms of life come our way let us do everything within our power to overcome and endure. We can then expect help from the teammate who never falters. The Lord can and should be our greatest source of strength and comfort. Part of the reason Christ "descended below all things" (Doctrine and Covenants 88:6) was so he can lift us above all things.

Let's be honest: some days tax us to our limits. Like I did on that Montana highway, we feel surrounded by raging winds of doubt, the bitter cold of fear, and the blinding snow of temptation. After doing all I could, I have fallen to my knees for relief, pleading with our Father in Heaven to help me through my current afflictions. I have wet my pillow at night seeking the balm of Gilead for the wounds within my soul. And I testify that the Healer of all wounds was there for me, just as he will be there for you.

When I was asked to help coach the United States Adaptive Bobsled Team, a group that contained some of the first amputee and wheelchair bobsled athletes in the world, I jumped at the opportunity. It was a great experience—though a lot harder than I anticipated. When I came onboard, the program was in a near-lawsuit situation in order to be allowed ice time at the Park City track. On my first day with the athletes, a news crew showed up to cover the story, which was a nice "Welcome, coach!" for me.

Getting bobsled into the Paralympics was our goal, and I believed it would take discipline, loyalty, good sportsmanship, professionalism, and personal responsibility within our program to help make that happen. Over the next few months I labored to turn the recreational program into a group of serious competitors who could (fingers crossed) represent their country in the near future. Some of the athletes took to this new level of training like fish to water, while others grumbled that it was too hard. What those complaining athletes couldn't see was that if they really wanted to compete for the United States on the world stage, then they needed to step up their game. History could look back on our example and how we achieved this feat of competing internationally.

While I was able to coach using much of what I had learned as an athlete, a lot of it had to be invented as we went along. From creating specialized training programs for each individual to developing new push and load techniques for amputee athletes based on their level of injury and model of prosthetics, I had to get pretty creative at times. The group's name was highly appropriate as I found myself adapting everything I knew about the sport to match this brave new world of a (hopefully) future Paralympic event.

I could probably write an entire book on the history of my time coaching these athletes, but I will summarize for the sake of time. All our hard work paid off and by the end of that first season we had gained the respect of the sliding community and the bobsled track staff. That was a win in and of itself.

The next summer I worked hard to plan and organize the first adaptive bobsled summer camp in the United States. This multiday event was filled with class time, physical testing, sled maintenance lessons, push and load practice and more. We had a wonderful turnout, and I still have athletes thank me for their experience. My favorite parts of the camp were the one-on-one sessions with the athletes or the late-night discussions on sled driving theory we had in the cafeteria. I never would have imagined that the program would self-destruct less than a year later.

I wouldn't be surprised to see a movie made some day about the challenges faced in moving adaptive bobsled forward; the behind the scenes drama would make for excellent viewing. You couldn't make up the things that happened to bring about the downfall of a program that I loved with all my heart.

Where to begin? A lot of the difficulties arose when the newer, younger, more competitive athletes began to stand up to some of the older, more veteran athletes (who also happened to be on the group's executive board). When I selected a team captain who was respected by the majority of the athletes, these older athletes were not happy, especially the program's director who happened to be another driver as well. I began to see a power struggle emerge that eventually led to a division within the program and my experienced voice became ignored. I saw grave danger written in the cards, but it wasn't until I witnessed what I felt were abuses of power and the completely unethical ways that some athletes were treated, that I knew I could no longer support the program.

The final nail in the coffin for me was the day it was announced that the program was being handed over to the coaches at the Park City track. It was a behind-closed-doors deal that had been forced upon the athletes, and me, and no one was happy. A meeting was held at which the athletes one by one stood up to say that they would not slide without Coach Holm. Just thinking of that moment brings tears to my eyes because those athletes were basically saying they would give up their sliding careers if I wasn't going to be their coach.

I knew that despite all the hard work I had put in and the accomplishments we had achieved, I couldn't do anything. I knew it was going to be a destructive blow to the American adaptive program for the time being, and sadly I had to watch everything we had worked so hard for fall to pieces. Many of the athletes I had grown to love left the sport in disgust, feeling betrayed and trampled. It was a tragedy.

I was devastated, angry, depressed, discouraged, and frustrated and had so many other emotions too. Disgusted was also high on the list. What was I to do?

Several options went through my mind. A lawsuit would only harm the athletes who still wanted to slide as we were held captive by the powers that be. We could take the story to the media; call on local, state, and national officials to intervene; contact legal representatives, including those who specialize in disability cases; and so on. Actually, an executive from a nonprofit that handled situations like this expressed interest in taking on the "case," but nothing felt right. The above solutions may have helped me feel better, but they would not have been better for athletes who had already suffered enough.

In the end, all I could do was turn it over to the Lord and ask him to take the wheel. I have only relayed one one-hundredth of the adversities that I and these wonderful athletes were asked to pass through, but a quiet part of me knew that if I exercised faith, it would all turn out somehow.

Do you wonder if the Lord is mindful of the trials you face? You have faith in his mighty power, but do you fear he won't hear your prayers for help in times of need? Are you like the woman in the New Testament who had an issue of blood and spent all her time and financial resources in seeking relief? Perhaps we should learn from this woman's faith.

As Jesus walked down the street, she "came behind him, and touched the border of his garment: and immediately her issue of blood stanched [or stopped]" (Luke 8:44). After doing all in her power for years, this humble daughter of God was willing to trust in the Savior's mighty power to do the rest. Whatever her anxieties may have been, she was willing to exercise "faith as a grain of mustard seed" (Matthew 17:20) in the Lord's power. As soon as she did so, her issue of blood was staunched or stopped.

We often think of blood as symbolic of life. When a wound starts to bleed, you get weaker, so let me ask you this: in what way are you "bleeding" emotionally, mentally, spiritually, or physically? What trials and afflictions are sapping your strength and weakening your body, mind, or soul?

Looking for things that are weighing you down is natural. As an athlete you constantly look for things that might be slowing you down or lowering your level of performance. The thing about adversities is that we usually don't have to try hard to discover them. Like an athletic injury, our afflictions have a way of making themselves known. For me it was losing the adaptive bobsled program that I had helped develop into a team with powerful potential. Whatever burden you may be carrying, I entreat you to remember the words of the same Savior who healed this woman: "let your hearts rejoice; for behold, and lo, I am with you even unto the end" (Doctrine and Covenants 100:12). He was with me until the end of that harrowing drive through Montana, he comforted me when my bobsled program imploded, and I know he will be with you until the end of the difficult path you are being asked to walk.

When I returned from my mission in March 2002, the Olympics had just ended in Salt Lake. I spent the following summer working at the track giving tours, hosting private functions, and trying to find out how my bobsled training would continue. While I was away my program had simply fallen apart. Few organized programs or clubs for bobsled athletes to train in were left in Utah. A quiet concern filled my heart. Were my sliding days over?

That was problem number one. Problem number two was that I didn't have a sled to use since our program sleds had been shipped back to the New York track. So I got to work first and trusted in the Lord to work it out from there. I knew I could hope and pray for God's help all I wanted, but unless I did my part as James taught, my "faith, if it hath not works, is dead, being alone" (James 2:17).

I set out to organize a program myself and began working with the track's manager and athlete coordinator, and at first it seemed like I was making headway. I put together a written proposal on how to pay for track time, who the coaches could be, and how the program would be structured. The plan was based a lot on the program my first coach had organized, with a few of my own creations added in. Additionally, I listed all the problems I could foresee and solutions for each one.

But the harder I worked, the more obstacles appeared in my path, which soon bogged my plans in a deep pit of "Let's put it off for another season." I felt like I was pushing my goal through a blizzard of foot-dragging, only this time I was having difficulty seeing any light to guide me. Everyone believed the program was a good idea, but no one took action to make it happen. I was frustrated.

October, November and December passed with no ice training, and I knew it was time to turn the problem over to the Lord. In my prayers I explained all that I had tried. I humbly admitted that I didn't know what else to do and that I either needed him to bless me with some inspiration or to reach forth his mighty hand and bring about a miracle. In retrospect, I guess the third option was to ask for patience to wait until the following season, but the thought never crossed my mind. Oops.

After all I could do, I was now looking for that tiny light of the Lord's guidance during the blizzard and honestly I didn't have to wait long. In January I was authorized to borrow a sled and train during some international bobsled training sessions and other open programs scheduled by the sport's national governing body. While it wasn't a weekly program with set times or coaching, it was a start. I may have only gotten a fraction of my runs in that year, but at least I got to train. Stubbornness won out, and the Lord came through. I knew that I had put forth my best efforts and had done all I could think of to overcome the trial. At that point I had to turn it over to the Savior and trust him, whether it worked out like I wanted it to or not.

I know some difficulties seem to overwhelm us like an emotional or spiritual Montana blizzard. We will have days when our hearts feel so broken and our lives so burdened that it appears there is no light at the end of the tunnel. It is in those times when we need to rely on the love of our elder brother and Savior Jesus Christ the most. His compassionate care is the tiny light that will help us stay on the right road.

I do not know what it is like to lose a child or a close loved one. I have never faced a life-threatening illness. I have not had to watch my home burn to the ground, nor have I ever experienced a natural disaster. I have, however, faced disappointment, heartache, depression, loneliness, fatigue, and many personal trials. And if I can testify of anything, it is that our Savior knows our strengths and our limitations, and he will lovingly stand by our side through all the tribulations we are asked to endure.

What task has the Lord given to you? What trial or obstacle has he asked you to "drive" through with faith, patience, and humility? Adversity often feels like a blinding and overwhelming blizzard in life, but we must keep our heads up and push forward with faith, which includes doing our part. Once we have done all in our power, we can turn to the Lord in full confidence and ask for divine assistance. The solution may not come in the manner or time we expect, but we will always hear him say to us, as he said to the woman healed in the streets, "Be of good comfort: thy faith hath made thee whole; go in peace" (Luke 8:48).

If you are facing a hard time in your life and feel as if there is nothing more you can do, I encourage you to turn to the Lord. When the trials of life bring you to your knees, start praying. You're already kneeling, after all.

I testify that Christ will always be our guiding light through the blizzards of life. He has been my best coach, supporter, and friend for all these years, especially during times of trial. I feel he extends to us the same invitation he gave to the Nephites gathered in the land of Bountiful in 3 Nephi chapter 17. "Have ye any that are sick among you? Bring them hither. Have ye any that are lame, or blind, or halt, or maimed, or leprous, or that are withered, or that are deaf, or that are afflicted in any manner? Bring them hither and I will heal them, for I have compassion upon you; my bowels are filled with mercy" (3 Nephi 17:7).

If you feel spiritually, emotionally, or mentally "afflicted in any manner," I encourage you to do all in your power to find a solution. Hold on to the victories you have already gained. If the answers for your personal blizzards don't come, turn to the Lord in faith. I promise you will find compassion, mercy, healing, and peace. He is the master of every storm (Mark 4:35–40).

CHAMPIONS KNOW TOMORROW IS ANOTHER DAY

If you've ever watched bobsled on TV, you probably noticed that most of the athletes could be described as "hulks": Big (six foot one or taller), fast (very), strong (not human) and extremely talented at what they do.

Well when I started sliding I was five feet nine inches and tipped the scales at 145 pounds, nearly seventy pounds less than world-class athletes. While my skill as a driver was increasing, my weight and height were flat-lined. No matter what I ate or how much I worked out, the numbers on the scale just wouldn't go up. That's a horrible trial, I know, but in a sport where strength and size are crucial to success, I felt physically inadequate and self-conscious. That I was only seventeen at the time didn't matter; I wanted to get bigger right then.

My wonderful coach offered some great guidance as did a few of the veteran drivers, but some other athletes and coaches were less than friendly with their remarks. I obtained a good understanding of the deep wounds one callous comment can make, and I vowed to take King Benjamin's words to heart and watch my thoughts, words and deeds (Mosiah 4:30) toward others from that point on.

An additional challenge was involved; one that the athletes and coaches who made those comments had no clue about. When the anxiety and depression got tough, my appetite was the first thing to go. It was a bit of a dual trial, but most people were only aware of the more visible one. As much as I wanted these "thorn[s] in the flesh" (2 Corinthians 12:7) to go away, I knew needed patience with myself and the Lord's timing.

So, I kept up with my training and did my best to eat well and slowly, ever so slowly, my weigh-ins moved toward 150 pounds and then finally 165. I left for my mission in March 2000 weighing a whopping 175, a weight I wanted to celebrate. I finally hit 195 pounds over a decade after I started sliding, and while it's an almost laughable "affliction" as you can tell, I worried about it for years. Could the Lord have changed me into a hulking Nephi-like athlete who belonged in an Arnold Friberg painting? Sure, but that would have deprived me of the growth, both physical and emotional, that I gained. I learned to love myself for who and what I was and not negatively view myself for who or what I wasn't.

I also learned that sometimes the patience the Lord asks us to have is the gift he wants to give. Given what Jesus went through in the Garden of Gethsemane (2 Nephi 9:21), he understands our silent cries that our "cup[s] may pass from [us]" (Luke 22:42). However, in his infinite wisdom, he knows that some trials must be passed through. As Joseph Smith once taught, "all difficulties, which might and would cross our way must be surmounted. Though the soul be tried, the heart faint, and the hands hang down, we must not retrace our steps."[22]

We knew we would face difficulties in this world. In premortality we were taught that trials would appear at the least-expected times in our lives, yet even with the knowledge of the pains and hard times to come, we all shouted for joy (Job 38:7) over our Heavenly Father's plan. So we were positive then. Why not strive to be positive now?

A mission companion, Elder Trampleasure, once taught me about the power of attitude when he told me a story of a rainy afternoon he spent tracting. Now when it rains in Honduras, it literally pours, and with few paved roads, you can imagine the mud and puddles we had to cross through, sometimes up to our knees. Well, Trampleasure said that as he pushed through one deep mud puddle, the thought occurred to him that he was getting drenched, muddy, and tired for the Lord. He stopped, and with a smile on his face, he looked up and told the Lord, "I'm doing this for you!"

That is exactly the kind of winning attitude we need to have if we want to win the game of life. We will face hard times, and we will face adversity, but we don't have to let it bring us down into the depths of sorrow. We need to do more than just endure with a grumpy face; we need to endure well. As the Lord reminds us, "Be patient in afflictions, for thou shalt have many; but endure them, for, lo, I am with thee, even unto the end of thy days" (Doctrine and Covenants 24:8). If a trial sucker punches us in the face, we need to get back up and punch right back.

Whether you are an Olympic athlete, a new parent, a business entrepreneur, or a newly called missionary, remember that a positive attitude brings positive results. Faith is optimistic, while despair is destructively draining. When adversity comes, I see many who fall into a deeply negative mindset, which indicates a lack of faith in themselves and the Lord. If adversity can make you fall to pieces, no wonder you feel like a victim; you've given up your power to choose how you react to your current circumstances. So think positively about your life, no matter what obstacles arise. As you increase in faith, you increase your power to faithfully face and overcome trials (even if it takes time to do so). Like an athlete lifting more weight in the gym, exercising faith during times of affliction will help us grow stronger. I'm not saying that will be easy, but the results for persevering are far more beneficial than giving up. No matter how long and hard the road may be, we must patiently trust in the Lord until the storm passes in order to obtain victory at all costs.

That being said, we are not weak, nor is our faith shallow if we struggle. Trials are meant to stretch and humble us, so it is natural to feel the strain. But while struggling, instead of giving in to despair, we would do well to exercise faith, perseverance, and perhaps even a sense of humor.

Let's jump back to that New York training trip to illustrate my point. Joe and I arrived at the Olympic Training Center in Lake Placid with wide eyes. Set in the beautiful Adirondack Mountains, the track is surrounded by breathtaking scenery. Driving into the park, we passed the biathlon area and saw a few athletes training. With the way the snow blanketed the ground and the trees, the scene looked like something off a postcard. As we pulled up to the training center and toured the facilities, we couldn't help but grin; we were living a dream, and the dream was good!

Over the next few days we were instructed in various aspects of our sport by great coaches. We met about a dozen other youth athletes from New York, and together we spent hours on the track, in the gym, and walking around town. Since we were all comparatively younger and new to the track, the coaches started us lower on the course. Joe and I wanted to go higher, but the coaches wisely said no as this was all done on the old Lake Placid track.

We both had a lot of fun on the trip, but of all the stories that I can tell let me focus on the best one of all, the Empire State Games.

The annual Empire State Games are like a state Olympics with events being held in dozens of categories, including bobsled, so at the end of our training camp, all the attendees were invited to enter, and Joe and I quickly signed up. We agreed to race together, even though some of the coaches tried to get us to compete separately. One coach said, "If you race separately, you'll get to take two medals home to Utah." But Joe and I were the only Utah athletes there and wanted to stick together. Besides, if we won, wouldn't we bring home two medals anyway?

The night of the race, Joe and I excitedly walked along the track, starting at the finish line and heading up toward the competition's start area so we could refresh our minds of the course layout. Along the path we saw the track crew spraying water onto the track so that it would freeze and create a fresh and fast layer of ice for the race. Or so we thought.

A large crowd of parents, officials, coaches, and athletes gathered around the starting line. For this race, the officials decided to handle things differently. Instead of having one driver and one brakeman per team, we were going to switch off and take turns driving and braking. Joe and I decided I would go first and he would go second, so when our turn came, we got in the sled and off we went.

The sled slowly picked up speed, and, for the most part, things went well. However, as we went through a few turns, the sled did not react the way it should have, and I felt I had little control. I hadn't been in the sport for too long, but I knew something was wrong.

Our run wasn't horrible, but as we crossed the finish line, I was frustrated. As we came to a stop, I jumped out of the sled and looked back at Joe. When he stood up, his lap and his seat were covered in slush. Boy, did he have an angry look on his face, but we both surmised what had happened.

Remember the track crew we passed who were spraying water onto the track's surface? Well, that afternoon and evening were rather warm, so there had been softer sections of the ice. Instead of a hard layer of clean ice, Joe and I had just gone down the track in the world's biggest Slushie. The sled wasn't responding like it should have, because the runners couldn't bite the softer surface.

Our current trial left us feeling pretty frustrated. We marched back to the start and told the officials what had happened. Under normal race conditions, a slush track is not acceptable, but this time the officials told us we would not be allowed a redo run. Gee, thanks.

Life's trials aren't just about things that happen; often they include things we wish would happen, like a temple marriage, a new job, a pregnancy—or a gold medal at a New York race, which because of rough track conditions, we had no hope of getting. I was disappointed, and Joe was getting angrier by the minute. He is an incredible athlete with a huge competitive streak. He wanted a gold medal just as badly as I did. So, understanding his frustrations, I grabbed his arm and walked away from the crowd so we could talk as a team.

Together we vented our frustrations, letting the trees and wildlife around us know what we thought of the race. After overcoming so many obstacles just to get to New York and working so hard during the camp, our chance of getting a medal had been flushed down the tubes. Joe was so upset that he threw his helmet into the bushes, which our main coach did not like.

Then it hit me (not Joe's helmet). We had worked hard. We had overcome a lot to get where we were. We deserved to have a good time and we shouldn't let the current trial ruin that for us. I decided I was going to have a good time, no matter how terrible the obstacles seemed. That's when my brilliant plan of positive humor hit me.

I turned and said: "Joe, this sucks. It does. But I don't want to go home angry and neither do you. How about we make a little wager?" (I don't approve of betting, but this was different). "Since you're driving the next run, if you beat my downtime, I will set you up on a date with my friend who is a cheerleader back home." May I remind you we were both seventeen-year-old high school boys with plenty of hormones to match. Of course he agreed. The more we talked, the more we cheered up, and soon we were laughing and joking around. The situation had not changed, but, through humor and positive action, our attitudes did.

Joe took his spot in the driver's seat, and I jumped in behind him. Our second run, which was half an hour after our first, was smoother and the ice harder. While you'll have to wait until the next chapter to find out what happened, I can tell you that maintaining a positive attitude made all the difference at the time. We went from anger to laughter, disappointed to cheery.

No matter what circumstances you may find yourself in, you can always find a way out if you keep your head and your attitude up. You can find ways to pay the bills. You can learn the skills you need to get the job you want. You can find time to play with the kids more. You can work on overcoming the bad habit that is keeping you from greater happiness.

As Amulek exhorted, let us "have patience, and bear with all manner of afflictions" (Alma 34:40). I'm not saying that an optimistic attitude will solve everything, but it sure goes a long ways toward giving us strength to press forward. By consciously choosing to rely on faith in the Lord, we can smile, even if only weakly, despite the bumps we encounter down the track of life. In doing so, I testify that we will find strength, hope, and comfort we need to endure to the finish line.

Besides, you never know. You might find a gold medal waiting at the end of your trial.

ALL THESE THINGS SHALL BE FOR THY GOOD

A common misconception I hear is that bobsleds go down the track on skis. Not exactly, but I can see why people think that. On the bottom of the sled, four steel blades called runners guide the sled as it slides down the track. They look like ice skates, only our blades are longer and round like your finger on the bottom. In competition you cannot apply any sort of coating or plating to runners, and they are anywhere from roughly three feet (two-man front runners) to four feet (four-man back runners) long and are about a half inch in width. They are curved upward at the ends while the main portion of the bottom of the runner is straight.

Let's dig deep and review some high school physics. Let's talk about friction. Friction is defined as a force that resists the relative motion or tendency to such motion of two bodies in contact. When you slide a glass across the table, there is friction between the glass and the surface, but if you poured some cooking oil on the table and slide the glass, it would move a lot more easily because the oil reduces the friction. In bobsled, since we want to go as fast as possible, we try to eliminate as much friction as we can because friction equals a transfer of energy. If too much of that happens we are going to slow down. So friction = bad.

One trick we use to eliminate friction is to take our sled's runners, flip them over, and clamp them on a stand or bolt them into the sled. Next we take sandpaper, place it in the palm of our hand, and sand the surface from one end to the other until it shines like a mirror. And this isn't just a one-time event. Before every race and training session, you work on your runners to clean them up because even the tiniest scratch on the sliding surface can affect your speed. It might be a miniscule amount, but when you can lose the race by one one-hundredth of a second, you do everything you can to give your team the edge. But this comes with a cost. The friction generated between the sandpaper and the metal surface of the runner heats up and can rub your skin raw if you're not careful.

Now, with this explanation in mind, let's look at adversity from an eternal perspective. Think of yourself as the sled's runner and life's obstacles as the sanding process. The sandpaper used to scrape off spiritual rust or the scratches of sin can be the trial you are facing right now. It will take effort, and you might get blisters, but in the end you will find yourself a polished surface like that of a race-ready bobsled runner. After hours of sanding, you know you're done when you can see your face on the runner's surface. In life, when God can see his face in ours, we are closer to being "done." Every adversity has a purpose and a time limit.

The prophet Joseph Smith was intimately familiar with adversity. From the first few weeks after the First Vision until his death, Joseph was persecuted, falsely accused, beaten, imprisoned, and slandered. No matter how incredible the revelations he received from the Lord, Joseph was ridiculed and second-guessed as a leader. His friends turned against him, and his family was nearly destroyed through the evil acts of the servants of sin.

During the winter of 1840, Joseph and other Church leaders were thrown into Liberty Jail in Missouri, a damp, cold pit that would serve as their prison for several months. During this time, they suffered from malnourishment and unsanitary conditions that lead to severe illness for several of the brethren. As if that wasn't enough, letters were brought to the imprisoned leaders that described the intense suffering of the Saints at the hands of lawless mobs. After reading the heart-wrenching descriptions of their afflictions, Joseph cried out, "Oh God, where art thou?" (Doctrine and Covenants 121:1).

My heart goes out to Joseph. Like so many of us, he trusted in the Lord completely and never failed to testify of the divinity of the work in which he was engaged. He had spoken with God face to face and had been taught by the Lord and his angelic ministers. He knew the destiny of the Church was to triumph over all other powers. And like so many of us, it wasn't that Joseph doubted. Indeed, his pleading cry demonstrates absolute faith that God exists and listens to our prayers. But his heart ached amid the trials, and Joseph sought peace and understanding. It was a plea for comprehension and enlightenment during a dark time.

The Lord tenderly responded with a lesson that can inspire us all: "My son, peace be unto thy soul; thine adversity and thine afflictions shall be but a small moment; And then, if thou endure it well, God shall exalt thee on high; thou shalt triumph over all thy foes" (Doctrine and Covenants 121:7–8)

How many of us in our times of trial have wondered, "Oh God, where are you? Why have you left me alone?" When we feel the abrasive nature of adversity sanding away at our weaknesses, we may cry out, "Father, are you still there?" We know he lives, but when the friction of tribulation heats up, we may wonder if perhaps he has forgotten us.

But Joseph was reminded, as we so often are, that God does not leave us alone in times of difficulty. Just as the Lord knew what lay ahead for the restored Church, he knows the gold-medal moments that await us and will lead us safely to them. When we truly come to understand this principle, we can "press forward with a steadfastness in Christ, having a perfect brightness of hope, and a love of God and of all men" (2 Nephi 31:20) no matter what we face in life.

Let me share the finale of my 1998 trip to New York and the Empire State Games, a story that I hope provides some peace during your periods of adversity and heartache.

After our bad first run down the track, Joe and I had our little talk where I challenged him to beat my time so he could win a date with my cheerleader friend. After he accepted, we walked back to the start with a different attitude. Yes, we were still in a bad spot, but we were going to have fun, despite the setbacks, and we planned to win our own private battle that night.

As we entered the sled for our second run, Joe and I were still joking about whether he could beat me. I tucked down into the brakeman's seat as we took off, and I immediately felt a difference in the track. The second run was much smoother than the first (we later concluded that the ice had had sufficient time to freeze). I smiled as Joe piloted the sled through the turns. The funny thing is Joe sometimes talks to himself while driving, which is pretty entertaining.

As we crossed the finish line, we both felt better about the whole situation. We figured we had lost the race, but in the end we had fun doing it, which is what really mattered. We got out of our seats, gave each other a high-five, and put the sled back in the storage area. With our heads held high, Joe and I walked back to the check-in area on a path that took us past the large scoreboard. Suddenly, Joe got excited. "Jeremy! Look at the scoreboard!"

Thinking we were dead last, I shook my head. "That's okay, Joe. I don't need to see it."

He grabbed my arm. "Dude, yes you do. Look!"

Just to humor him, I paused to look up at the results. I had to take a second glance. And a third. Was I reading that right? Right there in big bright lights it said, "TEAM HOLM USA . . . #1" My jaw dropped. We actually won? I couldn't believe it. I guess my first run wasn't so bad after all.

We were both in shock and overwhelmed with excitement; the grins on our faces were probably visible from space. I'm not sure if we walked, ran, or floated back to the check-in area where we found out it was official. The team of Holm and Sisson had won the three-hundred-pound combined-weight division of New York's 1998 Empire State Games. And yes, Joe beat me and thus won his date with my cheerleader friend.

But our trials were only beginning to work out for our good.

Thirty minutes after the race, the crowd gathered in front of the scoreboard and it didn't matter who we were or where we were from anymore. Parents, officials, coaches, and athletes all enjoyed the moment. There's just something about a bobsled race that can bring people together.

Joe and I, feeling rather on top of the world, kept looking over at the medals podium, and it finally hit me. We had overcome the obstacles, worked hard during the camp, made the best of a difficult situation, and now we had won.

One by one the teams were announced along with their finish times and rankings. Since there were two divisions, we had to wait until the end. I don't even remember if it was cold while we stood there. My body felt on fire, and I couldn't stop smiling.

The other athletes parted the way to let us through, and Joe and I took our place on the center podium. As the official came over to distribute the awards, we clapped each other on the back and stared at those metal objects hanging from our necks. After all that had happened, somehow, someway, we had done it. Things had worked out for our good.

It almost seemed like a movie, but it was my movie, and it was happening on a beautiful Lake Placid night. I realized that of all the many lessons that Heavenly Father was trying to teach me during that trip to New York, the most important one was that he cared. Just when I thought my hopes and dreams had been crushed because of adversity, a loving Father taught me that his ways are better than my ways. Even though it may feel like adversity ruins things, as Paul wrote, "all things work together for good to them that love God" (Romans 8:28).

Standing out there on that New York mountain, surrounded by the crowd and the flashing cameras, I knew without a doubt that God loved me. He had been with me the whole time, even when I wondered as Joseph did, "Oh God, where art thou?" I felt he was leading me to greater things than I ever thought possible. Tears filled my eyes as they began to play the national anthem over the park's speakers. As the whole crowd turned to face the American flag floating in the night breeze, my hand covered my racing heart. To have the national anthem playing, with the Spirit so strong, and a gold medal hanging around my neck . . . it was perfect. I felt as Paul, who said, "I have fought a good fight, I have finished my course, I have kept the faith" (2 Tim. 4:7).

That medal reminds me that adversity is a teacher, not an enemy, and that the joys God has in store for us are truly beyond imagining. As Job wisely said, "[The Lord] knoweth the way that [we] take: when he hath tried [us], [we] shall come forth as gold" (Job 23:10). In this case I came forth with the gold.

I thought I had fully learned this lesson after my New York experience, but Heavenly Father soon provided me with another dramatic, though a bit more hair-raising, lesson.

TAKE A KNEE; YOUR COACH IS ON HIGH

The phrase "beggars can't be choosers" describes the life of many competitors in the Olympic arena, especially new bobsled athletes. Not only do you usually get borrowed equipment, you accept whatever funding you can find (if you need a good cause to donate to, let me know), and you go where the coaches tell you and do exactly what they say (that part never changes). You quickly learn, as the prophet Samuel taught, that "to obey is better than sacrifice" (1 Samuel 15:22).

When I started coaching, I gained new respect for every previous coach, leader, and teacher I ever had. Taking on the instructor's mantel, I tried to lead using the same methods of motivation, guidance, and support they used to help me become the person I am today.

One of a bobsled coach's biggest responsibilities is (logically) to teach their drivers a turn's best drive-lines, the ones that will give their team the edge. Remember, not all bobsled curves are constructed alike, so each one has myriad potential drive-lines. Coaches and athletes may watch videos, study whiteboard schematics, or walk the course to talk about what to do at each point.

I found teaching the adaptive athletes I worked with to be a completely enjoyable experience . . . usually. Sometimes I felt like a parent trying to keep the family happy while separating team-siblings who weren't getting along. At times I had to find ways to push athletes in the right direction, even if they thought what I asked was difficult. I quickly learned which participants really wanted to be taught and develop their talents and which were content with staying where they were.

The athletes who accepted the most difficult of tasks were the ones who progressed the quickest. Because they trusted in me, their coach, they pushed themselves through the challenges and found themselves faster, stronger, and better equipped. It was a real example of faithful adherence to winning principles, even when they are difficult, helping prepare for desired "blessings."

Now, I'm not a perfect coach; I worked constantly to improve my skills and knowledge, and I made plenty of mistakes. As a group, we faced the continued challenges associated with new organizations and an innovative take on the sport. I admit I felt a heavy responsibility for the athletes under my charge. I know every parent, Church leader, business executive, Scoutmaster, team captain, coach, teacher, and missionary understands what I'm describing. Despite our weaknesses, we do the best we can to serve those in our care. While the athletes didn't always listen or do as I asked, I was proud of their efforts and achievements.

"Not withstanding my weakness" (2 Nephi 33:11) as a coach, I came to appreciate just how lucky we are to have someone watching out for us during times of adversity, someone who pushes and guides us to our full potential. Our "coach's" vigilance is as eternal as his love, and when he asks something difficult of us, we can move forward with faith, knowing that it will be for our good.

Let's be honest: sometimes during our struggles we feel like all we can do is hang on. As you can imagine, crashing in a bobsled is an intense experience. The world quickly turns upside down; the sound is incredible, and the forces are intense. To protect yourself as a driver, you tuck in the nose of the sled, so the world in a sense goes dark because all the light is blocked out.

Does your life seem dark right now? Are the trials placed in your path blocking out your emotional, mental, or spiritual light? If your days feel like an out of control bobsled, are you holding on to faith like your soul depends on it (which it does), all the while wondering what your Heavenly Father is trying to teach you? In those moments let us remember that the Savior is the coach; trust him.

Adversity is an instructor, at times even a brutal spiritual trainer who pushes our hearts and minds to grow and develop beyond what we think we can handle. But while we may have no clue when our trials will end, we do know that they will work out for our good and that God is in control until they do.

And as Latter-day Saints, we are blessed to know that our eternal coach is right beside us every step of the way. The task, then, falls to each of us, as it did to the athletes I coached, to decide if we will accept the challenges and invitations to learn, grow, and better ourselves, or will we fall away into despair, fear, and bitter loss.

If you are struggling with a soul-stretching trial, decide now to draw closer to the Savior. Turn to the scriptures and the words of the living prophets. Devote more time to prayer and meditation. Listen to inspiring music and attend all your church meetings. Conscientiously choose to draw near unto the Master, our coach who desires to instruct and help us reach our highest potential. It all comes down to the lifeline of faith.

Before some races or training sessions I would go into the museum at the Park City track and watch a movie on one of their flat-screen TVs, which helped me prepare myself mentally for the ice. One night I watched a movie that had old ocean sailing vessels in it, and I learned that whenever a storm was coming on, sailors would tie a rope around their waist and then "lash" or tie the other end to the main mast or some other sturdy anchor on the ship. This kept them from being swept overboard by the wind or waves and as I thought about it, I realized that this is exactly what we need to do when it comes to the storms of life. We need to firmly "lash" or tie ourselves to the gospel of Jesus Christ no matter what storms or waves of adversity come our way.

And while the tempest may rage around us, as it did for Christ's disciples on the Sea of Galilee (Matthew 8:23–24), we can rest assured that he has the power to calm our troubled hearts and lives. It may not come when we want it to, but in his own due time the Lord will stretch forth his mighty hand and we can feel him say unto our trials as he did to the storm, "Peace, be still" (Mark 4:39). While I am limited as to what I can do as a coach for my athletes, the Savior has no such constraints. When troubles come, we can "Be still, and know that [he] is God" (Psalm 46:10) for though we may fear or struggle for a time, he will not leave us to face the trials alone. As Elder Jeffrey R. Holland testified, "Considering the incomprehensible cost of the Crucifixion and Atonement, I promise you he is not going to turn His back on us now."[23]

Like an athlete caught in a slump we may struggle for a time, but the important thing to remember is that we can get past trials. And when we do, we will be stronger and will appreciate the gospel, the Atonement, and our own worth even more because of what we have been through. Like the love an athlete has for their coach after winning a big race, we will feel a deeper appreciation for the Savior during and after trials.

I hope in those times you'll remember that the human heart has a fire inside that will burn amidst any trouble. It is the spark of divinity that pushes us to reach upward, grab hold, and start climbing so we can enjoy the view of victory over adversity in this life and the next. And best of all, our best friend, even Jesus, will be there the entire way if we invite him into our lives.

Perhaps I can illustrate this with the final segment of my 1998 New York story. After winning the race, Joe and I were proud of ourselves and each other. We had held on to our goals despite the obstacles and had come out on top.

As amazing as hearing the national anthem with gold medals around our necks was, nothing beat our flight home. We decided we were going to wear those big shiny medals as we got off the plane. Airport security stopped us when the medals showed up on the X-ray machine. "What are those?" they asked, to which we replied, "Oh, those are just the gold medals we won in a bobsled race in New York." They waved us through without a smile. You can't impress everyone.

Once we began our descent into Salt Lake City, Joe and I took our medals out and put them around our necks. Some of the other passengers gave us sideways looks, but, hey, this was our party. You're only young once, right?

I can only imagine what we looked like walking down the gangway—like conquering heroes with big medals around our necks and huge grins on our faces. I'll never forget the loud cheer of our families as we entered the main hub. Seeing our parents and siblings standing there with smiles on their faces and love in their eyes made the trip that much more worth it. Every trial, every setback, and every discouraging thing that happened melted away as we walked into the arms of those who loved us.

We were home.

I truly believe it is going to be like that when we pass from this life. We won't have medals around our necks, but I believe that when we walk through that final doorway from this world to the next, we'll be greeted by people who love us very much. Every pain, struggle, and adversity we faced in this life will melt away. Those memories will be replaced instead with love, peace, and the joy of knowing that we made it, that we overcame, and that we are home.

I know it can be hard sometimes. But through my small experiences, I hope you have been able to find comfort and strength and draw closer to the

Healer of all wounds, even our eternal coach Jesus Christ. I testify that the Lord is intimately aware of you and that he loves you so much. I know that no matter how alone we might feel, he continually cheers from the sidelines and calls for us to keep moving forward, even if it means finding strength we never knew we had.

In times of trial, when our lives and hearts feel broken, let us remember that Jesus' earthly father, Joseph, was a carpenter. From a young age, the Savior learned how to repair and build up, the two things he desires to do for us at every stage of our lives. He will never forget us. "Behold, I have engraven thee upon the palms of my hands; thy walls are continually before me" (1 Nephi 21:16).

Let that inner fire of faith burn bright on the cold and dreary days. Look at life through eyes that are full of courage and spirit. Wipe the sweat from your eyes, brush off the dust, and rise to victory. Life, like bobsled, can be full of twists, drops, and sudden bursts of pressure. Just like I tell people when they are about to take their first bobsled trip, "Just hang on and enjoy the ride!"

When this mortal ride is over, we will understand something that every athlete who has ever won a race knows. When you stand on that medals podium or take that trophy in your hands, all the pain, suffering, and struggles melt away. Instead of looking back on our trials with regret, in that joyous celestial moment we will know with our whole being that it was all worth it.

DIVINE WORTH: DISCOVERING INNER GOLD

"Do you know how much you're worth?"

As I think about all the times my friends, family, teammates and leaders have asked me that question, I realize that some days I still struggle with an answer. Oh, I factually know about the good things I have done with my life, that I matter to people and that I am a son of God, but that firm foundation of belief in my self-worth is a work in progress sometimes. Perhaps you can relate.

I debated writing this chapter for months before, after careful thought and prayer, I realized that what I'm about to talk about was (a) a good introduction to a section on self-worth, (b) it might be of service to others who similarly struggle, and (c) it would just be background information to story I told in the introduction of almost taking my life.

Even so, talking about a topic like this is challenging. It's one thing to stand in front of crowd and put on my "game face"; it's even easier to appear strong and composed when you write because no one can see any face.

But the problem with that image is that it's incomplete. For years friends and associates have said that my life was so awesome because of bobsled, my talents, and so on. They thought I "had it all together." While I agree with the first notion and laugh at the second, more was going on than they could see. These well-meaning individuals would comment on how strong my testimony seemed, how deep my faith was, how popular I was, and how well I did in class. I was the "all-American boy" in the eyes of others since I grew up in Oklahoma (America's heartland), was an Eagle Scout, a pretty good student, talented, funny (I had my moments), pursued some lofty goals, and appeared to have serious direction for my life. I never got into drugs, alcohol, or smoking, and I tried to avoid trouble even when my friends or teammates wanted to do something "fun" (which usually meant something stupid). The Lord has helped me accomplish a lot with my life so if anyone thought my life was perfect, it's because they saw all the blessings I had received from him.

But here's the catch: most of us only show our good side to the outside world. We hide the not-so-perfect stuff deep in our hearts where we think it is safer.

Behind the public image that I began to perfect in high school, there was a hidden world of deep pains, crushing inadequacies, and sometimes crippling anxieties. I was a young man fighting something I didn't comprehend. I didn't understand why others were so happy when I hurt inside. I didn't understand when I broke down in high school and the MTC due to the depression and anxiety. Even after I came home to resume normal life, I couldn't understand why my emotions sometimes seemed out of control. I felt weak, broken, and like a failure. Most of all, I couldn't understand why God didn't seem to care. Why, if I was trying so hard to be good, would he let me suffer? Why, if he was so powerful, would he let me be overwhelmed by a darkness I couldn't fight? I must have been doing something wrong. I must have angered God.

During my eight weeks at the Missionary Training Center in Provo, Utah, I was blessed with incredible spiritual experiences, but I also struggled so much that we almost decided I should come home for a time. Thankfully, through many prayers and priesthood blessings I was able to endure and serve with some of the Lord's best in Honduras and Belize. But even during my two years, I had days where I struggled, a battle that continued into post-mission life when anxiety and depression still knocked me for a loop occasionally. I continued to wonder what I was doing wrong. Wasn't I worthy of a miracle? Wasn't I worth saving?

I understand if this chapter feels heavy, but I wanted to share some of my own struggles with feelings of self-worth so you'll know that I've been there. When the questions arise in your heart about whether you matter in this world, whether you have a mission to fulfill or a purpose in mortality, when you feel insecure or doubt your own abilities or potential, I understand what you're going through.

And for those of you who may be fighting similar mental or emotional demons, please don't give up. I promise it gets better because there is hope through the Atonement of Jesus Christ. If you find yourself severely struggling from depression or have thoughts of harming yourself or those around you, while I hope you find encouragement and strength through my experiences, a skilled professional can help you learn to cope with your "thorn in the flesh" and find the joy and peace that you desire and deserve.

Have I found that joy and peace? Yes, though my battles may be a lifelong journey. Like so many in today's world who suffer from similar mental and emotional struggles, I felt alone, that I was surrounded by people who wouldn't understand and would be ashamed of me since I was "broken." Remember, I spent much of my youth around athletes who seemed larger than life. When I compared my inner adversities to their (seemingly) perfect bodies, minds, and lives, I felt inadequate. I wanted to live like an Olympian in everything, which is one of the reasons I tried so hard to be appear perfectly strong. I guess that was how I dealt with my problems, by trying harder. I think I was afraid to admit the truth. In high school and during my twenties I was worried about the stigma that surrounds mental disorders. I worried about what would happen if the truth became known.

And I was definitely worried about how this all affected my bobsled career. What if a coach or a sponsor found out? What if I had a tough day in the middle of a competition? What if my struggles ruined the efforts and dreams of my teammates? The inconsistency and unpredictable nature of anxiety and depression have wreaked havoc with my athletic efforts for years.

Now, after years of research and striving to find answers with the help of wonderful professionals and Church leaders, I understand that this ailment affects millions of people around the world. I'm not as alone as I thought. It can touch even the strongest and brightest of lives, including many elite athletes and plenty of good, faithful Latter-day Saints. For me it was a battle against anxiety and feelings of deep inadequacy, but for you it might be one of hundreds of treatable and manageable mental illnesses.

Do you know how much you are worth? Even with a testimony of the gospel I questioned my value in God's eyes and in this world. I was a good person who managed to do some great things, but I lived with great burdens. The funny thing is, despite my reservations about my eternal worth and whether God cared, I knew he was the one source I could always turn to for help.

I want to make it clear that it was during the darkest of times that I came to appreciate the light of the gospel and what it teaches about our divine worth. We always talk about the Atonement redeeming our souls, but it was during these personal battles that I found Jesus saving my life.

When I asked, "God, do you really care about me? Am I worth anything to you?" I testify that the answer has always come back yes.

God has reminded me time and time again just how much worth I had. Case in point, it was during my earliest bouts with depression that I first became involved in bobsled. When I was wondering most about my value and worrying about my future, God showed me that he valued me as his son by blessing me with a sport that probably less than .1 percent of the world's population has ever experienced.

For me, bobsled was literally a lifesaver and a direct testimony of my personal worth in God's eyes. It's a thought that my coaches and fellow athletes probably won't understand. My sport helped me find a stronger self-respect and provided me with courage and mental strength to fight the feelings of anxiety and low self-worth. On the darkest days, bobsled was the torch that helped me feel the light. Whenever I sat in a sled or put on a piece of sliding apparel, I felt peace. The hope the Olympic spirit gave to me helped me stand against the gloom and better live my life in the way that God wanted me to. I guess you could say that "USA" became a personal "CTR."

On days when I wondered why heaven was picking on me, instead of being angry God would provide the most beautiful experiences on the ice. Whether it was an answered prayer that helped me drive perfectly down the track or a special sport-related opportunity that arrived at just the right time, I came to know God through bobsled. Not to sound sacrilegious, but the bobsled track became my personal mountaintop where I spoke with God and learned from him. Moses went to Sinai. I went to Bear Hollow in Park City. Moses brought back the sacred Ten Commandments. I came home from the mountain with gold, silver, and bronze medals, objects that I feel are personal gifts from God because he knew how much they meant to me. Some in the sports world may mock this view, but I cherish my bobsled experiences as opportunities to draw closer to heaven's throne.

Do I know how much I am worth? I'm learning. As I stood there on the ice or in the snow on so many cold nights, I felt warmth in my chest as I spent time praying or reading a scripture or a talk before I raced or trained. I still struggled, but the bobsled track became a sacred place where I could go to walk, talk and slide eighty miles per hour with God.

It was through these experiences on the ice that I came to feel his love and find the strength to stand. When anxiety made me feel alone, I knew I wasn't. I testify that God was there for me and on the days when I felt like I was losing hope, he extended his mighty hand to rescue me from the raging rivers of loneliness and fear. Through sacred experiences too numerous to list, Heavenly Father has taught me where my true value lies: I am his son. Far too often we listen to what the world teaches about "value," or what Satan wants us to think of ourselves (obviously not much). Things like money, car, position, physical appearance, popularity, and relationship status have no effect whatsoever on my eternal worth. God loves me for who I am, not for what my paycheck says or if I won the race or not.

The ideas or objects we tie our feelings of self-esteem to are often fleeting, whereas the gospel teaches that our divine worth is eternal and therefore unchangeable. Self-esteem comes from opinion—those of ourselves or others—whereas our worth is defined by God himself. The adversary uses the media, popular trends, and even the people around us to negatively influence our opinion of self. We need to see ourselves as God sees us, not as the world sees us, which even as disciples of Christ we can be guilty of doing. When we truly understand who we are as children of God, when we really see ourselves as his beloved sons and daughters and gain a testimony of our divine heritage, we will never doubt our worth again.

When we realize our divine worth never changes and that God's love for us is unconditional and everlasting, we will be able to stand amid trial, temptation, persecution, and even terrible loss and know without a doubt that we are loved and valued by God. As his children we have a royal heritage that makes any earthly title or social achievement, even an Olympic gold medal, pale in comparison.

But what does it mean to have worth? To me, when I was struggling with anxiety and depression, I thought that if I truly had worth, then God would heal me. I had the idea that my worth was based on whether my inner hurts went away. Do you ever do that and say, "If God loves me then he will ________ ?" Maybe its basing how much you think God loves you on whether you get the job, whether you are single, or whether you enjoy good health or even wealth. The problem with this line of thinking is that it says our value fluctuates, which it does not. We need to understand that our divine worth is not conditional; it is a statement of fact (Acts 17:29).

As I previously mentioned, in the ancient Games at Olympia, the winner received an olive wreath, while the second and third place competitors went home empty-handed. And when the modern Olympic movement was resurrected in 1896, the victor received a silver medal while the bronze went to whoever came in second. The first gold medals were not awarded until the 1904 St. Louis, Missouri, Olympics, and 1912 was the last time the gold medal was made of pure gold. Today's gold medals are actually sterling silver covered with a thin coat of pure gold. The things you never knew about the Games, right?

Modern athletes would probably scoff at the idea of competing for a simple olive wreath, but the ancient Olympians considered it a prize beyond measure. Similarly, those Greek athletes from Olympia may scratch their heads at the idea of a medal, while our modern competitors have been trained to want gold even though the silver medal was the big prize from 1904 to 1912.

My point? Any value or worth that is based on mortal perceptions or social definitions is temporary at best. You can be the victor today and lose tomorrow's race. This may affect how you are viewed as an athlete, but it never affects how much God loves you. You may have a great job today but lose it tomorrow. You may wonder if life is worth living today and experience a deep, loving experience tomorrow. Again, it doesn't change how much God loves you or your worth. This knowledge can bring a deep sense of happiness, self-confidence, and personal satisfaction, whereas basing our feelings of worth on something like clothes, a paycheck, or a bigger home is akin to building our emotional houses on shifting sands instead of eternal rock.

Am I of worth because I bobsled? Because I wrote a book? Because I have a job, served a mission, and have good friends? And if so, does that mean I am of less worth when I struggle with anxiety? When I make a mistake or sin? When I face a trial or lose a race? Do you see the danger in basing our feelings of self-worth on the world's view or on whether or not we are spiritually, physically, socially, mentally, or emotionally flawless?

I think the apostle Paul understood this concept quite clearly. The societies in which he lived struggled with the same desires for worth and wealth, value and vindication that we face. Perhaps he even saw one of Rome's changed versions of the Olympic Games (they became known as the Gladiator Games). I think Paul knew that everyone wants to understand if their life and existence has real meaning and worth. In his epistle to the people of Rome, Paul wrote:

> For I am persuaded, that neither death, nor life, nor angels, nor principalities, nor powers, nor things present, nor things to come, Nor height, nor depth, nor any other creature, shall be able to separate us from the love of God, which is in Christ Jesus our Lord. (Romans 8:38–39)

Nothing—no win or loss, blessing or trial, obedient decision or sinful act—can separate us from the love of God nor affect our worth in heaven's eyes. Yes, our choices can separate us from the spirit and ultimately Heavenly Father's presence, but even then he does not stop loving us. He loves the rich and poor, the famous and common, the winner and the loser. In God's opinion, their value is the same. If we really ponder this eternal truth, we will understand the power of the Lord's words when he told Oliver Cowdery that "the worth of souls is great in the sight of God" (Doctrine and Covenants 18:10). And if your worth is great in the sight of God, then no other opinion matters.

Every soul we encounter in this life is of infinite value and is loved by the God who gave them life. Whether we are the president of the company or a janitor who keeps the building clean, each of us is treasured equally in the eyes of God. And when it comes to answering the question, "Who am I?" we can answer with certainty, "I am a child of God."

When I feel inadequate, I can hold fast to the truth that I am a son of the living God and that he loves me. When I wonder about my worth, I remember the words of the psalmist, "All of you are children of the most High" (Psalm 82:6). The ancient Greek Olympians were competing to win the favor of the gods, but the psalmist reminds us that we already have God's favor because we are his sons and daughters. So the next time you wonder what your value is, I pray you'll remember that you are worth more than any gold medal, any job title, or any social status. And it doesn't matter what the other athletes or the kids at school or your coworkers say. Your divine worth does not change. Ever.

In sports, sacrifice and victory go hand in hand. To win the big prize, you must be willing to give everything and often a victory is valued more highly because the sacrifice to achieve it was greater. I say this because we are the prize that Christ and our Father in Heaven value above all and to "win" us, God gave his Only Begotten (John 3:16), and our Savior gave his mortal life (1 Peter 2:24). They are the champions, yet they desire to place an eternal crown on our heads (James 1:1).

So when the cold winds of adversity or temptation blow, when the discouraging clouds of sin or mortal sorrow fill the horizon, let us stand boldly and say with Paul, "The Spirit itself beareth witness with our spirit, that we are the children of God: And if children, then heirs; heirs of God, and joint-heirs with Christ" (Romans 8:16–17.) I pray, as a champion of the Lord, you can always answer that question, "Do you know how much you are worth?" with a resounding, "Yes!"

DISCOVERING THE CHAMPION WITHIN

Prior to the 2007–2008 season, I received a phone call from a dear friend who has always been a big supporter of my bobsledding efforts. I knew something was wrong when, in a quavering voice, she said, "I'm not doing so well, Jer. Can we do dinner?" As we sat down to eat, I noticed the pain in her eyes. Her radiant smile was absent and her shoulders slumped.

She went on to recount her struggles with depression and low self-esteem, two things I was intimately familiar with, but then she described a death-defying tango with an eating disorder. My heart broke as I listened to this beautiful and talented daughter of God tell me she was afraid that her eating disorder was going to take her life. With tears flowing, she looked me in the eye and said, "I don't want to die."

"How does someone get this broken down?" I wondered, an ironic question since I've had similar feelings about my own self-worth. Over the years, this dear friend and I have had many discussions about our struggles. We are kindred spirits, but as I listened to this amazing daughter of God, I couldn't help but feel angry at society for helping her to believe that unless she weighed "this much" and looked "that thin," she wouldn't be gorgeous, loved, or valued. What we believe about ourselves is ultimately our choice, but sometimes enough is enough.

It must break our Heavenly Father's heart to see how successful Satan has been in lowering feelings of self-worth in this world. Does it really take some physical trait, some material possession or social status to have value?

Having worked with several nonprofits that educate the public on healthy eating and mental habits, including efforts to positively influence the lives of our youth, the statistics I see are heart-wrenching. The numbers of suicides, eating disorders, steroid use, drug abuse, pornography addiction, alcoholism, and other dangerous habits are alarming. As my friend shared her struggles, I couldn't help but wonder what was to be done? My soul ached for her and all those like her, and I realized that the best solution was to help bring her feelings of worth more in line with heaven's view.

After a long talk, we decided that she should go to a hospital where I was later able to provide a priesthood blessing that lifted us both. The love of heaven that poured out through the power of the priesthood that day was a healing balm for her heart.

Truth be told, however, a part of me understood what she was experiencing since I have had similar doubts about my own physical appearance. Bobsled is physically demanding, so to compete with arguably some of the fastest and most powerful athletes in the world, your body has to be in top shape. As I mentioned previously, from the moment I first became involved in the sport, I constantly worried if I would ever measure up physically. In a sport where the best athletes are arguably some of the most skilled competitors in the world, yes, I had self-image concerns.

For the latter half of my teens and into my twenties, I was introduced as "the bobsledder and future Olympian." It was difficult at times not to feel pressured to succeed. From the moment people found out I was involved with sliding, they innocently began to ask questions about whether I would go to the Games, what I did for training, if I was going to win the gold medal, how much money I made competing, and so forth. I began to translate my involvement with bobsled as an "if/then formula." If I competed at the top levels of the sport and won medals, then I would be of high worth and happy. If not, then no dice.

To make matters worse, this type of thinking is almost encouraged by some in my sport. It was an all-or-nothing mentality of "If you aren't competing, then you aren't really 'one of us.'" I remember when one coach pulled me into an office and told me flat out that I needed to go out and raise more money and do more competitions or I should quit. No ifs, ands, or buts about it. The worst part is that I believed him. I began to wonder, "If I don't step it up, if I don't perform better, maybe I should get out of the sport." Although I enjoyed the game, I translated his words into a definition of and requirement for my worth as a bobsled pilot. Our sport was once considered an event for the socially elite, but nowadays it seems like an event for the physically elite only, which makes me a little sad. I have seen athletes who delighted in the sport who perhaps didn't measure up and were treated with less respect. But that is a discussion for another day.

I began to translate this need for success as a kind of pass code to continuing in the sport. If I didn't do well, I should "quit the club." So the more I worried about succeeding, the more I worried about my body, and so the cycle began, and around it went in a death spiral that actually prevented me from progressing in a lot of ways through self-sabotage.

My concerns about my physical appearance transferred over into my social life as well. I kept telling myself that "If only I could have bigger arms and chest and stronger legs, then I'll be attractive and better in my sport." So I slowly worked my way up to 160, 170, and finally 195 pounds. It's embarrassing, but when I hit that mark I felt like I could accept myself more. It was an okay goal to have health-wise, but basing my value on physical appearance was definitely a mistake. So as I listened to my dear friend sitting across the table I understood where she was coming from with her eating disorder.

Although I vehemently disagree with steroids and believe that they are cheating (not to mention dangerous), at times I could almost sympathize with those who use them. Many athletes feel the pressure to win so badly that they turn to performance enhancing drugs to give them the edge. And it isn't just limited to professional sports or the Olympics themselves. Steroid use among high school students more than doubled from 1991 to 2003 and over 6 percent of the fifteen thousand students in grades nine through twelve who responded to a 2003 survey acknowledged taking steroid pills or shots at least once.

I never touched performance enhancing drugs, but some days I wished there was a quick fix for my body issues. And having gone through this experience, I know that body image is not the only area that Satan attacks our self-esteem. He is a master salesman who unfortunately sells us a lot of insecurity, even amongst Latter-day Saints who are so kind to others, but brutal to themselves.

Do you ever have times when discouragement creeps in and you worry that you aren't good enough in some aspect of your life? You want so badly to be valiant, brave, faithful, perfect, Christlike, kind, obedient (the list goes on), but you secretly fear that you are falling short. Maybe you want to be the best teacher, the best spouse, the best parent, the best neighbor, the best housekeeper, the best missionary, the best scrapbooker, the best student, the best bargain shopper, the best scriptorian, the best cook, the best team supporter, the best home or visiting teacher, the best ward member . . . wow, that is a lot of "bests."

I would be surprised if right now in your life you aren't feeling the pressure and strain to be the best at something. And I bet there is a nagging voice in the back of your mind telling you that until you reach that "best" level, you won't be good enough. As Latter-day Saints, we may know that our divine worth cannot change, but unfortunately our self-esteem is another matter.

The biggest mistake my friend and I made—and maybe you're doing this as well—is that we were so busy comparing ourselves to others that we failed to base our feelings of worth on God's definition of our value. We kept saying we were in last place physically when our Father in Heaven held us high as champions.

As a coach, you have to be careful how you approach the issue of development. On the one hand you encourage your athletes to grow in body, mind, and technique. On the other, you want to make sure they do not become discouraged about themselves and their abilities, which is a surefire way to invite a loss on the field of play and the field of the heart. Some coaches would argue that pointing out an athlete's flaws helps them overcome or correct them (which is true), but the caveat is this has to be done constructively lest the athlete become so self-conscious that he or she cannot focus on the game or lose motivation and confidence to even play. That is what my friend and I were doing toward our physical appearance and our worth: losing the desire to play.

What does this have to do with spirituality? There is a fascinating relationship in sports between an athlete's state of excitement and the body's response. When a competitor is preparing for an event, the brain's hypothalamus kicks into gear and tells the endocrine system to start producing the hormones that get the body ready for action. But here's the kicker: if the athlete's level of excitement is too low (that is, he or she doesn't want to win or believe he or she can), the body reacts with a low-level response. If the athlete's excitement and anxiety is too high (that is, excessively scared to compete), then their body produces an overly high level of adrenaline and similar hormones. In both of these cases, the results are less productive than an athlete who takes a middle-ground approach that blends excitement, desire, and confidence evenly. This middle ground is the sweet spot that so often is called being "in the zone."

Here's the problem with Satan's tactics: when we believe we are not measuring up, at first we may try harder. Our level of excitement goes up because we are feeling inadequate (of less value) or like a failure (also of less value), which drops our confidence bit by bit. When this happens in a sport, some athletes will become desperate and may try to win at any cost. They want a victory, but they are losing hope that they can make it happen unless they cheat or play unfairly.

Can you see the danger? If we feel like we need to somehow earn or obtain our value then perhaps Satan can get us to do something desperate like develop an eating disorder or take steroids for example. And what if we become discouraged about our self-worth? Same thing; Satan can use our moments of despondency and sadness to tempt us into doing something spiritually hazardous. We may give into peer pressure, dive into an addiction or move away from the Church.

And the adversary is pretty smart so he won't attack our self-worth outright. The biggest avenue of his wicked campaigns against our feelings of self-worth is the media. All you need to do is spend one evening watching TV or walking the magazine aisle in the grocery store to see that his whispers are everywhere. He is working overtime to get us to believe how we have to look, what we have to wear, or what we should possess so we can have value and be happy.

Satan doesn't care that we were a gold-medal mom this morning. He just makes us feel bad that we accidently burned dinner. He doesn't care that as an academic champion we got straight As last semester. He wants us to feel terrible about the one test we bombed. He doesn't care if we won last week. According to him, the second-place finish this week just doesn't measure up. In his eyes, we will never be good enough. Unfortunately, he got me to believe it. He got my friend to believe it. Maybe he's gotten you to believe it as well.

So what's the answer? We find the spiritual "zone" through the middle road that the gospel outlines. When we experience a high-level of spiritual excitement (faith), which leads to a deep desire to follow Christ (obedience) we will feel an energizing dose of confidence that is based on a true understanding (knowledge) of our eternal worth. We will have a motivating aspiration to become our best, but also we possess a realistic understanding that our mistakes and shortcomings do not affect the status of our value in God's eyes. We will take our spiritual "victories" and "losses" with a grain of salt, realizing that both are guideposts on our mortal journey.

This healthy mind-set allows us to continually strive to "do all things whatsoever the Lord [our] God shall command [us]" (Abraham 3:25), yet be confident enough to turn to him with our sins and weaknesses to be "perfected in him" (Moroni 10:32) without becoming discouraged. When we can view ourselves with this eternal perspective then we will have a greater respect that God made us in his image (Genesis 1:27). We may have a wrinkle here, a gray hair there or perhaps a few post-holiday pounds, but those and any other things we dislike about ourselves become lost in the unconditional perspective of God's love.

Four things affect the outcome of your performance in sports: motivation, confidence, effort, and technique. If your motivation is low, then your effort will be low, which in turn affects your confidence and technique. If your motivation is high but your confidence low, then your technique and effort will likewise suffer. What if your motivation, confidence, and effort are all at high levels, but your technique is bad? Same thing. Every one of the Olympic and world-class athletes I know strive to include these four factors into their game-winning strategies, but did you know that the gospel encourages us to do the same?

Think about it. With faith as our spiritual motivation, then a stronger faith means a deeper desire to follow Christ, or an increased effort to do what is right. And how do we know what is right? Because our eternal coach has revealed the only techniques that leads to eternal victory in the form of the gospel (Acts 4:12). Having confidence in ourselves gives us strength to act on our faith by following the proper technique that leads to exaltation. No wonder Satan tries so hard to make us feel like we are falling short. If we lose sight of our true value (lowered confidence) than we may let our faith (motivation) and works (effort) slip, thus affecting our ability to follow the gospel (proper technique).

My friends we cannot afford to let Satan's lies lower our spiritual motivation or confidence. No outside opinion can change our worth in God's eyes; why should they change it in our own?

In December 1998 I won a perfect birthday present for myself in the form of a third-place finish at the Christmas Classic bobsled race (I would have preferred a "Silver [or] Gold" as the holiday song says), but our coaches decided to hand out paper certificates in place of medals. Years later, during a Utah Winter Games race, my teammate and I placed third, but this time we received a bronze medal. If you place the paper certificate and the medal side by side you may think that the bronze medal has more value than the third-place certificate, but the reality is they represent the same thing: a third-place finish. They look different, feel different, weigh different, and smell different, but underneath it all they have the same worth.

When we let go of our insecurities, when we stop comparing ourselves to others, and when we realize that its okay to make mistakes along the way, then, and only then, will we see that life is not about keeping up with the Joneses (even if they win gold). It's about keeping up with the Christ. And the Savior doesn't compare you to him. All those things we think we need to have, to wear, or to be in order to matter really don't mean a thing in his eyes. Someone with expensive clothes and someone who shops at the thrift store have the same eternal value. An Olympian and an overwhelmed parent are both loved and valued by heaven for who they are and who they can become.

Yes, we are here on this earth to learn and grow and part of that process means learning to overcome our weaknesses, frailties, and faults. But when an athlete joins a team or program and shows up to practice willing to learn and work, a good coach is equally willing to teach and correct. Our Savior has invited us time and time again to bring our weaknesses, burdens, and struggles with self-worth to lay them at his feet (Ether 12:27). The greatest thing about our eternal coach is that the door to his office is always open and with his help we cannot lose.

The next time you feel like you are falling short, remember to be patient and kind with yourself. You are of a member of the Lord's team with value beyond measure. Yes, we all want to do and become our best, but when those desires become harsh taskmasters that rob us of our confidence and desire to live as spiritual champions, maybe we should step back and reevaluate just what we are basing our opinion on.

To God we will always be of more worth than any gold medal, imperfections and all. When we discover that his is the only opinion that matters, we will come to see our value in an entirely different light. We will find that the things that the world tells us we need to buy or become really aren't all that important. When we each look in the mirror, we will see God's child looking back. It's not about the wrinkles, the few extra pounds, the medals on the wall, or the clothes in the closet. No, "if [God's opinion] be for us, who can be against us?" (Romans 8:31).

Unlike a bobsled competition, exaltation is not a race. I'm not competing against you and nor you against me, so why do we compare ourselves to each other? I'm convinced that when gratitude for our lives, including who we are in them, takes precedence, we will experience a peace and joy that no medal or title can bring. Confidence and patience will replace inadequacy and fear. Love, for ourselves and for others, will become a guiding light.

I testify that our value is great, unchangeable, and unshakable and when that fact really sinks in, nothing else will matter. We are all champions in God's eyes with the potential for great things.

SELECTIVE HEARING: I CAN'T HEAR YOU

A highly competitive sport like bobsled would be incomplete without a fair amount of "trash-talking," which can be hilarious. Trash talk is a time-honored tradition that employs a more . . . primitive aspect of sport. It involves the verbal expression of what could be termed "sparring." If the actual sporting event is a contest of strength, speed, and skill, then trash talk could be described as the contest of wits (I never said mature wits).

Mainly consisting of boasts for yourself and team or insults directed toward opposing players, staff, or even fans, trash-talking can range from good natured to downright nasty. While I imagine trash-talking has been around competitive events since the beginning of time, its underlying purpose has been to get into the head of your opponents and undermine their confidence (remember that little fact).

Ask any athlete and he or she will probably agree that trash talk comes with the territory. Even so, you have to be careful how much you let it affect you. One negative comment from an opposing player or fan can throw off your concentration and plant the seed of doubt in your mind. Coaches, administrators, trainers, and sports psychologists strive to help athletes build up mental defenses so these comments will have little or no affect.

I mentioned that trash-talk can be good natured, and nowhere is that more true than among bobsled teammates. Something about working together toward a goal brings teammates closer together and brings out hilarious comments that in fact demonstrate respect, care, and friendship. As a pilot I have sat back and laughed while listening to the good-natured ribbing that goes on between my teammates as we prep the sled. But if an athlete from another team tries to trash-talk one of your teammates, watch out.

I bring all this up because Satan is quite possibly the best trash-talker the world has ever seen. Unfortunately, his words are designed to do more than just get into our heads; they are calculated to reach our souls.

How does he do it? Basically anything that makes you feel of less worth is Satan "trash-talking" you. He will cloud our opinion of ourselves with fears, inadequacies, mistakes, and shortcomings, and choosing to believe his trash talk instead of listening to God's voice is dangerous. The risk, as many athletes have discovered, is that if we allow our shortcomings to become more powerful than our successes, then our self-esteem can suffer. We may become discouraged, barely lifting a finger in our behalf. I have seen this happen on the bobsled track, at my work, and in the Church. Those negative messages we play in our head can do serious damage.

A few years back while at the Calgary track my teammates Jared and Alex were taking a two-man sled down the course. Jared made a slight driving error, and the sled flipped over in the bottom third of the track before turning right-side up a few turns later, so they actually finished the course.

Now Jared was fine. He felt a little chagrined since we made sure to do a little trash-talking about his crash. Alex on the other hand suffered an ice burn on his shoulder, but the real damage was done to his mind. After this crash, Alex wouldn't get back in the sled. He gave excuses about not feeling well and being too sore, but we all knew there was a deeper reason: he was understandably scared of getting hurt again. The more Alex thought about it, the more his mind dwelt on the possibility of crashing again. The fear built up until he was paralyzed by it. Instead of learning from the experience and bettering himself like Jared was trying to do, Alex let his mind dwell on the crash and wasn't able to progress and reach his full potential.

Satan knows that if he can get us to become so afraid of failure, or even worse, afraid that we have already failed, our desire to progress will drop and he will rejoice over his victory. The adversary is our opponent on the field of life, and he wants us to lose confidence and faith so we will give up. If this happens, then we might stop trying so hard to win the game by gaining eternal life. After all, if you truly believe you have no chance at victory, how hard are you really going to play?

Now think about that for a second. We've been talking about our worth and eternal value in the sight of God. Having this knowledge can give us great strength and motivation in life, *but* if Satan can "mess with our heads" through negative trash talk, our desire to let our lights shine may decrease proportionally.

How do we defend ourselves? To put it simply, through selective-hearing.

Many wives say their husbands have selective hearing because he can listen to the game while magically missing her request to take out the trash from two feet away, but let's talk about selective hearing of a more beneficial kind.

When it comes to sports, I use "selective hearing" to describe an athlete's ability to choose the voices he or she listens to, whether internal or external. Do you listen to that opposing player who insults your ability, or do you listen to the encouraging shouts of your teammates? Do you focus on the opposing team's fan who is holding up a negative sign, or do you focus on the cheers of support coming from your side of the stands? Do you listen to the negative commentary from the pregame show hosts or do you instead focus on the motivating words of your coach? As an athlete you have to be careful because one negative comment at the right time can bring down a decade's worth of training if you let it get to you. Imagine preparing for an Olympic event and having an opposing team's coach tell you how terrible you were during your last competition. You can choose to ignore his words, which most of us would, or you can let them fester in your mind and rob your will.

Selective hearing works for us in the spiritual realm as well. We often say that Satan knows what buttons to push to tempt us, but he also knows what our deepest fears, insecurities, and weakness are. It may be a feeling of doubt, an unkind comment from a neighbor, or perhaps a recurring thought in our mind, but these negative messages are designed to keep us from playing our best.

Satan even tried to trash-talk the Savior and "get into his head" during his sojourn in the wilderness. After forty days of fasting and prayer, the adversary tried to play mind games with Jesus and cast inner doubt upon himself. In Luke chapter 4 verse 3, Satan says, "If thou be the Son of God . . ." If. The adversary's only purpose was to cause Jesus to doubt himself, his abilities and his life's mission. "Are you sure you're the Son of God? Maybe you're not." Have you ever had an experience where Satan tried to get you to doubt yourself or even your divine heritage?

The adversary tries again in verses 5–7 when while standing on the top of a high mountain they "beheld all the kingdoms of the world" (verse 5, Joseph Smith Translation). Satan tells the Savior, "All this power will I give thee" (verse 6). "If thou therefore wilt worship me" (verse 7). Satan was trying to build upon his earlier efforts to cast doubt on the Savior's divine role. "Well, if you're not the God of Israel, even Jehovah, then you need me to give your power and fame and wealth."

He does this with us all the time. Satan tempts us to take moral shortcuts and do what is prevalent in the world because, hey, then we'll be popular, rich, famous, and happy. His game plan is simple: (1) Get us to doubt our worth, and (2) Lead us away from God, who has promised to give us everything anyway. Satan is like an opposing player who says, "Hey, throw the game in my behalf, and I'll let you hold my trophy for a little bit." I think I'd rather win the trophy myself.

Whatever the adversary is causing you to feel insecure about, use selective hearing and ask yourself how God feels about this issue. Does he love you less because you might not look like the girl on the cover of the fashion magazine or because your car isn't as nice as the one next to you at the stoplight? Does he love you less because you are single or because you aren't making cookies for someone's birthday, writing your talk two weeks in advance, and volunteering four hours at the nursing home down the street?

We know the answer without a shadow of a doubt (though doubt is exactly what Satan is after). As the psalmist so beautifully asked of God, "What is man that thou art mindful of him? . . . For thou hast made him a little lower than the angels, and hast crowned him with glory and honour" (Psalm 8:46).

We should always use spiritual selective hearing to focus on God's voice and opinion because his love for us is as perfect as his judgment. Don't let Satan's trash talk convince you that you aren't good enough. As much as Lucifer wants us to believe otherwise, as children of God, our worth is not up for debate. God made *me* to be *me* and *you* to be *you*, and he loves us both with a perfect, unconditional love.

I learned this lesson one summer a few years ago while working at the bobsled track as a tour guide. I took people around the park to show them all the different sports and venues like the Nordic jumping hills, the bobsled, luge, and skeleton track; the freestyle skiing pool; and so on. I met so many wonderful people up there who have no idea how much they impacted my life. One of these individuals wasn't a visitor to the park but rather a coworker named Gil.

We all loved working with Gil, but I'll never forget a comment he made one afternoon that has stuck with me after all these years. Between tours I was standing in front of our host area leaning on the counter with Gil on the other side as we chatted about our lives. He asked about the upcoming bobsled season and my future goals in the sport. I answered that of course I dreamed of the Olympics, but I also wanted to finish school and start a family. I expressed that I wasn't totally sure what I would do and that I also had fears that I wouldn't be good enough as an athlete to make it.

Gil sat back in his chair, looked me right in the eye, and said, "Jeremy, you don't have to go to the Olympics to be important." His comment was almost like a slap in the face, a wake-up call to my soul, which was not doing a good job with selective hearing at the time. Gil's wise response presented me with an alternative perspective. Satan had been using negative trash-talk on me to turn a wonderful thing like bobsled into a harsh task master that determined my self-worth, but Gil's comment reminded me that my worth wasn't based on whether I went to the Games; it was inherent.

I had mistakenly believed that if I didn't reach a certain level in life (the Olympics) I couldn't be as happy. I was basing my worth on a thing, a status. I came to realize that even if I didn't (or did) make it to the Olympics, God would still love and value me just the same, as would my friends and family. Sure, some people would see me as less because I never went, but that is their decision. Gil's comment reminded me that when that big day comes, God will whisper, "I love you, son. I'm proud of you."

Selective hearing is powerful. If Satan can get us to focus on worldly definitions of worth, then he triumphs. His trash-talking can leave our self-image on shaky ground because let's be honest: sometimes we don't win or get everything we want. Sometimes we don't measure up to the actor on the screen, the successful neighbor up the street, or the coworker who seems to lead a charmed life. Sometimes heaven answers "no," and sometimes the lesson we need to learn can only be taught through adversity or loss. It can be easy to interpret all this as a statement about our worth, but here's the kicker: if instead we choose to focus on God's voice and his definition of our value, then nothing that happens (or doesn't happen) can touch our self-respect or self-esteem.

Whatever our personal "Olympics" are, we should remember that these things do not change our eternal value in the eyes of the Lord. His is not an interest of where we serve so much as it is how. Is our worth really based on how big our home is or how popular we are when ours is to look to the kingdom where "the least shall be heard amongst the greatest" (Luke 1:48), where there "are many mansions" (John 14:2)? Bishops and primary teachers, CEOs and secretaries, Olympians and weekend warriors, we will all share the same inheritance if we but prove faithful and endure to the end.

Looking back, my unhappiest times in bobsled came when I based my enjoyment (and self-worth) on whether I won. Of course I wanted victory, but problems arose when I allowed that desire to overwhelm my love for the sport itself. Satan trash-talked me by saying, "If you don't win, God must not love you, and maybe you should quit because you're not worth enough in the sport or in his eyes."

No wonder I was so gloomy; I was using selective hearing to listen to the wrong voice. I let myself forget who I was and why I should be content, win or lose. It wasn't until I separated my worth from the "quest for gold" that happiness found its way back into my heart. I had to stop listening to Satan's lies and start thinking that a medal had no bearing on my eternal worth. I spent time drawing closer to my Heavenly Father and feeling his love for me, whether I won or lost. I stopped worrying so much about what others thought about my success (or lack of) in the sport. I went back to the basics and focused on improving myself as an athlete and as a person. It should come as no surprise that I found myself enjoying the sport once more.

Beliefs are powerful things that drive both positive and negative results. They can either lead to greater happiness, strength, and peace, or they can lead us down mental, emotional, and literal paths that end in regret. The trick is to base our beliefs on true and eternal principles instead of the fleeting lies of this world and the adversary.

For example, as an athlete, what you believe affects your performance on the field and how hard you train off it. Like the saying goes, "If you believe you can or believe you can't, you're right." So here's the question: what false beliefs is Satan trying to trick you into thinking? Go ahead; make a list. Then, next to each negative belief ask yourself if what you're thinking based on gospel principles. We can use eternal truths to help gauge our beliefs about ourselves, kind of like a test runner.

In bobsled, a test runner (officially called the reference runner) is posted in the start area one hour before a competition begins. Remember how officials do a temperature test on our runners before we go down the track? They use the test runner to gauge what temperature our runners should be at when they have been in the cold air for a certain period (we're allowed a four degrees Celsius difference). But teams can use that test runner to their advantage.

Race protocol dictates that teams must have their sleds to the start one hour before the competition begins, but runners do not have to be on the sled for another half hour. Since officials post the test runner's temperature one hour before the race starts, that gives each team thirty minutes of data to help decide which set of their runners they will use based on that temperature (plus the average outside air and track ice temperatures). Why the decision? Teams that can afford to have multiple sets of runners that do better at different temperatures. So that test runner becomes the keystone of the decision, because after runners are on the sled and the thirty-minute mark passes, you can't swap them out without race jury permission.

The eternal principles and truths revealed in the gospel of Jesus Christ must be the "test runner" upon which we gauge our beliefs about ourselves. If what we feel about our worth is "several degrees" off from what the Lord has taught then we know our beliefs are incorrect.

Each of us is a champion of the Lord, a chosen son or daughter of our Heavenly Father who was reserved to come down at this day to help build the kingdom. I may or may not be viewed as a winner in bobsled (or life) by the world, but my value as a child of God will never change. Ever.

Through trash-talk the adversary tries to convince us that we are losers. He wants us to forget that we are meant for eternal thrones, dominions, and principalities, and I fear too many of us are okay with that. It's not that we are settling for second or third place; no, Satan wants us to believe that we are meant for last place and that must break our Heavenly Father's heart when he sees so many of his children living below their noble birthright. God wants us to live up to our divine heritage, and he works to remind us of that through daily blessings, spiritual comforts, moments of joy, and feelings of love. While Satan sends negative messages through the media and society's falling standards, God is constantly trying to help us realize just how much we are worth and how much he loves us. Which voice are we going to listen to?

I have fallen victim to the adversary's negative talk. Plenty of times I didn't feel good enough or thought I had failed. When I started writing these chapters on self-worth, I thought about a box of medals I have stored in a dresser drawer. Taking a break from writing, I pulled the box out and started going through the medals one by one and I asked myself, "Would I be worth less if I hadn't won this? Was I worth more because I had?" I looked at my medal from the New York Empire States Games and the Utah Winter Games set. I held two silvers I got from local races and a big gold medal from the first ever Utah Governor's Cup. I looked down at all the others to review the race experiences behind each one. As I folded the ribbons back around the medals, I quietly felt the spirit unfold a lesson.

If we were to compare my involvement in bobsled to mortality, then the medals were the parts of that life that I was proud of, that I was confident about. The losses, however, were like the parts of my life that I was self-conscious of, that I didn't like, that I wished had never been given to me or that I wanted to change.

And it hit me. Whether it is a gold medal that someone else won, the trimmer figure of the person sitting next to us, or some talent we wished we had, whenever we focus on our "losses" (the things we aren't happy with) we find ourselves forgetting about the countless gold medal-blessings God has given us.

Today I choose to focus my "selective hearing" on my blessings and divine heritage, the "gold medal experiences," rather than the losses or inadequacies. By learning to see what God sees we can find all the "championship" aspects that he loves about us. Satan's lies will melt away and his trash-talk will simply be words on the wind that float away in the breeze of God's grace.

As one who has spent many cold nights out in the snow, I know that even a tiny flame can make a difference. I believe we have a spark in our hearts that can never be extinguished, one that even Satan can't put out. It is the flame of deity, the flicker of godhood that reminds us of who we really are. And in those quiet moments the spark of divinity beckons us to higher ground. Are we listening?

If you ever wonder about your self-worth, kneel down and ask God to help you to feel his love. After all, "where there is no vision, the people perish" (Proverbs 29:18), so when we can't see what God sees our heart can perish. Only with his help can we see clearly through the fog of Satan's trash-talking and the illusions of this world.

Anyone who has been in the Salt Lake Valley during winter has probably experienced what we call an inversion. An inversion occurs when high pressure from the upper atmosphere pushes down on the lower pressure of lesser elevations. The result is that all the smoke, pollution, and dust in the air gets trapped in a dirty, cloudy layer that covers the whole Wasatch Front.

One afternoon I was driving down from Park City through Parley's Canyon, a drive that I have made too many times to count. As I was listening to some music and minding my own business, I suddenly rounded a curve in the canyon and had a clear view down into the inversion-covered valley, which gave me pause.

Salt Lake City looked like it was buried under a blanket of filth and I was astounded by the sharp contrast between the lower layers of gray and brown pollution and the upper atmosphere, which was crystal clear and a remarkable shade of blue.

As I contemplated the stark difference between the dirty lower layers and the clear, clean upper sky I realized that I was looking at a metaphor for mortality. We have two choices before us all the time, two voices we can listen to. The lower voice/layer allows the world and Satan to direct our opinions of ourselves, thus covering our self-image in a filthy and polluted fog of lies. But the higher ground, the cleaner air, is where we can see ourselves as the Lord does.

I hope we make a conscientious effort every day to ignore Satan's trash-talking and keep our feelings of worth at clean higher levels. When we look in the mirror, I hope that we always remember that our potential is not weighed in pounds, dollars, or gold medals. It is measured in eternities.

YOUR TEAM BELIEVES IN YOU

Remember who you are!" We have all heard that phrase before, especially you young men and women (don't roll your eyes just yet). From an athletic standpoint, for a good reason our coaches challenge us to focus on who we are and who we represent.

Over the years I have been blessed to associate with Olympians from as far back as the 1964 Tokyo, Japan, Olympics to the most recent Olympiad held in London, plus some who are preparing for the 2014 Sochi, Russia, Winter Games. Occasionally my journalism background takes over and I find myself "interviewing" these friends and colleagues about their Olympic experiences. Their stories of triumph, courage and sacrifice are truly inspiring and have given me much to strive for (although a few of their anecdotes are best left unrepeated).

These champions have competed in winter sports like bobsled, luge, skeleton, biathlon, freestyle aerials, snowboard-cross and Nordic ski jumping to summer events like gymnastics, volleyball, handball, wrestling, track and field events. Their backgrounds and personalities are as varied as their events, but one thing they all remember fondly is the opening ceremonies. It wasn't just the pageantry, the artistic displays or even the roar of the crowd. Although they phrased it differently, their favorite part was often the opportunity to walk out into that stadium with their teammates as representatives of their countries, sports, team, communities, and families. It was the realization of a dream that had great power because of what and whom it represented.

Many athletes use the Olympics as a visual that is imagined over and over in the years leading up to the Games. It is a mental latchkey that accesses the hidden reserves of mental, physical, and emotional strength needed to push through the challenges of training and competing for years to qualify. One reason walking into the opening ceremonies has such a powerful impact is because it is a literal declaration that the athlete has finally made it.

The pursuit of the Games is tough, very tough for hopeful athletes, but the thrill of representing their country and their loved ones provides them courage and strength. The lesson we can learn from this is that regardless of the fears, trials or anxieties you face, you can find great strength by remembering those who support you and those you represent, or when you remember who you are.

"Remember who you are" is a phrase that holds more power than most of us realize. When we remember who we are and who we represent we can feel great desires to better ourselves and achieve greater things out of respect for ourselves and those we represent. So this principle is important when it comes to our feelings of self-worth, but it isn't about ego; it is about bringing honor and glory to God and valuing ourselves and those around us as his children. This ideology unfortunately seems lost in many of today's professional athletes who focus on their egos first, their bank account second, and their legacy third. This fixation on "me, me, me" instead of "remember who you are and who you represent" goes beyond sport and has led to selfishness and self-aggrandizement becoming practiced more than sacrifice, dedication, loyalty, and respect. Remembering who you are is a reminder that the name on the front of the jersey is far more important than the one of the back.

Great coaches and leaders understand the emotional and psychological power that comes from mentally acknowledging your association with a certain team, group, or community. We all define ourselves based on the groups we belong to, the company we work for, the sports team we play or cheer on, the ward we are in, the charity or political organization we support. We love to align ourselves with groups/teams that share similar interests, goals, or beliefs.

There's more to it than the social aspect, but I'm not talking about worldly pride. Satan tempts us to feel superior when we obtain a certain title or membership within a specific organization. We are all children of God no matter who or what we represent, and that means more than any mortal label. Should we respect our achievements and those of others? Yes, but never at the expense of our value as sons and daughters of God.

So here's my question: who do you represent? Maybe you have never represented your country and family at the Olympics, but what groups, causes, companies, social circles, and teams have you aligned yourself with? Do they bring you closer to Christ, or will these associations slowly eat away at your spirit? Remember, you cannot play confidently on a team you feel is wrong. Go ahead and make a list.

Now being part of a team usually includes a uniform, and, for me, wearing anything with USA or an American flag on it has always felt like a challenge to live up to the high ideals of this great country and the standards of the Olympic movement. So what uniforms do you wear? And do you bring honor to those uniforms?

One of the greatest uniforms I have ever worn has been that of the Boy Scouts of America. I continue to draw strength from the legacy of the Scouts, and I strive daily to honor to this "team" that as an Eagle Scout I am still a part of. The traditions and principles of Scouting have helped me become the person I am today and I encourage all Scouts, past and present, to honor this "uniform." Living with this desire can help us remain trustworthy, loyal, helpful, friendly, courteous, kind, obedient, cheerful, thrifty, brave, clean, and reverent. My fellow Scouts, remember who you are.

Another uniform that taught me the value of respecting myself because of those I represented was that of a missionary. While serving in Honduras and Belize, I grew to love my fellow laborers in the vineyard, my teammates who worked so hard for the Lord and devoted their whole body and soul to the work. For most missionaries, the desire to bring honor to the Savor and to avoid dishonoring his name or his Church is a strong deterrent against Satan's temptations. The white shirt and black name tag were as much a declaration to the world of our identity as they were a reminder of whom and what we represented: the Lord, the Church, and the gospel.

Now, while many of the groups or "teams" we represent have uniforms, name tags, or some identifying item that can be worn and then removed, we must never set aside our identities as representatives of the Savior and his restored church. We cannot choose to forget who we are out of convenience.

I think the Lord understands this concept quite well, which is why he reminds us over and over again that we belong to and represent some pretty wonderful teams. The "uniform" we take upon us through baptism is eternal. Ponder what it means to be a member of The Church of Jesus Christ of Latter-day Saints and to belong to a fantastic (though imperfect) ward or branch. Think of your priesthood quorum, Relief Society, or Young Men and Young Women, but most of all, think of your Savior and your Father in Heaven.

When temptations arise, ask yourself: Do I really want to disappoint my loved ones whom I represent? Do I really want to dishonor the "uniform" of a disciple of Christ? On the flip side, when you are feeling discouraged or of low self-worth, the love of the Lord, your family, and your friends can remind you just how amazing you really are.

Remember that list of those you represent? I want you to carefully review each answer and ask yourself: does this association lift you up, and is it in line with who you want to be and who God knows you are? Put a line through anything on your list that is currently hurting you because those are the associations/teams that should be eliminated from your life. The Lord has asked us to stand in holy places, and that includes surrounding ourselves with good people, causes, and organizations. This may sound harsh, but as an athlete you work hard to eliminate negative influences from your life because you don't have time to waste or energy to lose fighting against something or someone that is holding you back from your dreams.

Negative "teams" and influences can lower your self-esteem and lead you into dangerous paths, so I promise that as you labor to eliminate them from your life, the Spirit will bring confidence to your heart and courage to your soul. I get it; pulling away from a bad "team" can be tough when it isn't the most popular thing to do, but I've always felt that those who go against the crowd and remain loyal to their covenants truly deserve respect and honor. Respect yourself enough to choose good teams.

Through my associations in bobsled and with sport philanthropy, I have learned to look at and respect myself though a lens of a purer light—heaven's light. This heaven-based view of myself motivates me to strive harder to do better every day. It pushes me to get up when I fall and to reach for loftier goals. It is a constant voice that seems to whisper, "Remember who you are and rise above the mundane so you can bring honor to God, family, and country."

It was in this state of mind that I began a habit that some might find rather amusing, but it had incredible significance to me.

Before my mission to keep in shape for sliding I often laced up my running shoes and heading out to pound the pavement or hit the running track. I would plug in my mp3 player (pre-iPod days) and go run or do sprint work. Since I was at school or work during the day, I had to either run early in the morning or late at night.

While running one night, my thoughts drifted to those I represented, like my friends, classmates, teammates, and family. Then it occurred to me that these weren't the only ones supporting me. My mind turned to Doctrine and Covenants 84:88, which says, "I will be on your right hand and on your left, and my Spirit shall be in your hearts, and mine angels round about you, to bear you up." As I continued running, I began to picture a group of tough stripling warriors running alongside me. Not all two thousand, mind you, just five or six. I imagined that as we ran they encouraged me to run farther and faster. I could almost hear their voices saying, "Keep going. We believe in you. You can do this!"

While my tennis shoes were among the Nephites, this scenario demonstrates how remembering who I am can bring great strength. It reminded me that I was part of the Lord's team, that I represented his Church, and that I was supported by angels. Strangely enough, I found myself enjoying the grueling workouts even more, because when I thought of all those I represented, I found strength to do more.

And it wasn't just heavenly teammates who helped me along the way. I am grateful for my incredible bobsled colleagues who have pushed me to be my best. Men and women like Lane, Adam, Joe, Randy, Travis, Mark, Steve, Matt, Don, Tracy, Katlyn, Don, Brad, Eric, Dave and Dan. The list goes go on. By remembering who I was/am in their eyes, I have found a greater love for myself as a son of God and a desire to represent them all with honor and distinction.

God has placed a sacred trust in each of us and has asked us to be teammates in his work to bring to pass "the immortality and eternal life" of our fellow men. When you remember who you are, you'll remember that God has a plan for your life, a unique mission that only you can fulfill. Heaven's trust is not meant to intimidate but to motivate. The Lord believes in us so much that he challenges us to be the "light(s) of the world" (Matthew 5:15). This knowledge can give strength and confidence when we understand that our Heavenly Father lovingly says, "I already trust you. I believe in you and know you'll do a great job with your time on earth."

My association with bobsled and the Olympic movement has been a life-changing, life-saving blessing. It taught me about who I am in the Lord's eyes, which has allowed me to see my worth and my life with a clearer vision. And we need clear vision when it comes to leading a championship life.

Satan, the master deceiver, is pretty good at diverting our attention from our divine heritage and potential. At times he dulls our minds and clouds our vision of self, but remembering who you are can give you strength to fight back. God believes in you enough to ask you to be a parent, a missionary, a bishop, a visiting teacher, or even a friend. Just as you have placed your trust in him, he has placed his trust in you. Take that trust and use it to power your life to greater heights.

Remembering that you are of immeasurable worth can keep you safe from harmful influences and temptations. Plus, actively recalling how much God loves you can push out Satan's lies regarding your worth, potential, beauty, intelligence. Burdens will become lighter, not because they disappear but because God knows your potential and he trusts you to stand tall and perform the specific tasks that only you can do. Each of us has a part to play in the competition of life, so we should always let our light so shine that others see our good works and glorify God because of it.

Remember who you are and who you represent. Make the most of everyday and live every moment like it's the fourth quarter. God's confidence in you reaches far beyond your own limited sense of the word. We just have to remember that he is cheering loudly from the sidelines, encouraging us to play with honor and self-respect. Even if you can't remember who you are, the Savior does, and he is calling you to win the game and inherit more than a gold medal.

His wants you to "win" an eternal crown.

CHOOSE THE RIGHT WHEN YOUR HONOR IS PLACED BEFORE YOU

Over the years I've noticed that champions of the Lord always seem to understand that while their worthiness may change, their worth does not. Come what may, good or bad, they know they are a child of God with unchanging value.

Now the caveat to this principle is that what we do and how we think and speak may not affect our worth, but it can affect how we feel. Our choices in life must reflect our eternal worth because even with unchanging value, sin is going to make us feel a loss.

Although I used non-gospel terms, I had the opportunity to teach this truth while participating in Utah's Gold Medal Schools. Sponsored by the Utah Department of Health this fantastic program encourages elementary school teachers, educators, and students to learn the importance of making healthy choices in diet and physical fitness. Just like the Olympics, Gold Medal Schools awards a bronze, silver, or gold medal if the school meets certain health and fitness requirements. It was great to watch entire schools get on-board, from students logging their miles walked to the lunchroom staff making changes to the menu. Even teachers and administrators get on-board with their own health and fitness goals.

I was honored to present the medals during special assemblies, but some principals asked if I would bring a bobsled to display and speak to the students, which I was happy to do, schedule permitting. This speaking circuit quickly became more than a few-word affair, however, as some schools dedicated entire assemblies for me.

When I asked principals for topics, they told me the students would benefit from a discussion on making championship choices in their daily lives. The underlying issues hardly needed clarification: with so many negative influences and messages out there, these young minds could use a positive example to stay on good and healthy paths.

This assignment weighed on me. I have been speaking to crowds since high school, but I kept asking myself how I could best teach the students to make the type of choices that bring greater happiness and self-confidence.

I reviewed the choices in my athletic career that brought victory and those that brought loss and regret, and then I thought about what made the difference. After some introspection I realized that it wasn't the one big decision, but the hundreds and thousands of tiny decisions that led up to the "main event." I decided to focus my remarks around just how important the everyday choices are in a champion's life. Whether in school, work, in sport or in our relationships, what we choose to do and how we decide to react can have tremendous impact on the outcome. As an athlete you can choose to obey or ignore your training and diet schedules. Will a recent loss crush you, or will you instead rise from defeat to become a future victor? Sports are great classrooms for the mind, body, and spirit, and bobsled has taught me that no victory ever comes without countless good choices made long before race day.

After several speaking engagements, I realized that the principles being taught were applicable to minds of all ages and areas of pursuit: how we feel inside is often the result of our decisions. Do choices change our eternal worth? No, but they can change how we feel inside and how we feel about ourselves.

A huge difference exists between self-esteem and self-worth, although we often use the terms interchangeably. Self-esteem is how we feel about ourselves, while our self-worth is how God feels. And whether you're an athlete or not, a healthy view of self is the result of constantly making choices based on both our values and our value. We can know we are children of God, but until we choose to live by this truth, we leave ourselves vulnerable to Satan's taunts and the world's twisted views and opinions.

As an athlete one of the most important steps you can take toward success is to take control of and accept responsibility for your thoughts, feelings, and actions, including thoughts, feelings, and actions toward yourself. The world says self-esteem comes from outward influences: money, fame, beauty, and success, and if you don't have them then you can't feel as confident or content. In my experience, I have learned that people are often the most unhappy when they base their choices on the pursuit of those temporary temporal things instead of on their eternal worth. Even gold medals can be lost or forgotten over time.

The most fruitful lives are led by those who grab a firm hold of their thought patterns, emotional circuits and time-management habits and use them to build a happy, productive life. But there's more to it than that! One thing I have learned from the champions I've grown up around is that when a decision comes along, happy individuals make a choice based on what is best in the long term and what best matches their internal value systems. If the outcome goes against what they believe or truly want in their lives, they respect themselves enough to say, "No."

Yes, choices have a big impact on our level of happiness and satisfaction in life. Our worth is unchangeable, but our feelings, including those toward ourselves, fluctuate on a regular basis. If we are down on ourselves, we feel sadness and discouragement. If we feel confident, then we feel a deeper happiness and calmness for life. The trick is to make good choices that lead to the later and avoid those that lead to the former.

While we all strive to maintain a healthy opinion of ourselves, the truth is that every one of us, even athletes, occasionally has a day or two (or twenty) that test our ability to believe in ourselves. Our struggles with self-esteem may be based on our physical appearance, our popularity level, our perceived mental capacity, and so forth. Underneath it all, what we think about ourselves is a choice. And while we need not become discouraged if we struggle with these mortal troubles, we must be cautious of another aspect of choice.

A popular phrase used by Olympic and Paralympic athletes and hopefuls says, "It's not every four years; it's every day." This powerful statement means that while the Games themselves appear on the world stage every four years, athletes make choices every day leading up to the opening ceremonies. But for me, the phrase came to serve as a reminder to make daily decisions that will help me move forward in life and prepare me for what the Lord has in store. But I saw it as a warning as well; Satan knows he cannot affect our heavenly defined self-worth, but self-esteem is another matter. He knows that while you can know you are of great worth to the Savior, when you have a day when you feel like a complete failure, it can be hard to unite what you feel with what you know. Because of this, Lucifer works to destroy us from the inside out by tricking us into choosing acts or thoughts contrary to our eternal value. We have all heard the phrase "moment of weakness," meaning we weren't our best in mind or heart when a decision was made. Can you think of an easier way to make us "weak" than to lower our self-esteem? A big trick in Satan's playbook is to make us feel so sorry for ourselves that we do something we'll regret. Low self-esteem can lead to a bad choice that leads to lower feelings for self and so the downward spiral goes.

If we believe we are worth what God tells us we are worth, then we can and should make choices that protect our self-esteem. If we want the blessings of heaven and the promised peace, confidence, and contentment, then we must live as champions of the Lord who choose the good over the bad every day.

A key philosophy of the ancient Greeks who founded the Olympic was called *arête*. Arête simply means achieving excellence of any kind, but perhaps a better description would be "living up to your full potential by doing the best you can." The Greeks used arête to guide them to better choices, actions and thoughts in all aspects of life, from sport to art, speech to thought, spiritual to physical. Arête was also a defense against actions, words or thoughts that would bring disgrace or prevent them from performing at their peak.

Wait, doesn't the gospel challenge us to do our best and to live up to our divine potential, our arête? And if so, like the ancient Greeks, shouldn't we make choices that protect our honor and virtue? If we want to feel as confident and happy as our eternal worth indicates we can, we must make choices that are in line with our potential, not our popularity or passions. We must build a champion's mind-set by defending our self-esteem by resisting Satan's lies because true champions know that doing wrong will never feel right and no matter how much the adversary wants to trick us, you can't feel good by acting, thinking or speaking bad.

Every day our senses are bombarded with the sights and sounds of lowered standards. And problems with our self-esteem usually arise when these false standards of the world conflict with the true standards of the Lord. If you want to feel lasting joy and have a deep confidence, choose to "play the game" within the rules the Lord has set.

Making our choices based on eternal principles will allow us to move forward in our spiritual "training." The greatest athletes I know choose to protect their minds and bodies so they can compete at full strength, which brings deep confidence in their abilities and potential on the track, the ice sheet, and the ski hill. Unfortunately, when we make decisions based on the world's standards, we are building our self-esteem on the sandy foundations of mortal opinion, which can actually leave our minds and hearts frozen to the things of God. And a winter sport like bobsled teaches you a thing or two about freezing (if you do not like the cold, then bobsled is probably not a sport for you).

During my second season, my mother dropped me off one evening at the Park City track's finish area where I noticed a fellow sled pilot, Ralph, who was busy chipping away at the base of the doors of his sled storage container. Our recent winter storm had dropped over a foot of snow by the container's base, and the mixture of warm sunny days and freezing cold nights had led to a buildup of ice around the container's doors, which were now frozen shut. So, with shovels in hand, we hacked away at the snow and ice until Ralph was eventually able to get his sled out from behind the frozen curtain.

I tell this story because Satan uses negative messages in the media and overly critical self-talk to build up mental, emotional, and spiritual ice around our self-esteem. When we are born, we have a naturally resilient opinion of ourselves. We feel genuinely happy about life, the future, and our value in the world. It isn't until those negative messages and critiques of our minds, bodies, or abilities filter in that this literally childlike innocence begins to change. I see this a lot when I speak at schools or to youth groups. The younger students have a bubbling enthusiasm for life, while many teens and young adults have begun to question their worth and their ability to be happy.

Our youth are at particular risk for this freezing of self-worth. They face so many negative messages about who they are and who they "should" be. It breaks my heart when so many young women and men feel they have to give in to immodesty or extreme lifestyles just to feel good about themselves. It must sadden our Heavenly Father to see his children make choices that so blatantly steal their self-confidence and self-respect. My young friends, defend your self-esteem with everything you have!

No wonder the gospel places such a high emphasis on individual worth. Like any good coach the Savior wants us to avoid the choices and decisions that rob of us the victories and growth he desires for us (Psalm 84:11). We must be on constant guard to protect our spirits and self-esteem from the buildup of Satan's emotional, mental, and spiritual ice. Just as my fellow sled driver was trying to get into that frozen container, so too are countless sons and daughters of God trying to dig through the negative thoughts and feelings they have chosen to believe or have had inflicted upon them in order to reach that inner core of self-worth.

We should never believe that we must choose sin in order to feel attractive or good about ourselves. We are made in God's image (Genesis 1:27) and are therefore beautiful and wonderful beings. Don't let Satan suck you in with lies. After all, choosing the ways of the world has never lead to a single victory that really mattered. When we base our choices on the Lord's teachings, we will be protecting our bodies, minds, and spirits. And champions always protect what they value most.

Our metal bobsled runners are incredibly important. We polish them smooth, keep them in protective cases, and generally treat them like our children. I've even heard rumors of drivers who put their runners in bed at night to keep them safe. And while that is a good example of how hard we should work to protect our self-esteem, another lesson should be learned here.

If we don't keep the runners clean, even the tiniest bit of moisture can cause them to rust if it isn't wiped off. And if that isn't cleaned up, the rust will eat its way into the metal and leave the otherwise smooth surface pocked, scarred, and flawed. And if the rust gets bad enough, it can take a lot of work to get them clean again. As athletes we have to sand runners for hours to get them race ready.

Just as a tiny amount of moisture can eat away at the metal of a runner, so too can Satan weaken our core image of self through the negative messages of the world and when we act on those false messages, well, our hearts can become tarnished. Bit by bit, inch by inch, Satan will lead us down paths of darkness until we find ourselves lost, confused, and brokenhearted. Like rust on a bobsled runner, the longer we let his influence stay with us, the deeper the holes that he inflicts on our spirits become.

Only decisions that honor eternal truths, principles, and moral values will lift our spirits, protect our hearts, and bring the blessings of righteous living. If there is something we are doing or thinking that is lowering our feelings of self-worth and happiness, let's repent. Let's invite the healing power of the Atonement to wash us clean and restore our feelings of respect and value. Remember, even champions make mistakes and poor choices occasionally, but they learn from them.

As the Olympic creed states, "the most important thing in life is not the triumph, but the struggle. The essential thing is not to have conquered, but to have fought well." God only asks that we fight well and endure to the end. That may mean enduring failure, mocking, mistakes, loneliness, illness, adversity, and imperfections, but by holding ourselves, and our choices, to God's standards, we will be like an Olympic torch, full of light and warmth. That light, that happiness, will shine brightly against Satan's darkness.

Never lower your standards in a vain attempt to find greater feelings of value. If we all possessed a perfect understanding of our eternal worth, then we wouldn't meddle in the foolish things of this world. I fear that one of the worst decisions we make, one that robs us of internal peace, is that we look at our peers and view their lives and successes as greater than our own. We allow our level of happiness and our feelings of self-worth to be determined by comparing ourselves to others. Here's my suggestion: don't worry about keeping up with the Joneses; worry about keeping up with Christ.

Start now to live up to your potential and value as a child of God. Choose to ignore the negative thoughts, messages, and temptations of Satan. Champions of the Lord must stand with a resolute determination to make decisions based on their divine worth. Look at your life from a gospel perspective. Look at what you have done and accomplished. You have every right to feel honored and proud. You are a champion in our Heavenly Father's eyes; to him you will never be second rate.

The definer of our worth would say to us as he did to Jeremiah of old, "I know the thoughts that I think toward you . . . thoughts of peace, and not of evil, to give you an expected end" (Jeremiah 29:11). A wonderful expected end, I might add. So follow Paul's counsel to the Roman Saints and "be not conformed to this world: but be ye transformed by the renewing of your mind, that ye may prove what is that good, and acceptable, and perfect, will of God" (Romans 12:2). Live worthy of your worth!

CHAMPIONS LIGHT THE WAY, EVEN IF ALONE

One cold Friday night during the 2005–2006 season I found myself sitting in the little building next to the start area (gloriously called the start hut) for a training session with the local bobsled and skeleton club.

Club time was always fun since it was a good mixture of veteran athletes and amateur sliders. Everyone was more relaxed and there was plenty of good-natured trash-talking between the athletes and even the coaches. The club was like a big family, complete with weird "cousins" and occasional drama, but overall everyone encouraged and pushed each other to reach their best.

Like a competition, training sessions have start lists that show the order each athlete or team will go down the track, so my brakeman and I were sitting in the building waiting our turn. The little structure was chock-full of spandex-covered bodies who huddled together to keep warm. Winter in Park City + clear Friday night + spandex = chilly, thank you very much. Speedsuits are fashionable (in our world) but not exactly insulated.

To pass the time, I spoke with a skeleton athlete friend in his midteens, which is not a terribly uncommon age for athletes to start that sport. I made a couple remarks that encouraged him to pursue his sport and goals. I began bobsled at about his age, so I knew what it was like to be surrounded by athletes who were older. I just wanted to help him become the great athlete that he desired to become.

Well, his name was called over the public address system, so he ran out the door to grab his sled and head down the track headfirst as crazy skeleton athletes do. As we all watched him push off, his dad, who was also in the room and had heard our conversation, said, "You know, he really looks up to you."

His words surprised me. I didn't feel like I had said anything special to deserve such admiration so I offered a quiet "thank you." I don't know if any of the other athletes heard what he said, but it stuck with me for the rest of the night, throughout the weekend, and to this day. I was grateful for the compliment and the respect, but why would anyone look up to me? It wasn't a question of my worth, but rather my worthiness for anything beyond the mundane. Maybe you can relate.

We all have days when we doubt ourselves, days when our dreams or the task at hand seem far larger than our abilities or strength. If you have wondered if you can really measure up, don't worry; you're in good company. Enoch felt inadequate because he was "slow of speech" (Moses 6:31). Moses worried about leading Israel out of Egypt because he felt he was not ready for the task, asking, "Who am I that I should go?" (Exodus 3:11). Jeremiah felt he was too young and struggled with his speech (Jeremiah 1:6). Moroni was troubled by the difficulties in writing on the plates and what effect this would have on future readers of the Book of Mormon (Ether 12:23). Even Nephi worried about his weaknesses (2 Nephi 4). You stand with the best if you ever feel inadequate.

After that training session, I struggled with my thoughts about my standing in the world. I felt undeserving of praise, although I have always tried to live a life that helps others come closer to Christ and become their best selves. And then it hit me: I have tried. I've tried to be a good athlete, a good representative of the Savior, of the Church, and of my sport. I've tried to encourage other athletes and help them pursue their goals, regardless of their skill level or country of origin. I'm not perfect, but I came to feel gratitude for the opportunity to influence this young athlete, one of God's children, in such a positive way in spite of my inadequacies.

My story is but a taste of the power our righteous (though imperfect) example can have on those around us. Our influence as sons and daughters of God can have a lasting and changing effect on the hearts of those we come in contact with. This is one of the reasons that I feel our Savior commanded us to "Let [our] light so shine before men, that they may see [our] good works, and glorify [our] Father which is in heaven" (Matthew 5:16). Indeed, Jesus spoke words of great encouragement when he said, "Ye are the light of the world" (Matthew 5:14). Talk about a call of the champions!

I smile when I think of being a light on a hill. Bobsled tracks around the world are lit up with stadium lighting, which allows us to train long after the sun goes down. Some of the newer tracks even have lights inside the turns.

But where exactly is this "hill" we are supposed to be shining our light from? Simply put, God asks us to let our light shine, "at all times and in all things, and in all places" (Mosiah 18:9).

He wants us to become a torch. An Olympic torch.

The Olympic torch is a powerful symbol recognized around the globe. While the main cauldron is lit during the opening ceremonies to indicate that the Games have begun, the torch relay symbolically sends a message of peace and friendship to all peoples and demonstrates a passing of the light of knowledge and spirit. What many don't know is that the torch relay is a modern invention. The first summer torch relay was in 1936 and the first winter relay in 1952. The ancient Greeks never performed this act, although in Athens there were religious-focused races with torches called *lampadedromia*. These races were held to honor the gods, especially Prometheus, who introduced fire to mankind. The first runner to cross the finish line had the honor of lighting a flame to the god being honored.

So if the torch relay represents a call to peace, brotherhood, friendship, and spirit, can we not, then, look at the gospel of Jesus Christ as a relay of sorts? Each of us carries the torch of testimony and spirit before us and therefore we can share that fire to light the fire within others. The trick is to let that light shine on whatever hill we may be on in life.

Many of us want our feelings of inadequacy and fear to go away before we take that big step in our life, or try out for the team or ask for that promotion. Maybe it's a Church calling or just a quiet prompting of the Spirit, but when an opportunity to let our light shine arises, we want the courage to come before we turn on the illumination.

But we can't delay; life waits for no one and as with my young skeleton friend, we may never know whose life we will influence for good. Our words and actions can be Olympic torches that lead others to Christ and help them find greater happiness. You may not understand how much good you can do when you let your light shine, but God does.

And here's the secret: when you stand as a champion of charity and faith, your feelings of self-worth will grow. When we serve others, when we are true to the gospel, when we have the faith and courage to be courageously compassionate while following our dreams, this is when we will find deeper peace and happiness. And I want to point out that a willingness to try, notwithstanding our weaknesses, demonstrates trust in the Lord.

One aspect of the Olympic torch relay that many have never seen is the official lighting of the flame. I'm not talking about the main cauldron in the

Olympic stadium; I'm talking the lighting of the flame in Olympia, Greece, at the twenty-six hundred-year-old Temple of Hera. A woman dressed as the high priestess offers an invocation to Apollo, sun god to the ancient Greeks, and then uses a mirror to focus the sun's rays and start a flame.

Thus the Olympic flame is lit using the sun. Our inner flame, however, can only be ignited and fanned by the Son, even the Son of God. It is natural to worry about our shortcomings, but we must never let our inadequacies overcome our incredible potential. After all, can't the weaknesses that we feel are holding us back be overcome with the Lord's help (Ether 12:27–28)? No wonder Paul so boldly declared, "I can do all things through him who strengthens me" (Philippians 4:13). We always stand tall when we stand with the Lord, no matter how small we feel.

Instead of letting feelings of inadequacy stop you from being your best, allow the Lord to make your weaknesses strong. You'll find that his help is more than adequate. And as you grow and let your light shine, you naturally help others to grow and glow. Do you realize how great and wonderful the things you can do are?

I think of the student who reaches out to a lonely classmate or a young man who turns down an offered alcoholic beverage. I think of a coach who teaches her athletes the true meaning of sportsmanship on and off the field, or a loving bishop who reaches out to the spiritually bruised and beaten in need of a friend.

Letting our light so shine before the world can inspire and guide others, even if doing so means we will be the lone light on the hill.

For many sliding athletes, once the race is over, they plan to head to the nearest bar or pub to unwind and celebrate. I have always been pretty clear that I do not drink, and most of my colleagues respect that. I was not trying to push my beliefs on others, but it reminds me that as a Latter-day Saint, our light always shines, so let it shine brightly. You may not be up "on a hill" wearing spandex and a helmet about to push a bobsled down that hill, but your goodness and spirit influences far more people than you realize.

I challenge you to live up to your divine potential and worth. Champions of the Lord cannot be afraid to do what is right, even if it is unpopular or appears difficult. The more you exert a positive influence, the greater your capacity will grow to listen to the Spirit direct you to those who need your example and help. Your light on the hill may just be the Olympic torch that guides those around you to their own dreams, and perhaps to spiritual safety.

But here's the catch: Satan fears your power. He knows the influence you can have on others, which is why he works so hard to make you feel inadequate in the first place. If we feel unprepared (inadequate) we will fear, but if we exercise faith and trust in the Lord, we can instead feel calm and unafraid (Doctrine and Covenants 38:30).

When a moment to let your light shine comes and you step up to the starting line, stick close to the Savior and give it all you've got. Let him guide your life and use your talents. Be an instrument in his hands and you can do great things. The Lord loves you for who you are and wants to your light shine even brighter. Stop seeing yourself as a spectator in mortality when the Savior knows you are a gold medalist.

Sure, we will sometimes wonder if our flame is going to die out. We need those times to challenge us like a good session in the weight room. On the days when the world seems too heavy, common men and women must look inside their souls to find uncommon courage and faith. Part of the reason the Lord challenges us is to help our lights burn brighter and to remind us of who we are.

One of Satan's main goals is to make us forget—to forget that we are of Israel, children of our Father in Heaven with the potential to become as he is. We forget that we have been saved for these latter days to help build his kingdom and hold back the tide of evil. Sometimes we forget the talents, attributes, and qualities we've been given. Satan seeks to pull down our self-image and cool our inner fires of hope and courage by convincing us that we are too weak, unworthy, and hopeless to make a difference.

Maybe you've had occasion to ask yourself, "Who am I to be a light on a hill?" You look at the Olympic torch of your life and wonder, "Why should I hold this up for anyone to see?" When the call comes to rise to higher levels in life, we must remember that it is okay to wonder if we are adequate, but we must never forget that we are capable. We are meant for bigger things in this world than hiding behind the bleachers so we can watch the world pass by instead of getting out there and playing the game we were sent here for. The Lord needs powerful champions to help move his work forward so when you feel like you're "too average" to make a difference, please do not let those feelings become your controlling emotions. Satan may be the source of inadequacy, but the gospel reminds us that our potential is heaven sent.

In my early life I never would have considered myself a candidate for bobsled. I hated roller coasters and I disliked sports outside of soccer. If you had told me when I was twelve that I would be a bobsled pilot someday, I probably would have laughed and experienced thoughts of inadequacy: "I'm not good enough to be a bobsledder" or "I'm average; the Lord would never call little me to do that." I still struggle with feelings of insufficiency at times. Who am to do this? Who am I to do that? Who am I to be a beacon on the hill for others to see?

And yet, here I am with over a decade in the sport as a pilot and coach. How?

I was reading in Jacob chapter 5 one day when the concept of inadequacy became a little clearer to me. By comparing our lives to the chapter's metaphor , we see that the Lord is pruning our hearts and spirits. And sometimes when we feel him pushing us to grow and let our light shine we say the same thing the servant said to the master of the vineyard, "How comest thou hither to plant this tree, or this branch of the tree? For behold, it was the poorest spot in all the land of thy vineyard" (Jacob 5:21).

In other words, we say, "Lord, I'm the poorest spot in this vineyard/ward/office/team. Why are you coming to me and asking me to do this task? You should ask Brother So-and-So or Sister Such-and-Such. They are much more talented, beautiful, poised, spiritual, and intellectual than I am."

When you have thoughts like these or moments where you doubt yourself, listen to the Lord's response to this servant: "Counsel me not; I knew that it was a poor spot of ground; wherefore, I said unto thee, I have nourished it this long time and thou beholdest that it hath brought forth much fruit"(verse 22).

Much like the miracle of turning water into wine, as we draw closer to Christ, he will take our weaker hearts and turns them into something stronger, something purer. He takes our spirits and molds them into the best they can be, the "best of the vine."

God doesn't ask you to do things you think you can do; he calls you to do things he knows you can do. We always hear that this generation was held in reserve to come forth in these latter days. What does that mean?

In a relay track and field event, a team is set up where the fastest runner is the last of the four athletes to run their leg of the race. Called the "anchor" position, this competitor has the crucial responsibility to either make up for lost time from the other three athletes or to maintain and increase a lead if they have one. Many would argue that the race can be won or lost by the team's anchor.

Brothers and sisters, we are running the anchor position in the relay of the dispensation of the fulness of time, and God trusts us to get the job done. Do not fear the tasks laid at your feet; fear the missed opportunities should you choose to ignore them.

To someone in your life, you may just be the bright symbol of hope that they need to rise up as champions themselves. The Lord believes in you and will stand by you as let your light shine. Go to those who need you. Reach out to those who suffer, who are discouraged, who are struggling with sin, or who do not believe in themselves. As you do so, you will become both a window and a mirror. A mirror because you will help your fellowman see who they really are, and a window because you will be a window to the Savior's love.

My friends, let your light shine as brightly as possible!

SILVER AND GOLD ARE GREAT, BUT HEAVEN LOOKS DEEPER

One of my favorite things about bobsled is the way it has brought me closer to my Heavenly Father and taught me about the gospel of Jesus Christ. I wanted to write this book to share the things God has taught me through sport because while they have all been sacred experiences, I wouldn't trade this personal relationship with deity for all the gold medals in the world. Because of this relationship, I know who I am; bobsled has taught me to see myself more clearly.

After my first two seasons in the sport, my parents and I decided I should try wearing contact lenses and enjoy clearer vision. I had been wearing glasses for a few years, but glasses are not conducive to bobsled since wearing them inside our helmets can be dangerous. If we crash, the lenses can shatter or the frames may break into pieces with sharp edges. So after a visit to the eye doctor, I found myself awkwardly trying not to poke my eyes out while learning to put contacts in.

It was worth it; when I took that first run down the track with my contacts in—wow, what a difference. I could see the details of the ice, the chips and scrapes and the drive lines from other drivers. I could see further into the turns and more clearly down the track. Things weren't blurry anymore; they were clear. Next stop: laser correction.

Now being able to see clearly is crucial because as a sled pilot I need to see what is coming my way at eighty miles per hour as quickly and as plainly as possible. Impaired vision just doesn't cut it out on the ice and mortal life is no different.

I'm not talking about our actual eyesight, although good vision is a true blessing. No, I'm referring to the way we look at ourselves and the clarity of our sight when we view others. Honestly some of us need a little corrective surgery when it comes to this.

Although they are rare, abuses of power exist within bobsled. These incidences often involved people who believed their positions of "authority" or experience in the sport gave them the right to exercise control over others or treat them with disrespect. Now I only mention this because in contrast the highest figures of authority in the universe, Heavenly Father and the Savior, have no desire to put us down or belittle our lives. In fact, these gods have stated that their main task is to help us become as they are (Moses 1:39) and even promised to help us along the way. And for that to happen sometimes we need to learn to see what they see in ourselves.

Sometimes we fail to see our worth clearly, when we feel that because of some physical, emotional, mental, or spiritual shortcoming we are "lame, or blind, or halt, or maimed, or leprous, or . . . withered, or . . . deaf." We become discouraged because we "are afflicted in [some] manner" (3 Nephi 17:7), because we aren't this or we aren't that. We look in the mirror with blurry vision and don't like what we see because when you get down to it, we aren't looking through heaven's eyes. We are looking through the world's or with our own imperfect sight. Just as I needed contact lenses to see more clearly, sometimes we need an outside opinion to help us change the negative thoughts or beliefs we have about ourselves—and that's okay! Even the Olympics have changed from time to time (the world did not hold the live pigeon shooting or the croquet competitions of the 1900 Games very highly).

Every bobsled track has a control tower similar to those found at airports. The control tower is really the brain of the track because every sensor, timing laser, camera, and speaker is tied into its systems.

Now tower operators use the cameras to keep an eye on every corner and straightaway of the track. I remember standing in the control tower as a coach surrounded by several "big wigs" who were there to see if one of our adaptive athletes had what it took to forerun for a World Cup race. It was interesting to watch the athletes go down the course from this perspective. From the control tower, you can watch teams push and load into their sled at the start and then flip through the cameras as they make their run. The more experienced tower operators can pick out the points where the team and specifically the driver make mistakes, or have close calls. While coaches are usually out on the track watching, we can sometimes use the tower operator's unique view to our advantage by asking what we did right and wrong. This outside perspective can help us see and perform more effectively.

Much like my vision before I put contacts in, sometimes our view of ourselves becomes impaired by the false opinions and trends of the world. When this happens, we may need the help of the tower operator of this world, Jesus Christ. With his assistance, we can learn to look at ourselves with all our strengths and weaknesses and see the incredible person we really are. We will love ourselves for who we are today and who we want to be tomorrow.

So what does our Savior think? What does he see when he looks at our lives and into our hearts? The gospel answers these questions with eternal truths that can help us look at ourselves more clearly. When we see what Jesus sees, we will love ourselves as he does. And if there's anything that I know to be true, it is that he loves us beyond words.

Jesus testified, "greater love hath no man than this, that a man lay down his life for his friends" (John 15:13). If your self-esteem is cloudy and dark, remember that Christ believed in you so much that he was willing to suffer in Gethsemane and die on the cross on Golgotha for you. You were worth that much to him then and you are worth that much to him now. Isaiah reminds us that the Lord has "graven [us] upon the palms of [his] hands" (Isaiah 49:16). When we look at ourselves through the healing lenses of the gospel, we can say, as the healed blind man, "whereas I was blind, now I see" (John 9:25). The trick is to stick with the eternal definition of our worth and ignore all the rest, even when others make that hard to do.

I was getting my two-man sled ready for a race a few years ago and I wanted to make sure that the articulation springs were still good. When I had taken them out to clean and re-grease them, I could tell by all the wear that they were several years old.

Now let me explain. A bobsled is essentially divided into two parts: the nose/cowl and the rear portion of the sled. This allows the front runners on the nose and rear runners on the back of the sled to enter and exit a turn with more fluidity. And since the sled is divided into two parts, it needs a connecting factor to keep it together on the way down the track. So inside the sled right in front of the driver's seat there is a good-sized center column that connects the front and rear of the sled via locking sockets. This allows the nose of the sled to "articulate" or move independently from the back. If a sled was sitting flat on the ground and you were to push on one of the nose's side bunks, the front of the sled would twist down to that side while the rear of the sled stayed flat. When you let go, the nose pops level again because of four internal springs.

It was those four springs that I noticed were worn down on my sled and had lost some of their tension. However, since this was a new area of sled maintenance, I wanted to get a more experienced opinion about whether or not I should replace them. So during a training session I asked one of the coaches to come take a look. This coach quickly pushed down on one side, said everything was fine, and promptly walked off as if I had wasted his time. I remember thinking, "Wow, thanks for caring." It appeared as though their level of interest for me and my sled was zero.

Now, I could have let it get me down. I could have let it affect my estimation of myself or my potential. He was a coach after all, so if he thought I wasn't worth taking the time to help, what did that say about me? But in the end I knew that while this coach acted the way he did, I had another coach on high who still cared and would always care.

If we want to see ourselves as clearly as Christ does, then we need to remember that he is a builder, not a destroyer; a comforter, not an attacker. He loves and gives strength and looks for the good while urging us forward. He is never too busy for us and his office door is always open.

That being said, we may have beliefs about ourselves that need to go. It may be something about our weight, our appearance, our ability, our intellect, our potential, or perhaps even about our standing in God's sight, but thoughts that pull us down need to be corrected immediately. So what do we do? How can we stop seeing ourselves in a negative light and instead see ourselves through Christ's eyes?

My first suggestion is to fill your mind and heart with truth. To do that you need to learn what God thinks about you. Read your patriarchal blessing. Ask your teammates, your family, and close friend, what they think God thinks about you. Ask your spouse, your seminary teacher, or your bishop what you are worth. Study the scriptures and search out the revealed doctrines about our worth as children of God since revealed truth is a sharp "two-edged sword" (Doctrine and Covenants 6:2) that can cut false beliefs about ourselves to pieces.

I also encourage you to ask your Heavenly Father through prayer about his love for you. If you ask with a sincere heart, God will answer you as he did me on November 28, 1999. My last pre-mission bobsled season had already begun, and after a particularly rough week I asked him to let me know if he loved me. I was feeling depressed in spirit and wondered if Heavenly Father really loved me, if I was special to him, and if I mattered in his grand plan. I had been reading Doctrine and Covenants 9:7–9, and as I studied the Lord's counsel to Oliver Cowdery, I found myself desiring a testimony about my worth in our Heavenly Father's eyes. So, feeling heavy of heart, I knelt down by my bed and asked, "God, do you love me?"

Brothers and sisters, I'll never forget the feelings of peace and comfort that filled my chest that night. I knew without a shadow of a doubt that God had answered me and that yes, I very much mattered to him. I knew that I was his son and that he loved me. I wrote the date in my scriptures next to the verses mentioned above so I would never forget the experience.

To see ourselves as Christ sees us, we need to eliminate any thought patterns, beliefs, or influences that keep us from that goal. When you say you are "too fat" or "too skinny," is that what the Savior would say? When you feel that you are "dumb" or "not good enough," is that how Christ feels? The Lord needs to be the standard that we test our thoughts and beliefs about ourselves against, and we must immediately remove any that are contrary to revealed truth. No matter what the world says, letting go of what holds us back allows us to fly.

One summer morning in 2008 my teammates and I were training at what we call the push track. A push track sits on a hill that mimics the contours of a bobsled track's start ramp. With two rails in the ground that we use wheeled bobsleds on, push tracks allow us to practice pushing and loading into the sled before riding down the small hill, up the crest of the next, then back down and up again to the start. To make it more effective, we set up timing sensors so we can better evaluate how we are doing.

My team and I had been practicing two-man pushes a good portion of the morning before switching over to four-man. There were quite a few skeleton athletes there who also use the push track, so we had some breaks. After a few hours things were winding down when my number-two pusher, Don, and number-three pusher, Brad, wanted to try one last push. Our brakeman, who I will call James, said he was too tired and opted to sit out. Guess it was going to be a three-man push.

We pulled the four-man sled onto the rails and set ourselves up on the wooden starting block. Our three-man push piqued the interest of a few of the others athletes, and, after we called our normal cadence (minus one voice), we took off. The push actually felt smooth, and I loaded into the driver's seat like clockwork. Down the hill we went and then up the next, then backward down the hill, and up again to the start.

We pulled our helmets off (we have to wear them on the push track) and walked over to the timing table. Abby, the athlete in charge of recording the times, seemed embarrassed. "You guys just pushed a half-second faster than you have all day." Brad, Don, and I traded looks before glancing toward our brakeman, James, who also heard the announcement. Or should I say, pronouncement.

Don, Brad, and I had taken the same sled we had been using all day and pushed it even faster without a fourth person. How? It was something I had known for much of the prior season, but James couldn't run as quickly as we could. When this occurs in bobsled, the slower athlete actually decelerates the push start. Imagine two runners who are connected by a rope tied around their waists. One is faster than the other. What happens when they start running? The slower runner holds the faster runner back. Same principle only in our case the rope is the bobsled itself.

In a way I wish this experience never happened. When we took that three-man push, James saw it and so did the other athletes. James knew what that push meant, and so did we. We needed a faster brakeman, which we found when Brad moved into that spot and another teammate Dan took over the number-three seat. A few minutes later James pulled me aside so we could talk. He let me know that since he had some new things happening in his life, he would like to step back into a more administrative role for the team. Considering the circumstances, I agreed this was the best course.

It's hard to make decisions like that, but if someone isn't pulling his or her weight and is damaging the entire team, something has to be done, and sometimes that means changing what isn't working.

So let me ask you this: what false beliefs do you have about yourself that you need to cut from your life? It may take time, and a lot of persistence, but replace those beliefs with thoughts based on your eternal worth as a child of God. Look at yourself through the lens of Christ's love. Would he say those things you are saying to yourself? Would he put you down for the things that you are beating yourself up over? I think you and I both know the answer.

Part of the reason the ancient Greek Games were so successful and continued for so many years was the judges. Originally known as *agonothetai*, or "game organizers," these judges became known as *hellanodikai*, or "the judges of the Greeks." The hellanodikai were responsible for protecting the purity of the Games, a job they took so seriously that for ten months prior to the games they lived in a special community in Elis, Greece, to study the rules and provisions of the Games from the *nomophylakes*, the "guardians of the law."

One of the greatest legacies of the hellanodikai is that they treated all the competing athletes the same. They were no respecters of persons (sound familiar? James 5:3) and they considered is a sacred honor to judge fairly. In their eyes, every athlete was worthy of respect and veneration even if they did not become the event champions. They were still winners for giving it their best.

While we are trying to do our best in the competition of life, I hope we remember that we have a Hellanodiko who judges fairly (2 Nephi 13:13), who does not love one more than the other (Romans 2:11), and who will give each of us a fair chance to win eternal glory (Mosiah 3:10). He is the law giver, the nomophylake that even now pleads our cause with our Father in Heaven to help us get there (Doctrine and Covenants 45:3–5).

If only you could see yourself as he does. Do we all have things we need to change? Yes. Do we all have sins we need to repent of? Definitely. But underneath it all, when we understand our true worth, we will stop treating ourselves as anything less than a child of the most high God.

The honor of crowning victorious athletes with their wreaths went to the most senior Hellanodiko who wore a purple robe. Because he was willing to wear the purple robe of the mocking Romans and allow them to nail his precious hands and feet to the cross, Christ is our "most senior Hellanodiko" and for that I am eternally grateful. He is my friend, my most trusted teammate and a coach that has never failed me.

I still struggle sometimes to see what he sees, but I testify of this: Jesus knows everything about you and me and he loves us just the way we are. When you are feeling down about yourself, please remember that the Savior himself said, "I will call you friends, for you are my friends, and ye shall have an inheritance with me" (Doctrine and Covenants 93:45). You must be something pretty special if Christ wants to spend eternity with you.

Don't ever let this world make you forget it.

GOOD TEAMMATES RESPECT OUR POTENTIAL

I want to smile when someone asks, "Do you drive the one- or three-man bobsled?" Occasionally I get asked about the five-man event, which died out in 1928. Five-man teams lay on their stomachs in a technique called "ventre-à-ventre" (belly-to-belly), which was thankfully banned around 1930.

So I simply state that I pilot *two-* and *four-*man bobsleds before explaining that if you're going down the track in a one- or three-man bobsled, someone did not make it in at the start (embarrassing and disqualified) or fell out on the way down (ouch and still disqualified). And if you have five, you have a hitchhiker.

So *two-* and *four-*man = *more than one*. If there is one thing bobsled has taught me it's that your level of success is highly dependent upon the people you surround yourself with. Regardless of strength or talent, no individual wins the gold medal without the help of coaches, trainers, advisors, administrators, sponsors, dieticians, sports psychologists, friends, family members, and everyday fans who support him along the way. Society idolizes the lone wolf, but if you want to become a champion, then pick championship-quality friends. As King Solomon taught, "Iron sharpeneth iron; so a man sharpeneth the countenance of his friend" (Proverbs 27:17).

We often raise a warning voice about choosing good associates to our youth, but the truth is we all have need of caution. Although false "teammates" sometimes come with enticements of popularity, fame, social gain, or perhaps even love and respect, we must be vigilant lest Satan use our desire for acceptance to lure us onto negative and destructive "teams."

President Gordon B. Hinckley counseled, "Choose your friends carefully. . . . Never lose sight of the fact that it is your friends who will lead you along the paths that you will follow . . . While you should be friendly with all people, select with great care those whom you wish to have close to you."[24]

We should be careful about whom we invite to be part of Team Mortality. Those we associate with will influence our decisions, which can affect how true we remain to our gold-medal pursuits, including gospel covenants. Just as a stone by a river becomes wet from splashing water, the longer we hang around a certain group of teammates the more they will affect our beliefs, actions, and desires. So how do we pick good teammates? I believe it all begins with respect.

Legend says the mighty Herakles (Hercules) declared that the Games be held every fifth year (four by modern calendars) to honor himself and his four brothers, which helped instill a sense of brotherhood. This emphasis on respecting teammates and fellow competitors continues in the modern Olympic movement. A main tenant of the Games is that the world can come together through peaceful competition designed to promote respect despite differences in language, culture, and/or religion. The Olympic spirit, then, models the gospel in that all are invited to partake freely (2 Nephi 9:50). As Joseph Smith said, "Friendship is one of the grand fundamental principles of 'Mormonism'; [it is designed] to revolutionize and civilize the world, and cause wars and contentions to cease and men to become friends and brothers."[25] Both the Games and the gospel encourage us to "love (our) neighbor as (ourselves)" (Matthew 22:39). The world says choose associates based on popularity, wealth, or fame, but the Lord reminds us what really matters is the heart (1 Samuel 16:7). In sport you may be from different countries, but you are equal on the competition field with identical opportunity to succeed. In mortality we have different backgrounds, but we are all children of God with equal opportunity to follow the paths of salvation.

I fear this principle of respect gets lost nowadays in sports due to our obsession with winning, so when I work with athletes I stress the importance of regarding their teammates as equals. No bobsled driver wins without his brakeman or pushers and vice versa. A winning quality found within all championship teams is a genuine respect and a desire to help each other become their best.

Similarly during mortality we must surround ourselves with a team of good influences who respect us and give us the strength to make it safely down the track of life. We need trustworthy colleagues who push us to become our best, support us, and lift us when we fall. Real teammates dream your dream and push you to achieve your potential. Is everyone we associate with going to be like this? No. But to become the champions the Lord needs us to be, we should use wise judgment to surround ourselves with teammates who strengthen us in the gospel and brighten our lives. Like a well-timed bobsled push, the respectful influence of good colleagues will move us forward.

Over the years I have trained, associated, and served with some of the greatest athletes in the world. I don't mean their physical prowess or athletic talents, though I'm constantly amazed at their achievements. No, I mean the greatness of their minds and spirits. These athletes are some of the most wonderful people I have ever met, such positive, courageous, and genuinely compassionate human beings. From gold medalists to world champions, national heroes to humble competitors, these "teammates" have blessed my life far more than I could ever express.

One such athlete was a literal teammate, Lane Mixon. Lane is a natural motivator who is upbeat, funny, and goal oriented. From the moment I met him during the 2005–2006 season, I knew Lane was the kind of athlete I wanted to slide with. The outside world would notice his strength and speed, but I loved working with Lane because of his dedication and attitude. Lane was constantly pushing himself to become faster and stronger and always checked to make sure I was doing the same. His excitement about the sport and his goals motivated me to work harder and stay positive about my own dreams. Whenever I had a bad run down the track, he was the first to get my mind back into a positive mode. I always knew Lane respected me in the spirit of true brotherhood, and I relied on his support time and time again. I cannot express how much I admire him.

Lane's friendship is but a representation of the caliber of teammates we need to surround ourselves with in life, people who respect us, lift our spirits, highlight our strengths, and help us overcome our weaknesses. As Christ taught, true teammates "lift up the hands which hang down, strengthen the feeble knees" (Doctrine and Covenants 81:5). And sometimes that means they have to respectfully remind us to live up to our potential.

As a speaker I often ask audience members about their dreams; I believe every person is inspired with ideas they should pursue. From career goals to athletic pursuits, academic dreams to artistic ambitions, there is no limit to what the human spirit can envision and achieve. We are children of the living God and as such possess an inherent ability to do amazing things, so we must be careful about false teammates who would destroy those ambitions. Good ones will *always* help us raise our light high.

When I started bobsled in 1997, I had yet to receive my auto driver's license, and since we lived in Sandy, which was forty minutes away from Park City, this travel itinerary was kind of hard to complete without (a) a car and (b) a license. Enter Mom.

My mom has always been an incredible teammate, especially during that first season. Despite the pressures of working part-time, raising four kids, and taking care of our home, Mom took it upon herself to be my personal bobsled chauffeur. We would leave an hour and a half before training started so we could arrive on time. Then, while I spent the next two hours on the ice, Mom usually read a book in her car or ran errands, then drove me home.

Mom was there for every race and never complained about my athletic dreams. I can only imagine the personal sacrifices she made behind the scenes to help afford the training, the competitions, and all the equipment, race fees, and other costs involved with such an expensive sport. The night before the 1999 Western Regionals, she stayed up late to hand-sew American flag patches onto the jackets I purchased for my team. I am where I am today because of everything she has done for me. Thanks, Mom! When I asked her why she was so supportive of a sport she was afraid I could get hurt in, she responded, "It never crossed my mind not to support you. You enjoyed it and it made you happy."

Now think back on a time in your life when a friend or loved one told you, "I believe in you." How much did that mean? Whether it was at your big football game, during your mission, or as you changed careers, doesn't it mean the world to have someone respect and support you? Real teammates like Lane and my mom support.

But that doesn't mean they should go easy on us. One of the greatest athletic trainers (also the most brutal) I ever had was Doug Hill. Tracey Anderson, a skeleton athlete, introduced me to Doug, and at first everything was great. We did some easy lifts, ran a few sprints, did some plyometrics—no big deal.

As the weeks went by, however, the exercises and drills turned into "I'm going to die" activities. I joked that we were in a boot camp run by a sadistic drill sergeant. People at the Jewish Community Center where we trained would watch us do exercises that I swear Doug made up. Mr. Miyagi had nothing on Doug as far as creativity goes.

Now, don't get the wrong idea. Doug was being the *best* kind of trainer you can have by choosing exercises that would increase our athletic ability and therefore our bobsled potential. My teammate Mark and I knew exactly what he was doing, and we trusted him with our health and dreams. In return he did more than push our physical limits. Doug constantly shared motivational thoughts and quotes, and he was always smiling (from enjoying the torture, no doubt). His positive attitude gave us strength to work harder. When he introduced us to other patrons at the gym, he proudly talked about our athletic dreams. I believe he did this to show us how much he respected us.

One week I had so much going on that I had to cancel a training session. Doug and I emailed back and forth to reschedule, but we kept running into conflicts. Doug finally wrote back, "Why don't we meet at 5:00 a.m.?" *Five in the morning?*

Now five o'clock isn't horrible, but to make it I had to get up around 3:30 a.m. My first thought was "He's nuts." But then I reviewed my goals and when I saw that Doug was willing to get up just as early to help me work toward them I couldn't say no. Doug pushed me to be my best, but he also sacrificed to help me get there.

I could go on and on about the incredible associates that God has brought into my life, but you get the idea. These friends, family members, fellow athletes, sponsors, coaches, ward members, and coworkers have become part of Team Jeremy Holm's Mortality. They are true teammates who have sought to build me up and help me pursue my worthy goals, and to them I give a heartfelt thanks.

I'm not suggesting that the only teammates we gather in mortality are those ready to die for us. But life, like a big competition, can be tough, and we need good people who respect us and will stick with us through it all. To become the champion the Lord knows you can be, surround yourself with teammates who support and encourage you in your dreams as you go about "doing much good." Choose associates who will help you be the light unto the world that God intends you to be.

Are your current "teammates" building you up and helping you become your best? If not, if they are negative influences that tear you down or weaken your gospel resolve, I suggest you reevaluate what their "friendship" means. As an athlete you cannot hold onto teammates who inhibit your chances for success.

I encourage you to *find* and *be* winning teammates in this life. Live in the spirit of brotherhood and respect both the gospel and the Olympics promote, for we are all striving for the same eternal goal. And this isn't a race for first place; the Lord has plenty of celestial gold medals to go around (see John 14:2).

TEAMMATES WATCH EACH OTHER'S BACKS

We give several things an almost treasure-like status in bobsled: our runners, our health, and our team/teammates. You would think that medals and trophies fall in this category, but although they are cherished objects, the memories and experiences of an athletic career far outweigh the tangible things that rust and fade.

We protect our runners due to cost and required upkeep and our health, for obvious reasons. As for our teammates, if you were going to dedicate your life to an Olympic-sized goal, wouldn't you be careful who you trusted along the way?

As you know by now, bobsled is a team sport, so you look for athletes who share your level of dedication, discipline, and determination. To be successful as a team, you must be able to rely on each other. Imagine what it would feel like to step onto the ice at the Olympics when you knew that one of your teammates did not want to win and was going to sabotage your efforts.

While we all desire to have and be good life-teammates, some people in this world really *do* want to sabotage our efforts. And they want to do more than steal a gold medal from us; Satan's followers want to rob our happiness and eternal salvation. Underneath their smile lies someone who for one reason or another comes "in sheep's clothing, but inwardly they are ravening wolves." (Matthew 7:15). They may want your money, your business, or sometimes just to "dig a pit for [you, their] neighbor" (2 Nephi 28:8) and push you in so they can get what they want.

I have seen this far too often in sports with athletes or teams who do whatever it takes to win, including tossing aside basic good sportsmanship if it will get them one step closer to the gold medal, championship ring, or competition trophy. Sadly, these individuals forget that any trophy or medal earned at the cost of their ideals and standards is no victory at all; it's a personal loss.

Real teammates, however, protect their associates no matter the cost. You can tell how much someone values his spouse, children, friends, the gospel, and his athletic teammates by the degree to which he strives to look after them. Most problems arise in marriages or within a group dynamic because this stops being the case. When you stop caring for those who matter most, you stop treating them like the champions they are.

A few years ago I began assisting the presidents of the Utah chapter of the US Olympians Association. Debbie Stark-Clark, one of the presidents, was kind enough to write the forward for this book. Debbie and Blaine Lindgren, another president who won silver in the high hurdles at the 1964 Tokyo Games, have been amazing mentors to me as we have coordinated service projects, charity outreaches, fundraisers, parade marches, dinners, show booths, and public programs with Utah's past, present, and future Olympians. As we worked for the growth of others and the promotion of sport and the Olympic movement, these wonderful spirits became precious parts of my life that inspired me to reach higher. My association with Debbie, Blaine and all the other athletes reminds me of the scripture, "A faithful friend is a strong defense. And he that hath found . . . one hath found a treasure" (Ecclesiastes 6:14).

To me the words "strong defense" indicate that true teammates protect you physically, mentally, and emotionally. I have been blessed through my friendship with athletes like Debbie and Blaine who have been a strong defense for me against discouragement, temptation, and fear. And over the years I have seen the way they protect and defend others in the spirit of Olympism because, and here is the key, *they value them so highly*. They are full of charity and love for their fellow man.

And while these great people are viewed by the world as almost-gods, we in the Church are surrounded by individuals who are striving for exaltation, which is to become gods. Do we treasure our good teammates and lift them like Debbie and Blaine do for others?

A bobsled team must be unified and stand as a strong defense for each other. It can be something as small as spotting for your teammate in the weight room or supporting each other during a public relations event or stepping in when another athlete starts to cause problems. A teammate who has got your back is "a treasure," especially since when you travel for a sport like bobsled your team becomes your family.

However, as any married couple can attest, a good teammate may not always believe in, or agree with, the same things you do, but they will at least respect your viewpoint. So, do your "teammates" help you live your beliefs, or do they try to turn you from them? In sports, breaking the "commandments," the rules, can get you disqualified, and the thing about team events like bobsled is that the whole team can lose if just *one* member breaks a regulation. You can have the fastest, most powerful teammate in the world, but if he or she won't follow the rules, he or she will do more harm than good. A teammate who pushes you to break the rules is a liability, because he or she can cost you the game, the tournament, or perhaps even your career. Similarly a group or individual that desires to lead us away from the safety of the Church is not a dependable association.

So real teammates help us stay true to our standards. Sometimes our so-called "friends" taunt us to give in and break the commandments, but in my opinion it takes more strength and is much cooler to stick to the Lord's rules. People who want you to sin are not real friends, so stand your ground as a champion with faith when someone seeks to tear you down spiritually, emotionally, mentally, or physically.

And as disciples of Christ we should be the kind of friend or colleague or spouse that is a "strong defense" against evil, discouragement, temptation, fear, and the pains of this world. Just as there is no turning back as a team, once we have started down the bobsled track, there is no retreat in the competition for salvation, no time-outs. Much like the Lamanites of old, Satan seeks to enslave mankind (to sin) so we will be as miserable as he is. To do our best we must find teammates who will help us stand firm against Satan's evils, teammates like the unknown soldier who stepped forward to defend his teammate, Captain Moroni, against a very real danger.

It's a story that doesn't get much attention, but in Alma 44 the Nephites and Lamanites fought a major battle on the banks of the river Sidon. The Nephites gained the upper hand, so Captain Moroni told his men to stop fighting and pull back. He only fought to defend his people, not because he delighted in the bloodshed (Alma 48:11).

Moroni told the Lamanites that if they would promise not to fight anymore, they could go home. Some wisely accepted and promised never to return. But not Zerahemnah; no, he was so full of wickedness that he threw his weapons down at Moroni's feet and said, "Behold, here are our weapons of war; we will deliver them up unto you, but we will not suffer ourselves to take an oath unto you, which we know that we shall break . . . but take our weapons of war, and suffer that we may depart into the wilderness; otherwise we will retain our swords, and we will perish or conquer" (Alma 44:8).

Zerahemnah had no desire to protect and care for his army; it was all about him. He wanted to conquer the Nephites, and if his soldiers had to perish to achieve his goals, well, that was just too bad. When Moroni told him that his only choice was to make the oath or perish, Zerahemnah grabbed his sword and charged. Just as he was about to swing, one of Moroni's soldiers stepped forward and smote Zerahemnah's sword "even to the earth, and it broke by the hilt" (Alma 44:12).

We do not know what Moroni's reaction was, but we can imagine how he must have felt toward this brave teammate who stepped forward to defend his captain. We may not have his name, but I am certain Captain Moroni never forgot this faithful friend.

I have had such courage displayed in my behalf during a particularly difficult time in my bobsled career. When I was coaching the US Adaptive Bobsled group there was an important meeting held in which my position as head coach was one of the main topics discussed. I did not know this beforehand and was not in attendance. I had driven straight to the track from my office where I received a text saying the meeting was going later than planned. I rushed to the track's start area to find the person in charge of ice time to ask (beg) for a later check-in so our teams could still train during the evening's session.

It wasn't until later, after I received another text saying the program's time was cancelled (and therefore mine wasted), that I found out what happened.

A few of the older (in age) athletes who happened to be on the board of directors did not completely agree with the way I was coaching the program. I was pushing hard to improve everyone's game and increase their level of competitiveness from club-level to competition-ready. The goal of the adaptive bobsled movement, after all, was the 2014 or 2018 Paralympic Games. These athletes needed to be ready if that truly was their goal.

Unfortunately this format naturally favored the athletes who were faster and stronger or were willing to put in the effort to become so. The "senior" athletes did not like feeling second-rate to "rookie drivers," even ones who were working harder and performing better. Sure, I made mistakes, but I gave everything to the group and in a single season with the help of a few others managed to improve the program greatly. I feel that the ensuing scenario demonstrates the kind of coach I tried to be.

When it was announced that I may be removed as coach, the program's team captain, Cody Reese, immediately stood and said, "I will not slide without Coach Holm." A second athlete, Brandon Larson, stood and said the same. Then a third, a fourth, a fifth, and so on until well over two-thirds of the program's active athletes drew the line in the sand (I mean ice) and gave their ultimatum. If I left, they would go too.

I had no idea this was going on. I was at the top of the track trying to negotiate a way for the athletes to slide after the meeting ran late, but when I found out what occurred and the incredible outpouring of support and defense that those athletes stood and gave for me, I was humbled. Looking back at what Cody did, I cannot help but draw a parallel to the soldier who stepped forward to defend Captain Moroni. Both selflessly put themselves at risk for someone they believed in and believed was worth protecting.

I am grateful for the protective influence of my teammates, literal and figurative, who over the years have helped me make right decisions and become a better person. Their love, faithfulness, and support mean the world to me and have guided me to be the man I am today and have been a strong defense against the storms of life.

May we choose gold-medal teammates who, like Cody and Captain Moroni's soldier, will help us to do what is right and be the champions the Lord wants us to be.

OLYMPIC-LEVEL COMPASSION

Over the years I have been blessed to make friends in sport from Australia, Canada, Norway, Japan, Jamaica, Mexico, and so on. No matter what language we spoke, the spirit of athletic camaraderie has led to relationships that will last forever.

One of my favorite memories involves assisting an Australian team prepare to race in the 2010 Vancouver Olympics. I loaned Jeremy (what a great name) Rolleston and his brakeman Jason the use of our four-man sled and coached on the side. Some of my teammates jumped in to provide a full crew, so to say thanks they bought us a case of beer only to discover that we didn't drink, which brought a good laugh.

Now, this experience doesn't involve any races, medals, or publicity, but I love this memory because of the service rendered. Of all the competitors I have met, the ones who stand out the most aren't those with the biggest names or the longest list of victories. They are the ones who demonstrate a championship-level of care and respect for those around them. One that stands is my teammate Don Osmond.

Yes, Don is the son of *the* Donny Osmond. We met during my sophomore year of college, and I found Don to be one of the best friends you could ever have. He was always the first to reach out to someone who needed support and always put forth the extra effort to say something nice about everyone. I will never forget the time Don flew home to Utah from New York in the spring of 2007, the season before he tried bobsled for the first time and blacked out on me. That's right, he blacked out as my brakeman on his first trip down the track, which is why he has the nickname "Blackout." But I digress.

We both had hectic schedules, but we made time for a quick dinner to catch up during his visit. It was during a trying time in my life, and Don could see that. In a truly Christlike manner, he listened as I explained all that was going on. He reminded me of the good in my life and encouraged me to find the happiness that the Lord wanted to bless me with. I left that dinner feeling refreshed in spirit because of Don's advice. His friendship reminds me of the French proverb, "A faithful friend is an image of God." Thank you, Don. You gave me the push I needed to get back out there.

Don's friendship reminds me that building any championship squad starts with people who care and share in our mutual goals. And while it is an honor to be part of a winning athletic team, it can never replace our membership in the "household of God" (Ephesians 2:1). We are blessed as Latter-day Saints because we are surrounded by loving neighbors, home and visiting teachers, Scoutmasters, living prophets, apostles, bishops, etc. When we enter the waters of baptism, we join a team of billions on both sides of the veil who "are willing to bear one another's burdens . . . mourn with those that mourn . . . and comfort those that stand in need of comfort" (Mosiah 18:8–9).

Truly association with the Saints is one of the greatest joys in this world, and Church membership allows us to participate on the greatest team on earth, for what squad has a greater intention than sharing the gospel, perfecting the Saints and redeeming the dead? And if love is the basic tenant of our faith, then love is the guiding emotion for our team. We want to win eternal life, which means being with those we love for eternity, but we also want to help as many of our teammates as possible to win that prize.

In this way the ancient Greeks were more gospel-like than our society's view on winning. The earliest Olympics emphasized effort, discipline of mind and body, and the perfection of the athlete's soul. True, Greek victors were heralded as heroes like today, but a major difference was that whether an athlete came in first or last every struggle was honored because it meant growth through courageous effort. In our modern view of athletic competition, it is kill or be killed, win at any cost. It doesn't matter that the silver medalist was only .01 behind the gold medalist—they still lost. This focus on caring for the winner alone has created a mountain of problems in the sporting world. If we think like this, then a gold medal means your life's work paid off, while a silver medal means your efforts were worthless. What a tragedy.

As Latter-day Saints we are to cheer/care for everyone, regardless of their title or status. While from a mortal perspective success is a marker for levels of respect, the Lord asks us to do better. When the disciples argued over who "should be accounted the greatest" (Luke 22:24), as if they wanted to know who would get the spiritual gold medal, Jesus corrected them by stating that the kings of the gentiles (earthly leaders) exercise authority over those around them, but "he that is chief, (should be) he that doth serve" (verse 26). This instruction is made all the more powerful because the Savior then humbly served by washing the disciples' feet (John 13).

When I think of my friend and teammate Don, I cannot help but see a type of the Savior's love and the way he expects us to live. To Don it didn't matter what your job or title was, how much money you made, or what kind of car you drove. He cared just the same. We should remember that one of the greatest tenants of the gospel is that the prophet and the Primary teacher have the same opportunity for celestial glory as long as they prove faithful. Titles, portfolios, and other earthly awards are not specie to be traded for exaltation. As Peter taught Simon, "the gift(s) of God (cannot) be purchased with money" (Acts 18:18–23). The scriptures remind us that all earthly possessions, even Olympic medals, will be left behind when we leave this world. No wonder the gospel is so focused on helping us move beyond selfishness and into a life that is full of service and love for our fellow man. At the end of the day, we all claim the title "Child of God," and that is all that matters.

I think that is one of my favorite aspects of bobsled. During any given ice session, you can have Latter-day Saints training alongside Catholics, Evangelists, Atheists, and Buddhists. You may have a pre-law student competing on the same team as a soldier, a personal trainer, and a general contractor. You can have twenty different languages spoken under twenty different flags all dressed in equally different uniforms. But take those *superficial* differences away and you are left with equality. We are all competing in the same sport under the same rules on the same ice. Each athlete is there to do his or her best, to pursue his or her dreams, and to represent his or her country.

Whether on the ice, in our homes, at work, or in our hobbies and pursuits, we all want "teammates" who genuinely care. No paycheck, gold medal, new car or job title can ever replace the satisfaction and happiness that comes from having even one good friend, one good teammate we feel Christlike love for. True teammates care not because of what we can offer; rather, these faithful friends and loved ones value us because they care for us unconditionally. To these wonderful mortal angels we have value simply because we are *us*; they focus on what's underneath.

During the 2006–2007 season, I acquired a set of four-man runners that needed a lot of work. Whoever had stored them for the past year or two had covered the runners with some unidentifiable sticky substance, then wrapped them in paper towels before leaving them in an outdoor storage bin. When I began to unwrap their mummy-like packaging, I shook my head. Rust had formed over most of the exterior, and the unknown sticky substance etched the pattern of the paper towels into the metal surfaces. To the outside observer the runners looked terrible, but I knew that underneath the ugly exterior was a set of blades that would help our times improve.

So we got to work. Using plenty of acetone and various tools, my teammates and I removed the hardened paper towel/sticky substance mixture before sanding the rough surfaces down until there were blisters on our hands. In the end, the once visibly damaged runners were smooth and clean. Their outside appearance may have been unfavorable, but what lay underneath is what really mattered.

When it comes to being a caring teammate to those around us, what do we look for? Do we notice clothes, social status, and even spiritual standing first, or do we strive to look at others through the loving eyes of Jesus Christ? This compassionate philosophy seems contradictory to the world of sports where so much focus is placed on being "tough." The Lord's mortal journey, however, was full of humble service. His example reminds us that what really matters is our worth as sons and daughters of God.

Basically the Lord asks us to practice good sportsmanship. When I watch a victorious athlete rub the other team's face in their defeat, I feel as though a greater loss has occurred. Is it bad to revel in a win? Of course not! Victories, no matter how small, should be celebrated with enthusiasm. However, everyone is deserving of respect. Athletes who understand this are the ones who shake hands with opponents post-game and thank them for the game. The media ignores the loser, while a real winner remembers that they, too, are deserving of admiration for the effort put forth in the competition. After all, "the important thing in life is not the triumph, but the struggle."[26] A gold medalist and the athlete who came in last place are still children of God, and that underlying value never changes with a victory or a loss.

I like those words, "underlying value," kind of like the value of those four-man runners we cleaned up; their value lay underneath what was visible. Similarly the Lord knows our true value, and that is what he bases his love for us on.

By its definition, *unconditional* means "without condition." The Lord and our Father in Heaven love us unconditionally, and when we learn to see others through their eyes, we will stop looking for what the world values (fame, material possessions, and beauty) and focus on being a teammate who lifts, inspires tolerance and promotes goodwill. After all, these are the main themes of the Olympic spirit and the gospel alike.

The Savior's parable of the Good Samaritan is a powerful example of sportsmanship/Christlike service. How often in life do we find ourselves feeling "stripped" and "beaten" by our trials, fears, or mistakes as the poor traveler was by thieves? We go on with our daily lives, passed by on either side by strangers and acquaintances who simply don't care or who pretend that nothing is wrong.

But think about how much it means when a Good Samaritan reaches out to lift and heal. My friends, we must open our hearts to the promptings of the Spirit and be good Samaritans/teammates who reach out to the lonely, the sick, and the afflicted. We can be the Lord's champions and build up those around us every day. Every person we encounter is a son or daughter of God, and the good sportsmanship that the Olympics promote can be a guiding light as we remember that each person's divine heritage is far greater than any earthly achievement.

As C. S. Lewis once said, "It is a serious thing to live in a society of possible gods and goddesses, to remember that the dullest and most uninteresting person you talk to may one day be a creature which, if you saw it now, you would be strongly tempted to worship . . . There are no 'ordinary' people. You have never talked to a mere mortal."[27]

The ancient Greeks held their games to worship the gods. It is my prayer that we can remember that we are surrounded by gods in the making. May we honor and serve those around us and remember that no matter what titles or social status a person holds (or lacks), they are not "mere mortals"; they are children of God.

Let us cultivate a spirit of forgiveness, patience, and Christlike love. It might take some effort, but it is worth it, especially in our marriages and families. Satan knows that a good team relationship, especially one bound by a temple covenant, can be a powerful influence in our lives, so watch out for his cheap shots.

Our earthly teammates are Heavenly gifts; treasure them. Let us forgive and forgive often. One of the greatest things about my teammates over the years is that not one has ever gotten angry over a mistake I made on the way down the track. Oh, sure, they may complain or give me grief if I bump a wall or come out of a turn too late and we flop down hard, but they have always kept it in the realm of a team error. "*We* came out of Turn Four late" or "What can *we* do better next time?" Knowing that we can overcome any mistakes as a team makes a huge difference. We are stronger, more open in our communication, and more supportive instead of critical. Of course we get frustrated sometimes, but we have always constructively talked about what we can do to better ourselves as a team. We aren't perfect, but every step forward means progress.

Speaking of progress, reach out to those who have grown away from the Church. A good "teammate" is always worth finding again, and your love, friendship, and example may be the lifeline they need to come back to the Lord. Sometimes we must reach beyond our comfort zones and our own circle of friends and bring in those who are wandering, no matter how imperfect they may be, because to God they are still champions of infinite worth.

Basically, when you take away all the hate, jealousy, and judgment, of humanity, what is left? Love. And love is better than any gold medal and worth more than any championship ring. As Moroni taught, we must "cleave unto charity, which is the greatest of all, for . . . charity is the pure love of Christ, and it endureth forever; and whoso is found possessed of it at the last day, it shall be well with him" (Moroni 7:46–47). Be a champion of the Lord; be a teammate who cares.

A FRIENDSHIP GREATER THAN SILVER AND GOLD

In bobsled instead of a steering wheel we use intricate guidance systems designed around carefully engineered resistance structures and a center axle pivot point. Ropes connect this system to two D-shaped rings the driver holds, which is how he pilots a sled. Pull left to go left, right to go right, and pull both back to go straight. The thing about bobsled steering systems is that they have an alignment, just like a car and teams check it regularly.

The alignment can be adjusted partially by fine-tuning what we call the "return bungees" inside the nose of the sled. When they are both tightened with the same amount of resistance, they help keep the front axle straight, like properly aligned tires on a car. But if one is pulled tighter than the other, the front runners will point off to one side, which leads to a few problems. First, if your alignment is off when you make a steering correction, you won't actually be driving like you think. If your alignment is off five degrees and you make a five-degree steering correction, you'll actually end up with a ten-degree difference. The second problem with misalignment is when you pull back on the ropes in a straightaway you'll drift to whichever side the misalignment favors. Ultimately, if you have a skewed alignment, you aren't in full control of the direction the sled is traveling; the uncorrected problem will always pull you off course. Bobsled lesson number forty: keep your sled aligned.

Like the steering system in a bobsled, those whom we spend the most time with will alter the alignment of our lives and therefore affect the direction in which we are headed. Bad influences can affect our lives like a misaligned steering system in a bobsled. Peer pressure can act like the tightening of one return bungee on a bobsled—you may find yourself heading in directions you never wanted to go.

After so many years in bobsled, I can't give enough credit to the friends and family members who have meant so much to me, who have helped me stay on track (literally and spiritually). However, when I think about who has been the greatest example of a true and loyal teammate, who has kept me aligned with the principles of righteousness, only one person comes to mind: Jesus Christ. He is the teammate that never gives up, never turns his back and never stops trying to help me reach my potential. Through bobsled, my mission, vacations, and so forth, I have had the opportunity to travel all over the world, and one thing that brings me absolute peace is the knowledge that no matter where I go, the Savior is always by my side.

For example, I was the only member of the Church on a trip to the Calgary, Canada, track in 1998. It was an amazing experience for all of us, but there was a personal aspect of my journey that increased my testimony and deepened my trust in the Savior.

While the other athletes watched TV during evening free time, I felt a desire to draw closer to Christ because I knew my relationship with him would give me strength and clarity as an athlete. So before bed I took my Book of Mormon to the empty cafeteria and read by the green glow of the soda machine. As I feasted on the words of the prophets in a place where Olympic athletes ate their meals, the Spirit filled me with a deep peace. During our ensuing training sessions, I felt that Christ was with me. I learned that it doesn't matter where you are; Jesus will be there to support and love you because he wants you to triumph.

As a teammate Christ has absolute faith in you and your abilities. He is there for every competition and training session of life. With unconditional love it is his voice that cheers and coaches the loudest from the sidelines and encourages us to do our best. He is the support we can lean on during our tough "scrimmages" or when we make mistakes on the field. When the game of life seems against us, the Savior is always for us.

Now good teammates challenge us to add another weight plate to the bar in the gym or run one more sprint on the track. They egg us on to push the sled harder or dare us to drive the sled faster. Well, when we stay close to the Savior, we gain strength to live as he would have us live, but we can rest assured that he is going to challenge us and call us to rise to our highest potential even when we don't feel ready for it.

Seven months into my mission, I found myself in a chapel in San Pedro Sula, Honduras, with about one hundred other missionaries. My companion was getting transferred, so I was anxious to find out who my new mission teammate was. Well, as my friend and former district leader, now an assistant to the president, called out my name, I was shocked to hear that not only would I be receiving a new companion, but I was also now a trainer, a senior companion, and a district leader, all in one shot. I went in a junior companion and came out overwhelmed.

My new companion Elder Billy Rodriguez became one of my best friends from the mission field, but even so I remember wondering what the Lord was thinking. Didn't he know about all my limitations, weaknesses, and inadequacies? When I expressed my concerns to our mission president Rene Oliva, he challenged me to read Joshua 1:9, which says, "Have I not commanded thee? Be strong and of a good courage; be not afraid, neither be thou dismayed: for the Lord thy God is with thee whithersoever thou goest." President Oliva reminded me that with Christ as my teammate, I had no reason to fear.

And yet, in mercy far greater than I deserved, the Lord has been there even when I was afraid. He was there when I feared that I could not make it through the MTC, when I feared that my life was over, when I wondered if I should give up bobsled, and on countless other occasions. He has been there when I won and loved me when I lost, in bobsled, the gospel and in life. It is only now, years later, that I have come to see that I needed bobsled in my life because of the way it brought me to the Savior. Jesus asked Peter to come to him on water; he asked me to come to him on ice.

So how do I thank him? It's easy to shake my teammates' hands or give them a man-hug after a race, but how do I thank the Savior? I follow his example and show gratitude through service to my fellow man.

As I mentioned earlier when I organized the first ever American adaptive bobsled camp in September 2011, one of my main goals was to connect with each of the attending athletes. It was a challenge given the busy schedule I had as camp planner and head coach, but I prayed daily for opportunities to serve each competitor and interested participant.

On the first day, after an evening session that focused on the basics of sled mechanics and maintenance, I kept my eye on one camp attendee, Koloa Wolfgramm, who had been quiet during the earlier classes and activities of the day. I silently wondered what he was thinking about this new sport (for him) and if he was really interested in pursuing it.

Well, I made it my goal to reach out to him. But how? The opportunity presented itself as the other attendees filed back inside for free time before dinner. Koloa and I were left alone outside with one of our two-man bobsleds, and I initiated a conversation to get to know him better. After a few minutes I had the thought, "Why not let him sit in the sled and try it?" So I invited him to do so and wow, what a change came over his face once he sat in the driver's seat. His eyes lit up and a big smile split his face as he blurted out, "Oh, wow!" He was hooked.

Koloa went on to become an excellent brakeman and an even better sled pilot before serving a mission for the Lord, the same Lord who was watching over both of us that Park City evening and knew exactly what we both needed for our individual athletic futures.

It is this relationship with Christ that made Moroni, Alma, Paul, and Joseph Smith so great, the same relationship that can make all of us great. When we develop closeness to the Savior, he can better lead us to great heights. Whether that means finding the strength to make it to the Olympics, go on a mission, or start a family, Christ must be the central member of our team on this earth. If we do so we will discover a teammate who offers peace, love, strength, and genuine concern. He believes in us so much that he offered his life to help us achieve the greatest goal of all: exaltation. Much like the miracle of turning water into wine (John 2:10), Christ can take our weaker, more tepid hearts and turns them into something stronger.

I know how wonderful it feels to walk out before the crowd with your teammates and climb onto the podium as the medals are placed around your necks while the national anthem plays. That, my friends, is a little bit of heaven on earth. But as nice as that experience is, there will come a day, after the race of life is over, when we will climb on divine ground and be crowned, not merely medaled, before a gathering of heavenly teammates. I know without a doubt that tears will fall when we are so rewarded by he who supported us through it all. When we see the Savior, the love in his eyes will melt away all our sorrows and heal even our most secret wounds.

I hope we surround ourselves with teammates who help us prepare for that day. Let us in turn live as champions of the Lord, champions who stand for charity, kindness, and respect. In this manner we can better honor the Savior and his own selfless sacrifice for us, the teammates he gave his life for. And at the end of the day, whether we "won" or "lost," there will always be one voice calling from Heavenly stands, the voice of a beloved teammate who cheers us forward to the finish line. Jesus is by our side every step of the way, and for that I am eternally grateful.

THE WORTH OF GOALS IS GREAT

Every once in a while we see a pilot fail to make it in the sled during the Push Start, which always makes me cringe because the sled becomes a ballistic missile heading down the track. Sometimes nothing happens and sometimes the sled and track end up pretty beat up. Regardless of the outcome, once an empty sled *starts* moving, it isn't *stopping* until the finish, which is a good metaphor for mortal life.

From birth to death we are constantly experiencing, learning, aging, and growing, but there is no stopping the mortal clock until the ride is over. But aspiration is the driver of our lives, and without it we can become pilotless "sleds" that just go wherever life takes us. The question is what direction do we want to travel in? We are not here to drift; we are here for gold, and goals can help us get there *if* we want to.

In February 1998, Randy, our coach, planned a race for the athletes involved in Utah's first youth bobsled program. Everything was brand new, and most of us only had a handful of runs on the ice in *tiny* sleds that were less than half the size of our normal two-man bobsleds. But we were excited to race and grateful that our loved ones came to support. Besides, we needed them. Back then our parents "volunteered" to help move our sleds around and get them out of the track at the bottom (our speeds were too slow to make it to the finish line.) The race started much lower on the track, near turn eleven of the fifteen-curve course so we hit mind-blowing speeds of about thirty-five miles per hour.

A part of me still knew the race was an opportunity to progress. I had taken my first ride down the track two months before and experienced a few weeks of on-ice training, so the competition was a natural milestone on my path to "greater glory." A quiet inner voice kept reminding me that this *was* a race and that I should get ready.

I met up with my parents and veteran sled pilot Bruce Rosselli, who had been competing internationally for years. Bruce helped me review some of the basics of sled piloting, and the more we talked the greater grew my yearning for victory. My *desire* to win soon formed my *dream* of winning, but I took it one step further because a dream is just a wish; a *goal* is a concrete objective. Well, that gold medal became my concrete objective, and I was willing to do my part to get it. True greatness isn't just handed to anyone, and potential always requires effort to be reached. Our ability to turn desire into intelligent action can mean the difference between victory and defeat on the ice or in mortal life so always go for the "goal-ed."

So if life is constantly moving forward, what are you going to do with the time you have been given? Like I did that February evening, most of us desire to do our best and reach our potential. We fought hard in the War in Heaven for the opportunity to come here, and we want to leave our mark in the world. We have righteous desires.

But desire, like faith, is not enough; we must *do*. Plenty of people want good things but never get off the couch to make them happen. To be the peculiar people that the Lord wants us to be requires (1) righteous desires, (2) setting goals based on those desires, and (3) taking the steps necessary to make our goals reality.

Since this would be my first bobsled race ever, I fought the pre-race jitters. Yet despite the butterflies, my *desire* to win was now my specific *goal*, and Bruce and I talked about how to make that goal happen, or what *actions* would bring success. Now it was up to me since our good desires and goals, when acted upon with real intent, can lead to great victories in life.

God did not send us to this earth to fail. Sure we may wander and lose a "game" here and there, but in the end he sent us to become champions. How are we honoring our divine heritage and our eternal potential? The Lord will hold us responsible for the ways we develop and use our time, talents and abilities (Matthew 25:14–30). Plus, if our ultimate desire is to become like our Heavenly Father, shouldn't we build our lives into something that he would be proud of?

For the race, my teammate Nick and I had good runs down the track, so after the competition we went to the awards ceremony at the Day Lodge, a building located by the new entrance to the park. I was surprised when our names were read as having won. First place in my first race? I could handle that. We grinned as the gold medals were placed around our necks, and I was grateful that Heavenly Father had helped me achieve my goal of doing well. I knew he expected me to do my best because anything less than that would be to sacrifice this beautiful gift we call mortal life.

We know we are of a noble birthright, a chosen generation that has been held in reserve to come forth at this time. What goals are we setting to progress and to help the Lord's work? God knows our potential; should we be surprised that he asks us to reach for it? As Elder Richard G. Scott taught, "The Lord has a purpose for you. . . . Discover it and fulfill it."[28] Righteous desires and goals help us discover that purpose and fulfill it. Just ask the brother of Jared.

After constructing the barges that would take his family to the Promised Land, this mighty prophet expressed concern that they had no way to get fresh air (Ether 2:19) and that there was no light within the vessels (verse 22). Here is a tiny nugget of gold found in the story. The Lord gave the brother of Jared a solution for the air problem (verse 20), but then he asked, "What will ye that I should do that ye may have light in your vessels?" Or in other words, "What is your solution to reach the desired objective?" I think the Lord was reminding the brother of Jared, and all of us, that the spark of light/knowledge/courage we need is often within us if we but look for it.

The brother of Jared's concern/desire for fresh air and light can be compared to our righteous desires, which bring freshness to our lives and light to the "vessels" of our hearts. Through experiences in bobsled, my mission, and everyday life, I have learned that great joy can be found when we set righteous goals that help us fulfill our part in God's plan since our spirits thrive on growth and development.

Let me be clear: I'm talking about taking our lives and making something of them while also serving those around us and building the kingdom. If acted upon, righteous desires and goals help us progress and become more like our Father in Heaven. And most of us have a desire in our hearts to do good things, sometimes even great things. We all have a bucket list of things we want to achieve. So what are we waiting for? Why ignore that flash of insight, that burning desire, or that clear vision of the soul? After years spent speaking and lecturing, I often see people hiding their dreams *from themselves*. They are embarrassed, as if the desire to do more with life is bad, and they bury their aspirations behind thoughts of "I'm not good enough" or "Who am I to succeed?" We sell ourselves short even when we know our eternal value, and I think this disappoints our Heavenly Father. Like any father, God wants his children to succeed and be happy, and we all want to be happy, right? I've never heard, "Hey Jeremy, I love misery. How can I be miserable?" Simple: don't believe in your dreams.

As spiritual beings having a mortal experience, our hopes and dreams represent a craving for growth and the opportunity to create. Could that be why we feel discouraged when we give up on those desires, because we know we are not giving it our best?

The optimistic and driven personalities of the athletes I associate with have brought light and joy into my life over the years. At first I wondered why they were so happy, but then I realized that their joy comes from listening to their heart's desires, and then they work their backsides off to make them come true. They also see a challenge in doing every little thing to the best of their ability. While an average man may be complacent in doing a "good job," champions are not satisfied until they have done their best.

But it all starts with a plan. President Howard W. Hunter said, "In order to accomplish the things we desire . . . we must have positive and definite goals in mind. Success in life . . . doesn't come by accident, but as the result of a well-defined plan and a concentrated effort to bring about a realization of the plan."[29]

In a way everything in the Church teaches us about goal setting. The gospel is designed to lift us to higher levels through faith, obedience, and the achievement of righteous goals and ordinances. It starts with faith/desire (like my desire to win that bobsled race) and continues through baptism, receiving the gift of the Holy Ghost, going on a full-time mission, marrying in the temple, partaking of the Sacrament, and so on. The gospel is a step-by-step process for eternal progression, and our worthy goals—whether spiritual, athletic, academic, financial, mental, or personal in nature—assist in that development. They move us forward, which is, by definition, *progress*.

But let's be honest: some goals require more effort to achieve than others, and that's where we get stuck. We have desires to do "much good," but instead of trying we say, "I could never do *that*." Maybe we are haunted by past mistakes or failures and believe they define our future, so we give up. Even worse, perhaps others have conditioned us to believe that we only deserve mediocrity. The result is we kill our goals before they get any traction, and if there is anything that pushing a several hundred-pound bobsled on ice has taught me it's that you need traction.

During the 1998–1999 season, I worked at the Park City track in the passenger ride program, which allowed customers to take a ride down the course in either a four-man bobsled or one-person sleds called "Ice Rockets."

The Ice Rockets were a blast (we may or may not have tied four of them together and gone down the track), but nothing beats a four-man ride. If you ever have the opportunity to take one, you won't regret it.

While working at the top of the track one afternoon, I learned about traction the hard way. Once the passengers were in their seats and the driver was ready, we grabbed the push handles and took off in a sprint down the start ramp. Most of the guys I worked with were also athletes, so we pushed for training and fun. Let's be honest: we were showing off.

But there was a problem. Since the sled was full of passengers, we could push at full speed but not jump in. The solution was to push the sled partway down the start ramp then let go and try to slow down before we hit turn one. That's where it got tricky.

As you know, in bobsled we normally wear special shoes made just for the sport that have several-hundred sharp spikes on the bottom. Well, I didn't have those yet, so I was wearing a cheap pair of sprinter's track spikes that just didn't cut it. I let go of the driver push bar and my world turned upside down. My feet slipped out from under me and I slammed down on my back on the ice so hard that my watch broke. I slid into the first turn as I tried to catch my breath and my pride.

As I got to my hands and knees, I shook my head to clear the cobwebs and turned to see the laughing faces of my coworkers. Then I took the fifty-meter "walk of shame" back up to the start area with all the customers, track crew, and my boss watching. Looking back on that experience, I have to agree: "Pride cometh before the fall."

I bought a new pair of bobsled shoes from my coach a few weeks later. Like the Grinch's heart they were two-sizes too small, but I didn't care. I was done eating ice.

Far too often when an idea or a desire pops into our mind or heart we quickly sweep the legs out from under it and push it down the track. We dismiss many opportunities without allowing them to gain some traction in our lives. It's tragic!

To accomplish our righteous desires and goals, we must give them traction through (1) faith in the Lord and his ability to help us achieve worthy goals, and (2) a strong belief in ourselves. If we lack one of these two fundamental foundations, we will lack the courage and willpower necessary to pursue our goals and will dismiss them instead.

Now, if you have reservations about your goals, are you doubting yourself or the Lord? Honestly, doubting either one is a waste of time, time that you don't have to waste (Alma 34:12). We can either let life choose what happens and therefore "slide by," or we can set and follow goals that will help us be the best that we can be and perform our own personal missions.

Elder Gene R. Cook said, "Many men go . . . go forth lost in the world with only a vague idea of what they would have from life. Some men decide what they want, commit themselves to obtain it, and in righteousness exercise their faith until they obtain [it]."[30]

Exercise your faith and let your righteous desires thrive. Don't worry about whether or not you can do it. With God all things are possible, so dream, and dream big. As President Gordon B. Hinckley said, "Believe in yourselves. Believe in your capacity to do some good in this world. God sent us here for a purpose, and that was to improve the worlds in which we live. The wonderful thing is that we can do it . . . Trust in the Lord."[31]

You can do great things with your life. You can be successful and impact the world around you for good. You can do all the great things that the desires of your heart are telling you to do, so write that book, get that degree, take your kids on vacation, memorize ten scriptures, start your non-profit, launch your new business, learn a new talent, and on and on. If fear holds you back, then put your fears on ice.

But how do we do all this? How do we take our righteous desires and turn them into accomplished goals? Well, in order to cross the finish line on a bobsled track, you have to take it one turn at a time. So let's take your righteous desires and figure out how to turn them into gold medal accomplishments.

CHOOSE A STAR AND FOLLOW IT TOWARD HEAVEN

I've heard a lot of people say how crazy a bobsled push start looks on TV, so I thought I'd explain how it works.

We practice pushing and loading into the sled on push tracks and dry land before we hit the ice. When a new athlete runs on ice for the first time, he may only take a few steps and load in. The next time, he takes a few more and picks up the pace. Finally he is loading in at full speed. What spectators don't see is that when you take four bobsled athletes that quickly load into a narrow bobsled with spiked bobsled shoes, occasionally we experience what I call "bobsled acupuncture." The spikes end up in the legs, back, and even shoulders of the teammate in front of you. Bobsled acupuncture is free, but so is the resulting punch from the spiked teammate.

Now the start ramp (or start track), where we push and load, begins at what we call the start (or push) block. The start block is about sixty inches wide and is partially frozen into the ice. We pull the sled in front of the start block and the team pushes off. And no, you can't start behind the block to get a running start.

Once we shout our cadence (audible queues to indicate we are ready), we push off the block and sprint through the push stretch. The push stretch is really dead area since our time does not officially start until we cross the first timing sensor about fifty feet later. After that we go over what we call the crest and begin sprinting down the start ramp, where we load into our sleds at carefully timed intervals.

But wait . . . who's driving the sled? If the pilot runs with the rest of the team, how does the sled stay straight during the push start? Well, beginning at the push block and running roughly two hundred feet are two grooves cut into the ice, appropriately called the "start grooves." These channels allow us to set the sled's runners into controlling tracks that keep the sled straight until the driver jumps in. Once the grooves end, the team is on their own.

The start grooves on the track act a bit like our parents and teachers during our developing years, but, like the end of the start grooves, there comes a time when we must walk on our own. As teenagers we start to define ourselves and develop our independence, which some do through rebellion and defiance, but for the vast majority of our wonderful youth, these years are spent preparing for missions, college, temple marriage, fulfilling careers, and further Church service.

So what happens when we've accomplished all the initial goals laid out for us by our parents, leaders, or the missionaries? What do we do when the spiritual start grooves end and we are in complete control of our bobsled, i.e. life? That's where those righteous desires and dreams come in. They become the "what's next?" once we turn them into specific goals.

Goals are crucial components of sports like bobsled. Coaches, trainers, sports psychologists, and nutritionists constantly work with athletes to set goals because they know that to stay motivated and increase their abilities, athletes need challenging ways to progress. And champions know that setting goals helps them develop their potential. Desires are the foundation, but goals and work build our dreams into success.

Concrete goals move our lives forward in productive and satisfying ways that bring joy and growth. Goals also allow us to serve the Lord and those around us, but we have to choose our goals. Heavenly Father may confirm our decisions or inspire us with ideas, but he will not force us to act, nor will he always tell us what to do (Doctrine and Covenants 58:42). He leaves much of life's "driving" up to us.

So what type of goals should we set? Here are two suggestions. First, while we know little about Jesus' childhood and youth, we do know he spent that time "(increasing) in wisdom and stature, and in favor with God and man" (Luke 2:52). By this example we can divide our goals into four main categories: wisdom (knowledge), stature (health/physical), favor with God (spiritual), and favor with man (social). My second suggestion for the setting of goals is to study the thirteenth article of faith. Is your goal honest, true, chaste, benevolent, virtuous, lovely, or praiseworthy, and will it do good to all men?

Ideas for goals can come in several ways. Perhaps we were inspired by a scripture or talk. Maybe the Spirit gave us a flash of insight of some course we should pursue. I find that ideas often flow during quiet moments of introspection. Sometimes the light flips on and says, "You really should do this." This can happen in the temple, in nature, on our knees, on a bobsled track, or just while driving home. If that happens, act. But I fear that too often we brush those insights aside as mere whims; be careful how quickly you push away inspiration. In addition, sometimes the Lord gives us specific goals and direction through our leaders, priesthood and patriarchal blessings, the counsel of friends and family, and the gospel itself. Stick to these objectives like glue.

As Latter-day Saints, we have a sacred obligation to seek out righteous and worthwhile ways to improve the world around us, but our Father in Heaven wants us to use our heads about it and is willing to help guide us if we but ask (Matthew 7:7). While a small goal may not need much contemplation, our larger goals require more thought, and we should seek to "first obtain (our) errand from the Lord" (Jacob 1:17) before we dedicate ourselves to them. But there's a caveat: we know we can receive confirmations to our decisions, but only after we have done our part through meditation and prayer (Doctrine and Covenants 9:8).

That being said, as a good coach the Savior may leave it up to us to decide what good things we will accomplish with our time, talents and resources. It's not that he doesn't care; rather, he cares enough to let us learn to walk on our own.

So let's try this. Grab a sheet of paper and write down a list of things you want to do in life. It can be to take a tenth of a second off your bobsled push start, serve a mission, get married in the temple, graduate from college, learn Italian, or even finish the vacation scrapbook. Anything that comes to mind is fair game, so don't let your mortal mind edit what your spirit is trying to say.

Now, from your list I want you to pick three goals that you want to achieve *within the next thirty days*. Circle them and then ask yourself why you want to achieve these things. Is it to better yourself? Is it to help someone else? Is it to further your talents? Is it to become more Christlike? Is it to help build the kingdom? Will it bring positive energy and happiness? Are you passionate about it? A lot of the time we know *what* we want. We might even know *how* to get it. But too often we fail to focus on *why* we really want it. I call this the Why-Because principle.

Why do we pray? Because we want to talk to God.

Why do we pay tithing? Because we want to be obedient and support the work.

Why do we eat? Because we are hungry.

Why do I want to achieve *X goal*? Because . . .

If our Why-Because formula is off-balance, then we will most likely fail to achieve even the best of goals. Figuring out the *why* of our goals is crucial *because* it gives us the motivation to pay the price necessary to achieve the objective. It also helps us decide if we really want to pursue a goal. The Savior taught the value of a Why-Because understanding when he asked, "For which of you, intending to build a tower, sitteth not down first, and counteth the cost, whether he have sufficient to finish it?" (Luke 14:28). We may not have all the money to finish our goal (yet). We may not have all the skills or abilities to do it either (yet). But if we have sufficient faith and determination to see things through (and work our backsides off) until the tower of our dreams is complete, then by all means let us proceed.

The Why-Because formula also helps us understand what gave the Savior the strength and courage to go complete his objective: his atoning sacrifice. Jesus accepted this sacred responsibility as "the Lamb slain from the foundation of the world" (Moses 7:47). But *why*? Why did he stand up in the premortal council and say, "here am I, send me" (Abraham 3:27)? Why did he endure the unimaginable agonies of Gethsemane (Doctrine and Covenants 19:15), the unlawful trials by the Jewish council, the mocking of the Roman soldiers, and finally the agonies of the cross? What is the Lord's *why* when it comes to accepting, embracing and fulfilling the role of our Savior? *Because* he loves us (Romans 8:37–39), and because of that love the Atonement was only one step (a crucially central one) toward his ultimate goal: to help us all reach exaltation and achieve eternal life (Moses 1:39). The Savior's love provided the desire and strength to volunteer for the most heroic sacrifice ever performed, yet Jesus still gave glory to the Father (Moses 1:19). The Atonement itself is a reminder that if you don't have a strong enough why-because formula, you might not have the drive to make it to the finish line of your goals.

Now the next step to achieving a goal is to decide whether or not it is a worthy one. Is it in line with gospel principles? Will it bring you closer to the Lord? I'm not saying that every goal we set has to be life-changing, but by actively weighing our desires against revealed truth, we can better evaluate the direction of our lives. This is a personal matter, and while others may not understand why you want to achieve a goal, all that matters is that it is important to you. If you honestly feel like it will help you progress and become the person the Lord wants you to be, go for it and let it be your guiding star.

Bobsled has taught me that maintaining a focus on what we want and why we want it can have tremendous impact on the outcome. We often throw around words like motivation, drive, enthusiasm, passion, ambition, and desire to indicate someone's willingness to go after a goal. And while those are great, motivation is only good for part of the journey. It provides the fuel for our progress, but there must be something else involved: dedication.

Dedication can mean the difference between victory and defeat in sport and the gospel. When you are truly dedicated to a goal, you will make any sacrifice necessary to achieve it. In the Church, when we talk about conversion we really mean our level of dedication to the Lord, our covenants, and our Heavenly Father's plan. The more converted/dedicated we are, the more likely our chances of reaching exaltation because we will sacrifice whatever the Lord asks of us and obey his words until the end.

Think about that as you read these words by the prophet Joseph Smith: "A religion that does not require the sacrifice of all things never has power sufficient to produce the faith necessary unto life and salvation; . . . It was through this sacrifice, and this only, that God has ordained that men should enjoy eternal life."[32]

Our level of success in life and the gospel will depend on how converted/dedicated we are to our objectives and how willing we are to sacrifice for them. The only difference between "I give up" and "I won't give up" is one word and a willingness to hold fast to the end, which we will discuss in the next chapter.

When obstacles come, are we going to lose hope and give up, or are we going to buckle down and get the job done? Champions turn their desires into dreams then goals, which, when paired with dedication, result in overwhelming success. There is no other way. Unless dreams are planted as goals, nourished by work, and cultivated through dedication, there will be no harvest. You have to give your best to achieve the best. As Paul counseled, "Know ye not that they which run in a race run all, but one receiveth the prize? So run, that ye may obtain" (1 Corinthians 9:24).

Bobsled teaches you a thing or two about running, especially running fast. Sprints, sled pulls, resistance pushes, and speed drills are a way of life for us. It doesn't matter if you're a driver, a side pusher, or the brakeman, get ready to make sprinting a new friend that you'll love to hate (said with only a tiny bit of sarcasm).

But running, and exercise in general, teaches you a lot about dedication.

You sweat, you ache, your muscles burn, and yes, sometimes you bleed. At what point do you quit? How many more forty-meter sled pulls do you want to do? How many flying one hundreds will you complete before going home? How bad does it have to hurt before you say enough is enough? It's all about your level of dedication.

One of my first experiences with desires, goals, and dedication happened one blazingly hot summer afternoon in July 1998. We're talking cook-an-egg-on-the-sidewalk hot. My coach Randy and I, along with a few other athletes, met at Cottonwood High School in Murray, Utah, to make use of their black-rubber running track.

Randy put together a particularly nasty workout for us that day that started with several short-distance sprints, then moved to forty (meters), then one hundred, one hundred fifty, and finally two hundred. Oh, and it gets better, because after a short break we did the same thing in reverse. But when a three-time Olympian gives you advice about your sport, you take it, and if he asks you to run until you puke, you do. So I did . . . and I did.

Partway through the second round, I experienced the wonderful lightheaded and nauseous feeling known to many athletes that only has one outcome: things come out. I barely made it over to the side of the track before I lost it, much to the delight of my coach and fellow athletes. "Did you throw up?" I nodded. "Good for you, man!" That's how we roll.

At that point I had a choice: pack it in for the day or finish the workout. I knew what my body wanted (to collapse), but my heart wanted to improve as an athlete. Maybe it was the lack of oxygen due to the sprints, but somehow I made the choice to get up and finish; dedication won the day. Did it make a huge difference in my life's outcome? No, but it did reinforce my willingness to stick to the task until it was done, a philosophy that helped me in high school, in college, in Boy Scouts, on my mission, in bobsled, and in life in general. Dedication is key.

So let's review. It all begins with *desires* to do something, which turns into *dreams*, which allow us to set concrete, specific *goals* that when coupled with *dedication* make a game-winning strategy. But wait, we're missing a crucial step: *effort*.

Standing at the top of the track, my main goal/objective is to cross the finish line as quickly as possible. In order to reach that main goal, I have to take each turn one at a time, thus dividing that big goal into smaller ones. To break it down even further, in each turn I need to decide where and when to steer, so the proper steering points become even smaller goals.

So, I have my **big** goal (a) get to the finish line. I have the **medium** goals (b) to help me achieve the big goal: drive each turn well. And then I have the **small** goals (c) to help me achieve the medium goals: drive each steering point in the turns properly. For all you math fans out there, it is something like C+C+C=B and B+B+B=A.

The setting and achieving of a goal is easier when you divide it into long-term and short-term objectives. The long-term goal is your big objective, while the short-term goals are the steps you need to take to reach the long-term goal. If my overall objective is exaltation, then I need to meet the short-term goals of baptism, temple covenants, tithing, and so forth. By looking at our goals in this manner, we can develop road maps that will help us plan the work required for their attainment. You achieve big things by breaking them down into more manageable tasks.

So let's look at those long-term goals you selected and use the following questions to create some small-term goals.

1. What will it take to achieve your goal? Be specific. Do you need to set up a diet plan? Do you need to read a book or take a course to learn more? Do you need to eliminate a bad habit?

2. **Who: Can you do this alone?** If not, who can help you? A family member, an instructor, a friend, a Church leader, a professional in the related field, or someone else?

3. **Where can you go to achieve this goal?** If you want to learn to kayak, is there a lake nearby? If you want to learn a martial art, is there a studio in the area? If you want to develop your soccer skills, is there a university camp that could help?

4. **When are you going to work on this goal?** Is there a specific hour or day of the week? Do you need to rearrange your schedule? Is there a deadline/time frame?

Now that you've answered these questions, find a quiet place where you can be alone and really think about those goals. How will you feel when you achieve them? Will there be satisfaction, joy, and the sense of accomplishment? Let those good feelings wash over you. Then I want you to think about how achieving this dream will change your life. Will you find improvement? Is it something that will help energize your life?

Back already? How do you feel? Are you confident that your goals are good things and are worthy pursuits? Then start planning your goal-map and get to work! Never fear the work. As Henry David Thoreau wrote, "if one advances confidently in the direction of his dreams, and endeavors to live the life which he has imagined, he will meet with a success unexpected in common hours."[33]

Dreams are great, but sticking to the task until you earn the gold is priceless.

STICK TO THE TASK 'TIL IT STICKS TO YOU

Anytime you set a goal, you can expect two things: first, you will have to work for it, and second, you will face obstacles. Like death and taxes, these two principles can be written in stone, though neither should intimidate us. We're Mormons; we don't quit.

Occasionally fate stares us in the face and opportunity knocks to invite us down a path of greater glory. In those moments we must stop dreaming and start doing because no gold medal was ever earned by someone who failed to decide and act. A dream or goal that is not committed to and labored for is like my unused 2002 Opening Ceremonies tickets—nice, but worthless.

Once we have set our goal, it's time to do something *very* important: commit. So let's talk about commitment (yes, single adults, I'm using the "C" word) because without commitment all our dreaming, planning, and goal-setting won't matter. Commitment is how we "endure unto the end" (Matthew 24:13).

Bobsled is demanding. It's *physically* demanding because you workout at high levels and can take a beating inside the sled. It's *financially* demanding since equipment costs and training/travel fees get pretty high. Plus, with all the ups and downs of sport, it's *mentally* and *emotionally* demanding.

So how do you get through all that? How do you keep going when you have no money for food because you spent it on training fees? How do you push through the pain of rehabilitating an injury? How do you sacrifice your time, body, and mind to a goal? You do it because you are *committed*.

We can best understand commitment by substituting another word that we discussed in the last chapter: dedication. To be 100 percent dedicated means you have committed yourself to finishing no matter what.

That's what I love about bobsled: once you are in the track, you are committed. There are no off-ramps, red lights, or ways to stop unless you crash or pull the brakes before the finish line, which is a big no-no. That is the level of dedication we must have when it comes to our goals. We must fight "a good fight" and "finish (our) course" so at the end we can say we "kept the faith" (2 Timothy 4:7).

Two men sat down to breakfast. One man smiled and said, "Well, the pig was successful."

"What do you mean?" his friend asked.

"Well," the first man said, gesturing to the bacon and eggs. "The chicken was involved, but the pig was committed!"

When it comes to our goals, sometimes we act like the chicken that made a small contribution of a few eggs and went on her way. We give some effort, make some sacrifices, but if something really tough comes up, well hey, we tried. We turn chicken.

The pig, however, gave everything he had to that breakfast. He was completely committed. While the story is a little silly, it demonstrates the level of commitment we must have toward our goals. Commitment is a promise that you will not quit until the race is won, a covenant to give everything you have to reach the finish line. Commitment strengthens us against the doubt and discouragement that Satan uses to get us to give up. He fears your potential, which is why he works hard to keep you from setting goals and working for their achievement. I have seen this on my mission, in my sport, and in the lives of those around me. Obstacles show up, doors close, and extra work piles up. It happens and it's normal. Push through.

Sure, the road to the top can be difficult and lonely. You may have to make sacrifices of time, money, and energies. Sometimes you have to put off fun for work, but commit and press forward. Look up, not to the side and never downward. Stay committed! When you feel the pressures and the frustration of setbacks, hold fast to your dreams and goals. It is always when you stand your ground that the light finds you.

At baptism and in the temple, do we not covenant/commit to obeying the commandments, following the Savior, and enduring to the end? Do we not commit to serve God through the use of our time, talents, and resources? Righteous commitment can lead to success in every goal-oriented effort. To remind myself of that fact, a few years ago I came up with a personal motto, written in Latin: *Aut viam inveniam aut faciam*. Basically it translates to, "I'll either find a way or make one."

So look at your list and ask yourself what trials or obstacles you may have to overcome to achieve your goals. You can't anticipate every setback, but it helps to be prepared (the Boy Scouts taught me that). Next, write down how you can overcome each potential difficulty. Goal: college degree. Obstacle: pay for college. Solution: apply for scholarships or student loans. Goal: family vacation. Obstacle: unemployment. Solution: polish your resume and job hunt like crazy. Get the picture?

Whatever your goal, where there's a will, there's a way. Correction: where there is faith-filled commitment there is a way. So review your goals and ask yourself, "Am I willing to commit 100 percent to achieving these desires? Do I want it so badly that I will do whatever I righteously can and hold true until victory is mine?" If so, sign your name next to each goal, thus contracting, even covenanting, with yourself that you will see it through until the end. That level of commitment brings serious power into our lives.

Commitment helps champions kindle a fire within. Do they feel the agony of failure or the chill of doubt? Sure, but instead of allowing those things to defeat them, champions build a shield-wall around their hearts. This wall of commitment is impenetrable, having been constructed of courage, motivation, and faith/hope. A committed heart can be the strongest place on earth when it is full of the right things. Champions are still just human beings. They may have some amazing abilities, but they still have to work hard and set goals. They are champions because they commit to being one.

During the 2005–2006 season, we started to have more races at the local level, which were great for extra practice and were fun. My brakeman and I decided to enter one of these races, and coming off a good week of training and a relatively recent win, we were both committed to success. We set our goal and dedicated ourselves to it, but just like clockwork obstacles appeared to challenge us.

I had "one of those days" that lasted for a week. Some things were happening at work, I was struggling to keep up with my homework, I had a nice stack of bills, and, the worst of all dating was awful. On race day when I woke up, I lay in bed and thought, "I don't want to do this today." I was whining, but in my defense it had been the week from . . . somewhere not so cold.

But that little voice in the back of my head got really annoying. "You're not a quitter," "You're better than this," and "You committed to yourself and your teammate, so get going." I kept telling the voice to go away, but it wouldn't listen. Finally, I threw the covers off the bed and said, "Ok, I'm going!" I got my gear together and grumbled the whole drive to the track.

We prepped our sled in the start area, which helped get my mind into race mode. Strangely, apparently some of the other teams had the same struggle I did because they didn't show up. I thought, "I almost took the easy way out, but instead here I am."

After our two competition runs, I discovered that we had won second place (barely edged out of first). As I held the medal in my hand, I whispered a prayer of gratitude that Heavenly Father had pulled me out of my sea of self-pity and allowed my commitment to my teammate and to myself rule the day.

But what if I hadn't gotten out of bed that morning? What if I hadn't been so committed that my spirit wouldn't let me quit, even when I wanted to? I call that medal my "commitment medal" because it reminds me that only through 100 percent commitment can we achieve our goals.

From a gospel perspective, commitment is an exercise of agency and faith. You choose to dedicate yourself to your goal, no matter what. Without commitment, the winds of adversity, temptation, or even self-doubt can wash our dreams away (Matthew 7:27).

Over the years I have seen a lot of athletes come and go from my sport. They may have started with hopes of money, fame, glory, attention from media and the opposite sex, and so forth. And some of them were really amazing athletes; they just weren't committed because the motivation behind their goals was weak. Things like lust, greed, and pride will never provide the level of commitment required to achieve a worthy goal. Those take love, courage, and a desire to progress.

After training one day, I came home and wrote down the following lines:

You must have faith in your dream before anybody else will.

You have to work hard before anyone else can push you.

You have to set goals before anyone else can support you.

You have to take chances before anyone will take them on you.

You must do what is necessary before others will sacrifice for you.

Some say that commitment and self-discipline are the same thing. I disagree. To me commitment is the mental decision to see the goal achieved. Self-discipline, however, is acting on your commitment. To be successful, commitment and self-discipline must go hand in hand.

Commitment is what drives a basketball player to show up to practice, but his or her self-discipline is what pushes them to work hard during practice. Commitment is what helps missionaries get up each morning, and self-discipline allows them to work themselves to exhaustion in the Lord's service all day long. As we read in James 2:22, "By works (self-discipline) was faith (commitment) made perfect." You can have all the dedication in the world, but until you put that power in motion through effort, your goal is nothing but a wish. Effort is what separates the dreams of today from the achievements of tomorrow. I call this the "Dead-Sled Principle."

Bobsleds are incredible pieces of machinery. Whether made in Italy, Germany, Austria, or the United States, each sled is crafted for speed with every part carefully engineered to provide the best results possible. Sleds are as much a part of the team as any athlete who races in it. They are smooth, sleek, and fast pieces of art.

But while that sled might be incredibly built and beautiful, until we get it to the starting line and push off, it's nothing more than a sculpture. Good to look at, but it's not going to win any races. In the end it doesn't matter how lofty our dreams of gold are; until we actually push off and get moving, our sled is no better than a pile of metal and fiberglass, hence the phrase "Dead-Sled." Dead, inert, motionless.

The harsh reality is that no matter how pretty you paint the picture of your dreams, nothing is going to happen until self-disciplined effort becomes involved. As President Marion G. Romney once said, "While the Lord will magnify us in both subtle and dramatic ways, he can only guide our footsteps when we move our feet. Ultimately, our own actions determine our blessings or lack of them."[34]

While serving as a Zone Leader on my mission, it was fascinating to study the level of commitment displayed by the different elders and sisters. I could tell which missionaries had committed to serving the Lord because they worked hard. The ones who lacked this dedication struggled more often and worked with less enthusiasm. I see this dynamic in sports all the time. When someone is committed to a goal we call it being "driven," but commitment is only a step on the path to success, not the destination. Yes, you've laid the crucial foundation of dedication, but without applied effort there can be no victory. "I want" never accomplished anything. "I will" leads to gold-medal outcomes. By exercising our agency through commitment and effort, we can live as champions every single day.

Let's get to work.

WHISTLE WHILE YOU WORK FOR GOLD

A week after my teammate Matt and I won the 2008 Utah Winter Games, we had another race scheduled called the 2008 Pioneer Cup. I wonder what the early saints would say about a bobsled race commemorating their sacrifices and faith.

To prepare, Matt and I, along with our other teammates Don and Brad, put in some focused practice sessions and made sure the sled was in tip-top shape. After the ever-necessary runner sanding, we felt like Team Holm was ready to go. However, on February 2, race day, I felt anything but ready; I felt horrible.

Winter flu season in Salt Lake City can be a beast, and I fell victim. I woke up on the morning of the Pioneer Cup and wondered who beat me up. I was sore, achy, and slightly feverish, and I wanted to sleep until the next Saturday. But I couldn't. Well, I *could* have called my brakeman and coach and said I wasn't going to make the race, but the stubborn side of me fought against it. I lay in bed for about an hour going back and forth until obstinacy won out. I got up, got ready, and made the drive to the track.

Matt, my brakeman, was great. We flipped the sled over on the stand at the Start, and he told me to go rest while he got the runners and shims on. As I sat (well, more like lay in a coma) in the start house, I wondered how we were going to do. That we were even racing was a personal victory, but what about the competition? We had been working hard the past few weeks, including for the Utah Winter Games win. We had done the sled and runner maintenance and all our off-ice training as well. It was time to put faith in the Lord's grace since we had done all that we could do (2 Nephi 15:23). Did I expect the Lord to help us win? No, but I had confidence that he could help us do our best under the circumstances, and that was enough for me.

As it turns out, it was enough for gold, although they didn't give any medals that day. While I did not bring home a physical reward, I obtained a valuable lesson regarding the pursuit of our goals: work makes the difference, and after we have done all we can, we can trust in the Lord's mercy.

Work is an eternal principle. After their removal from the Garden of Eden, Adam and Eve were told, "In the sweat of thy face shalt thou eat bread" (Genesis 3:19). It is only through effort that we can hope to progress in life and achieve our goals. The Lord himself set the great goal for us when he said, "Ye are therefore commanded to be perfect, even as your Father which is in heaven is perfect" (Joseph Smith Translation—Matthew 5:48). This is not a suggestion; it is a commandment, one that we cannot possible achieve without a willingness to work (and a lot of mercy).

Now the original Greek word for *perfect* means "to be complete, finished, or fully developed," and while some argue that this level of perfection is impossible, we know, as Nephi did, that "the Lord giveth no commandments unto the children of men, save he shall prepare a way for them that they may accomplish the thing which he commandeth them" (1 Nephi 3:7). In my opinion the setting, laboring for, and achievement of righteous goals is one way we can grow and become more like our Father in Heaven, thus obeying the mandate to become perfect.

As a people we believe in being industrious and self-sufficient, two traits that allow us the freedom and ability to learn, develop, and serve the Lord. Like the early Saints, we should "not idle away (our) time, neither (should we) bury (our talents) that (they) may not be known" (Doctrine and Covenants 60:13).

I know that excuses appear easy, but only effort gets results. You can either picture failure or you can visualize and work for success. As President Thomas S. Monson says, "Work will win when wishy-washy wishing won't."[35] No one can achieve your dreams for you; they can love, support, and encourage, but it's up to you to pay the price. Do I want fast runners? Then I need to sand them. Do I want the sled to drive well? Then I need to do the maintenance. Do I want to push faster? Then I need to hit the gym and the sprint track. Goals are good, as is commitment, but without effort there can be no success.

There is truth in the saying, "we make our own luck." While everything we have comes from the Lord (Mosiah 4:19, 21), God expects us to set goals and commit to laboring toward their achievement (Alma 37:34). Nephi had to labor to construct the boat that would bring his family to the promised land (1 Nephi 17–18). Joseph Smith had to labor in "the work of translation"[36] of the Book of Mormon. Even the Savior had to labor to fulfill his atoning sacrifice in Gethsemane and on the cross. Desires, dreams, and commitment without works are dead.

This was something I struggled to get some of the adaptive bobsled athletes I coached to understand. They had good desires for the sport, such as competing for the United States in the Paralympic Games. They wanted to have faster pushes and quicker downtimes and to land big sponsors and get new equipment and funding. The problem was not with their dreams—it was the lack of consistent effort, and I made some of them mad when I pointed this out. They wanted good things and were even committed to good things, but I couldn't get them to see that dreams remain dreams until they are purchased through effort. Some athletes just believe they can magically obtain the strength and skills necessary to win even though they slack off at practice or in the gym.

This actually caught up to one athlete. He was a "standing driver," which meant he had a prosthetic on one leg that allowed him to run and jump into the bobsled (wheelchair drivers are "seated drivers" since they begin seated inside the sled). Our program was invited to provide forerunners for a race, which was a great opportunity for the adaptive bobsled movement. This particular driver and his brakeman had taken a couple of runs down the track that day, two I believe, when their turn came up again. I helped the brakeman move the sled to the push block, waited for the buzzer to go off, and rolled the sled down into the start grooves. I moved around to the back of the sled and began recording with my digital camera so we could watch the start later.

The brakeman, Cody, was an excellent pilot, but due to scheduling he was unable to qualify as a forerunner and was professional enough to brake for his program teammate. He was a hard worker, on and off the ice. Cody attended nearly every training session and was putting in a lot of hours in the gym. But the driver of the sled he was riding in . . . not as much. When I asked him why he wasn't working out harder so he could push faster, he said, "Just give me a faster brakeman."

These two athletes got ready, called their cadence, and took off pushing. Everything appeared to be going well until they got past the crest of the start ramp where the track starts to go downhill. A few steps later the pilot jumped to load into the sled and caught his foot on the edge of the sled's cowl. We all watched in shock as he promptly fell over the *other* side of the sled with his push bar still up. Cody saw his driver fall then debated what to do before kicking out of the back of the now empty sled. He did not want to go where that train was heading.

While they both made the long walk back to the start (neither was hurt), I switched the camera off and walked over to where the race director was standing. Since our program contained some of the first adaptive bobsled athletes in the world, we wanted a good standing in the sliding community. Thankfully the experienced race director understood that "it happens," but he mentioned exactly what I was thinking: the driver had fallen because he was tired. He did not develop the full stamina required to take that many runs. I'm not trying to embarrass this athlete in any way (which is why I never mentioned his name). We all knew that he was not the first nor will he be the last pilot to miss loading in. However, what stood out to me was that this all could have been avoided had that athlete done more physical work.

How many of your goals never got past the "I want to . . ." phase? How many have you let go because you became tired or lost interest right before the finish line? I call this the "80/20" rule: we put in 80 percent of the effort required, but for some reason we give up instead of finishing that last 20 percent. We start down the bobsled track of our dreams, but pull the brakes and get out a few turns from the finish line. How sad! Again, it is only through continuous, dedicated efforts that we can obtain triumph in life and success in our desired goals. Be 100 percent tenacious, not 80.

Victories really aren't won in the moment an athlete crosses the finish line. They are won during the months and years that lead up to the competition. A lack of effort-filled preparation will lead to a lack of success on race day and even the Day of Judgment (Alma 34:33). Working toward a goal is the preparation that makes the impossible become possible. And it's what gives us self-assurance as well.

I think every athlete knows what it is like to have a game they did not feel ready for. It can be pretty tough to have confidence in these situations. As the Lord declared, "if ye are prepared ye shall not fear" (Doctrine and Covenants 38:30), but as with all eternal principles, if we fail to prepare for game day through careful planning and effort, we have no such promise (Doctrine and Covenants 82:10). And feeling ill-prepared for a race because you wasted your chances to prepare is horrible.

But let's focus on the positive. I want to tell you about a time when efforts and preparation led to a great outcome. Let me tell you about Operation Snowflake.

Operation Snowflake has to be one of my favorite bobsled-related experiences (so far). It occurred in March 2009 on the last day the track was open that season, but let me lay out some background first.

My team had focused heavily on four-man for about a month when the president of the local bobsled and skeleton club approached me with a talent-scouting opportunity for Getty Images, which provides some of the most beautiful stock photos in the world. Chances are within the past twenty-four hours you have seen a Getty photo in a news report, in a magazine, or on TV. Well, with the Vancouver Olympics roughly two years away, Getty wanted to update their library of winter sports photos that companies could purchase for marketing pieces or media outlets can use for event coverage. Operation Snowflake was a photo-shoot for bobsled and skeleton images, and my initial role was to help select athletes and coordinate sleds since I had sport experience, was on location, and knew the athletes.

I took my camera to one of our final training sessions, and, as you can imagine, everyone wanted to be involved. I took headshots for the producer, but in the end she asked who I thought should be in the shoot. That's where the work and preparation element comes into this. As I thought about all the Utah-based sliders, I had to decide who could handle a professional photo shoot, who had the talent to make it look good, and most of all who had the experience to make the shoot successful. I felt blessed because the athletes I recommended also happened to be friends, which is why Operation Snowflake is such a fond memory. Plus, after reviewing my recommendations, the producer asked if my four-man team and I would be available for the photo shoot. Since we had been training all season, they wanted us to participate. Everyone's hard work was paying off, *literally*.

The day of the shoot was absolutely beautiful. The sky was a deep blue, the sun was shining, and the temperature was perfect. I felt like I was surrounded by family. During the catered breakfast at the top of the track, I looked at my teammates, Don, Brad and Matt, and then over at my old teammate Joe, who would drive the two-man sled, and his brakeman, my friend Nick. Two more friends, Matt and Tracey, were the delegated skeleton athletes for the shoot.

The Getty crew treated us like celebrities, which was fun, and, of course, there was good-natured trash talk going on between the athletes and even among the photographers. We spent several hours at the top doing simulated push starts and sitting in the sled like we were going down the track. The greatest thing about the shoot was the feeling of team unity for all of us that day. It was surreal.

One of the many humorous experiences included my brakeman Matt telling Don and Brad to keep their heads down and in line with mine out on the track. They swore they had been doing so the whole time, and during lunch one of the photographers plugged his camera into his computer to review the day's photos. As we all crowded around the screen, he scrolled through breathtaking shots of our team traveling through a turn. Suddenly he stopped on one, looked at Matt, then back at the screen and said, "Hey, isn't that you with your head up in the back of the sled?" It was a great shot that ended up making the final cut, but in the photo Matt's head was up, whereas Don's and Brad's were down. A picture is worth a thousand words, and that one gave us a thousand laughs.

Operation Snowflake was great, but none of it would have been possible for any of us had we not put in the time and work *before* the opportunity arrived. Our years of on-ice efforts made that dream-day possible.

No, success does not happen on the day of competition. But what happens when our efforts aren't working, when our work isn't as effective as we originally hoped? Simple—we adapt and improve our efforts so they can bring better results. We fix the chatter.

Chatter in bobsled refers to the audible sound a loose runner makes as a sled goes down the track. Our four runners sit inside "shoes" that connect the runners to the axle, and while we bolt, the runners into the shoes, sometimes there is lateral (side-to-side) movement of the runner within the shoe itself, which causes "chatter." Chatter causes a bit of friction between the runners and the ice, which can slow you down. Not by a lot, but when you could lose the gold by one-tenth of a second, every little bit counts.

One solution to runner chatter is to use what we call "shims." Shims are small pieces of thin sheet-metal that slip between the runner and the sled's shoes with a bolt running through both. When you tighten those bolts, the shims help the runner remain solid in the shoe. Chatter gone.

But there's more. Let's say that when you set your runners in you notice the center lines don't match up on one side. Maybe the front right runner points inward by a miniscule amount (this can be tested with lasers). You can adjust how many shims sit by the front runner bolt and how many sit by the back in order to get your runner alignment back on course.

Correcting less-effective efforts toward our goals is not only normal, but it is also recommended. Patience is one thing, but beating your head against the wall is another. Champions know that goals require effort, but worthless effort is wasted energy. Work hard, but work smart too. Don't be afraid to adapt and make changes if you need to.

Our Heavenly Father wants us to make the most of this life and dream big dreams. We must be willing to work and hold true until they are achieved, because if we remain faithful, do our best, and trust in the Lord, we can hold our heads high since we gave it everything we had. Any good athlete understands that fighting hard and leaving nothing on the table brings a deep sense of satisfaction, confidence, and peace, regardless of the outcome. So don't get discouraged if things don't happen right away; be patient and persistent. You will get tired. You will face discouragement. You will want to quit. *Don't.* As former heavyweight boxing champion Jack Dempsey once said, "A champion is one who gets up when he can't."

Pray as if it was up to the Lord; work as if it was all up to you. Your gold-medal moments in life are waiting; go out there and get them.

ROAD MAPPING OUR SUCCESS

I have some good news and some bad news. The good news is that now your mental toolbox is full of winning practices to help you achieve your righteous goals. The bad news is that many righteous goals have been lost through the mismanagement of those same skills. How? Simple: by not following a good track map.

In bobsled a track map is a schematic that displays the course's layout. They can be pretty basic, but some of the more detailed ones include the outbuildings and nicknames of the different turns. When you look at a thorough map of the Park City track, turns six through ten are labeled "Albert's Alley" (after Prince Albert of Monaco), turn eleven as "Wasatch," and turn twelve as "Olympic." A Vancouver track map may label turn one "Slingshot," turns twelve through fifteen "Gold Rush Trail," and turn thirteen the infamous "50/50," because the opinion is that sleds have a 50 percent chance of successfully making it through.

When mixed with effective track walks and video examination, a track map can help sled pilots review the sequencing and design of turns. Think of it as a cheat-sheet that helps a pilot program his mind with what to expect. But what if he never had a track map to memorize the order of the turns? What if he could not take a track walk or review video to study the individual turns? I'm betting his first few runs down the track would be pretty rough because, and here's my point, he had no way to judge where he was on the course.

The failure to follow a plan is one of the greatest demolishers of dreams that I see in people's lives. They have wonderful desires to do something good, and they set and commit to specific goals. They even work hard, but at the end of the day, they are missing a crucial component of winning strategies: a focused way to track their progress.

I've heard it said that athletes live or die by their ability to set goals and track their headway. Tracing our progress can motivate us and keep us on course until the end. If your goal is to run six miles, once you hit mile three, recognizing that you're halfway can help you find the physical energy and positive mental state to finish.

Let's give a visual to the concept. I have two brass bookends from the 1980 Lake Placid Olympics, which have tremendous sentimental value since I was born that year and the inspiring USA vs. Russia "Miracle on Ice" hockey game happened at those Games. But if we compare these bookends to the setting of a goal on one side and the achievement of the goal on the other, then the books in between represent the steps we need to take to complete the journey. A tracking sheet allows us to see and follow those steps.

Like Latter-day Saints, bobsled athletes are a record-keeping people. We track our workouts so we can see progress in the gym. We track our diet so our nutrition maintains top form. Many pilots maintain a notebook where driving notes are made after each run. Some athletes use journaling to track their mental and emotional development. We do all this because if you don't know where you were, how can you possibly know where you want to go?

Several methods are available for tracking progress. Some people use a checklist that leads up to the completion of their goal. Others use the calendar on their phone to schedule necessary actions. I have seen sticky notes on mirrors or fridges to remind someone of what they need to do that day. One of the easiest is a simple to-do list. One of the devices I implemented to track adaptive athletes' progress on the ice was to post an old dry-erase board in the storage bin where we kept our sleds. After each session if a team sets a new PR (personal record), they write the new push start time, their downtime and their top speed. Then we all celebrate.

A tracking sheet is a great way to take a big goal and visually break it up into smaller steps that ultimately lead to that big objective. When I'm going through the first turn of a track, I'm not thinking about the bottom; I am focused on the current curve. Once I get through that turn, I will mentally cross it off my progress sheet and focus on the next turn and the next until I cross the finish line. As the prophet Joseph Smith once taught, "When you climb up a ladder, you must begin at the bottom, and ascend step by step, until you arrive at the top."[37]

Tracking our progress helps evaluate how far we have traveled toward our goal and what step(s) we need to take next. Recording achievements also increases our confidence as we complete each step. Sports psychologists call this "shaping," which means you celebrate and acknowledge every successful step you take toward your end goal. Basically, shaping is used to reinforce the positive completion of a desired action. So, what steps should you applaud in the pursuit of your goal?

Remember the list that I had you draw with your short- and long-term goals? Start there. Study your objectives and ask yourself how you can best chart your efforts to successfully move from one short-term goal to the next. It might be a chart on the wall that you check off when you successfully complete some specific action, or a jar you drop a coin in every time you achieve a short-term goal. Something that works for me is carrying around a three by five card that lists the day's goals. Find what works for you and use it to keep you on task. I say that because most people do really well when they first set their goals, but two weeks later the goals become forgotten memories. Your tracking sheet can be a physical conscience that says, "You're so close. Keep going and finish the next step!"

Let's try something. Find the first short-term goal on your list and circle it. Next, I want you to do it. That's right, put the book down and go. No excuses. Make the phone call, find the class schedule, buy the book you want or text your running partner. Be Nephi and "go and do." I'll be here when you get back.

Now I'm betting that you feel at least an inkling of satisfaction for taking that first step. Whatever you just did moved you toward your goal. You did something to progress and make yourself better. Now cross that goal off of your sheet and write, "Done!"

That is one of the reasons for a tracking sheet. You need a plan on paper or on the computer or your mobile device where you can celebrate each successful victory. So let's chart your progress. Be sure to list all the steps it will take to reach your end goal and include a way to check them off once you complete them. If you will do this, you will find greater motivation and a deeper desire to reach loftier goals.

My friends, celebrate your victories. I know from my own experience and from studying the lives of Olympic champions that goal-setting has power to lift us up. So don't just slide by in life. Climb! Don't be afraid of failure nor the work that will have to be done. A little sweat never killed anyone, plus the view from the top will change your life.

Don't wait for the situation to be "perfect" before you start; life never is.

Drop the excuses and pick up your dreams. When you have exhausted all possible options for progress, pray for more. Never give up. I know that by doing this you will increase your opportunities for success, for serving the Lord, and for building the kingdom of God.

ENDNOTES

1. Bruce R. McConkie, *Mormon Doctrine,* 2nd ed. (Salt Lake City: Bookcraft, 1966), 264.
2. Jeffrey R. Holland, "An High Priest of Good Things to Come," *Ensign,* Nov. 1999.
3. Bible Dictionary, "Prayer," 752.
4. J. Devn Cornish, "The Privilege of Prayer," *Ensign,* Nov. 2011.
5. Richard S. Van Wagoner and Steven C. Walker, *Book of Mormons* (Salt Lake City: Signature Books, 1982).
6. McConkie, *Mormon Doctrine,* 581.
7. Lawrence Corbridge, "The Way," *Ensign,* Nov. 2009.
8. Thomas S. Monson, "You Make a Difference," Apr. 1988.
9. David O. McKay, *Man May Know for Himself,* comp. Clare Middlemiss (Salt Lake City: Deseret Book, 1969), 22–23.
10. Gordon B. Hinckley, *Stand a Little Taller* (Salt Lake City: Eagle Gate, 2001), 8.
11. McConkie, *Gospel Doctrine,* 218.
12. Bruce R. McConkie, *A New Witness for the Articles of Faith* (Salt Lake City: Deseret Book, 1985), 236.
13. Joseph Smith—History 2:29
14. Harold B. Lee, *Stand Ye in Holy Places* (Salt Lake City: Deseret Book, 1974), 243–44.
15. Robert D. Hales, "The Covenant of Baptism: To Be in the Kingdom and of the Kingdom," *Ensign,* Jan. 2001, 6–9.
16. "Choose the Right," *Hymns of The Church of Jesus Christ of Latter-day Saints,* no. 239.
17. Joseph Henry Thayer, *Thayer's Greek English Lexicon of the New*

Testament: Coded with Strong's Concordance Numbers (Peabody, Mississippi: Hendrickson Publishers, 1996).
18. "How Firm a Foundation," *Hymns*, no. 85.
19. Holland, "An High Priest of Good Things to Come."
20. Winston Churchill, first wartime address, September 4, 1914, Guildhall, London.
21. Winston Churchill, speech, June 4, 1940, House of Commons, London.
22. Joseph Smith, *History of The Church of Jesus Christ of Latter-day Saints*, edited by B. H. Roberts, 2d ed. rev., 7 vols. (Salt Lake City: The Church of Jesus Christ of Latter-day Saints, 1932–51), 4:570.
23. Jeffrey R. Holland, "Broken Things to Mend," *Ensign*, May 2006.
24. Gordon B. Hinckley, "A Prophet's Counsel and Prayer for Youth," *Ensign*, Jan. 2001, 2.
25. Larry E. Dahl and Donald Q. Cannon, *Encyclopedia of Joseph Smith's Teachings* (Salt Lake City: Bookcraft, 1997).
26. The Olympic Creed.
27. C. S. Lewis, *The Weight of Glory*, rev. ed. (New York City: HarperCollins, 2009).
28. Richard G. Scott, "Learning to Succeed in Life," Sept. 15, 1998, BYU Devotional.
29. Howard W. Hunter, *The Teachings of Howard W. Hunter* (Salt Lake City: Bookcraft, 1997), 259.
30. Gene R. Cook, Lima, Peru, area council meeting of the Andes area, 1980.
31. Gordon B. Hinckley, youth fireside, San Diego, California, Mar. 24, 1996.
32. Joseph Smith, *Lectures on Faith*, comp. N. B. Lundwall (Salt Lake City: N. B. Lundwall, n.d.), 58.
33. Henry David Thoreau, *Walden* (Boston: Ticknor and Fields,1854); also http://www.goodreads.com/quotes/443071 (accessed December 6, 2013).
34. Marion G. Romney, "The Basic Principles of Church Welfare," in Conference Report, Apr. 1981.
35. Thomas S. Monson, "Great Expectations," CES fireside, Jan. 2009.
36. Joseph Smith History, 1:68
37. *Teachings of Presidents of the Church: Joseph Smith* (Salt Lake City: The Church of Jesus Christ of Latter-day Saints, 2007), 268.

ABOUT THE AUTHOR

Jeremy C. Holm is a renowned author, motivational speaker, bobsled athlete and coach, journalist, graphic designer, and advertising consultant.

Jeremy Christian Holm was born in Phoenixville, Pennsylvania, on December 22, 1980, and he grew up playing soccer and baseball while dodging tornadoes in the Oklahoma City suburb of Edmond, Oklahoma. He is the son of Jeffrey and Candy Holm and has one older brother and two sisters.

Jeffrey Holm was the founder of High Performance Coatings, Inc. (HPC), an international company that was involved with numerous world-championship auto racing teams and high-level industrial, military, marine, automotive, and aviation projects for over thirty years.

From an early age, Jeremy had a deep love for reading and creativity, two passions that were continually motivated through his inspiring teachers at Will Rogers Elementary School in Oklahoma, Brookwood Elementary in Sandy, Utah, and later Churchill Junior High and Skyline High School in Holladay, Utah, where Jeremy graduated in 1999.

After graduation, Jeremy chose to serve a Christian mission for The Church of Jesus Christ of Latter-day Saints to the countries of Honduras and Belize from March 2000 to March 2002. After his two years of service, Jeremy returned home and attended college at Brigham Young University and Salt Lake Community College, where he graduated in print journalism, an area of study that only fueled his love and honed his talent for writing.

Jeremy also began in the exciting winter sport of bobsled in January 1997 on the then newly constructed Park City, Utah, 2002 Winter Olympic track. After that fateful ride down the course, Jeremy was hooked and went on to train and race in both two- and four-man bobsled. In 2010, Jeremy was asked to coach the United States Adaptive Bobsled Team, thus allowing him to develop and coach a program that contained some of the first Paralympic bobsled athletes in the world.

In 2008 Jeremy formed the Athlete Outreach Project (AOP), an organization designed to use the influence of Olympic and world-class athletes and hopefuls to inspire others, serve in the community, spread hope, and assist nonprofit organizations in their causes. Since its inception, the AOP has been involved in countless fundraisers, motivational events, school and hospital visits, teen education programs, neighborhood service projects, and more.

After spending over fourteen years as an athlete, speaker, presenter, and philanthropical organizer, Jeremy decided to put his writing skills to use and has since written *The Champion's Way*, a motivational and inspirational book designed to help readers achieve their full potential and live a gold-medal life.

Jeremy currently resides in Salt Lake City, Utah, where he is a highly sought after graphic and web designer and advertising consultant. When he isn't busy with his lengthy-list of responsibilities, Jeremy enjoys visiting local public schools, juvenile correctional facilities, Boys and Girls Clubs, and countless other organizations to help others discover the champion within.

NOTES

NOTES

NOTES

NOTES

NOTES

0 26575 13675 3